shelter in ... Nikunau Island
So we headed for the island
W.N.W. On getting close to the land
we met with a strong current
running E.X.S. Saw a small
boat shed in lagoon and
ran up to it. hoisted burgee
and stood in. At 4 p.m. we
double reefed the mainsail &
put a reef in the staysail.
Two natives came off in a canoe
there are 26 men & 8 women
on the island. They make copra
and dive for pearls. Looking
very squally to wind'ard and
the moon which is half has
a big ring around it. At 8.30
p.m. we stood away to the N.X.W.
cleared the island and headed
N.E. still heavy sea on. Pumps
and Lamps attended to.

The Sea Journal

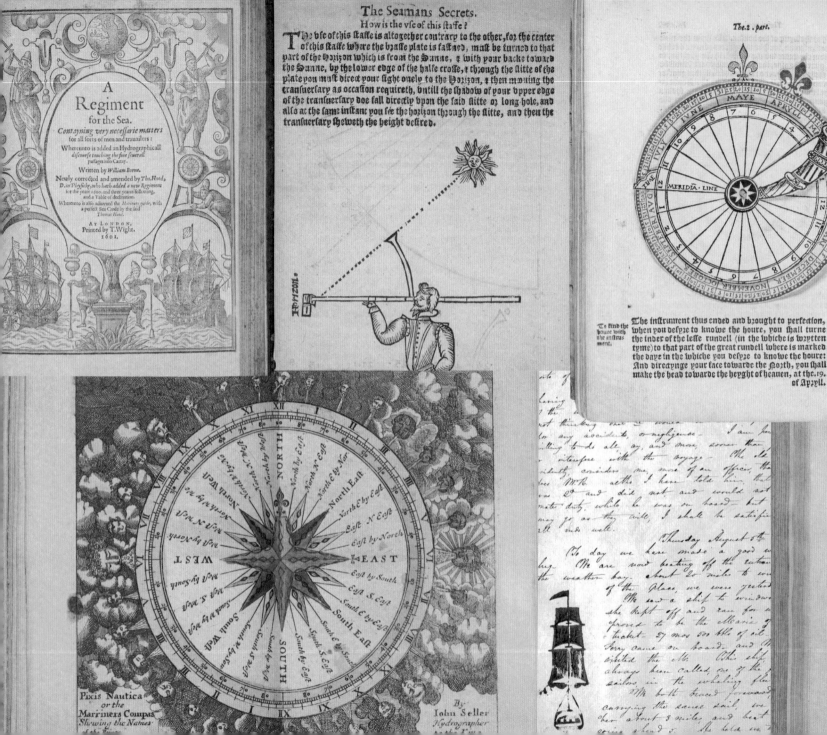

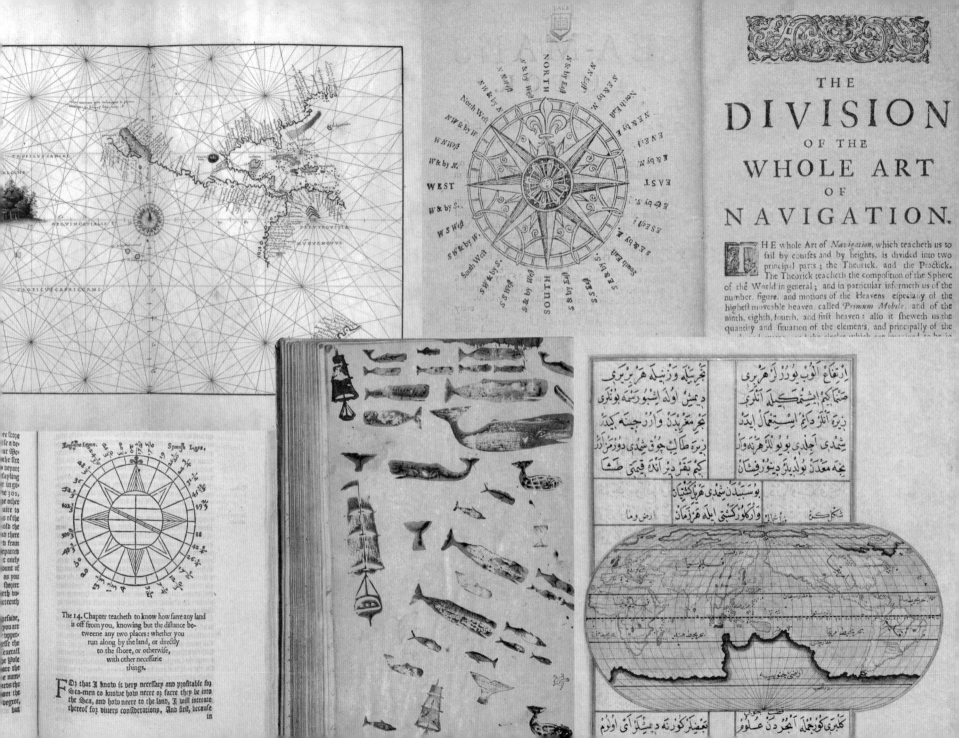

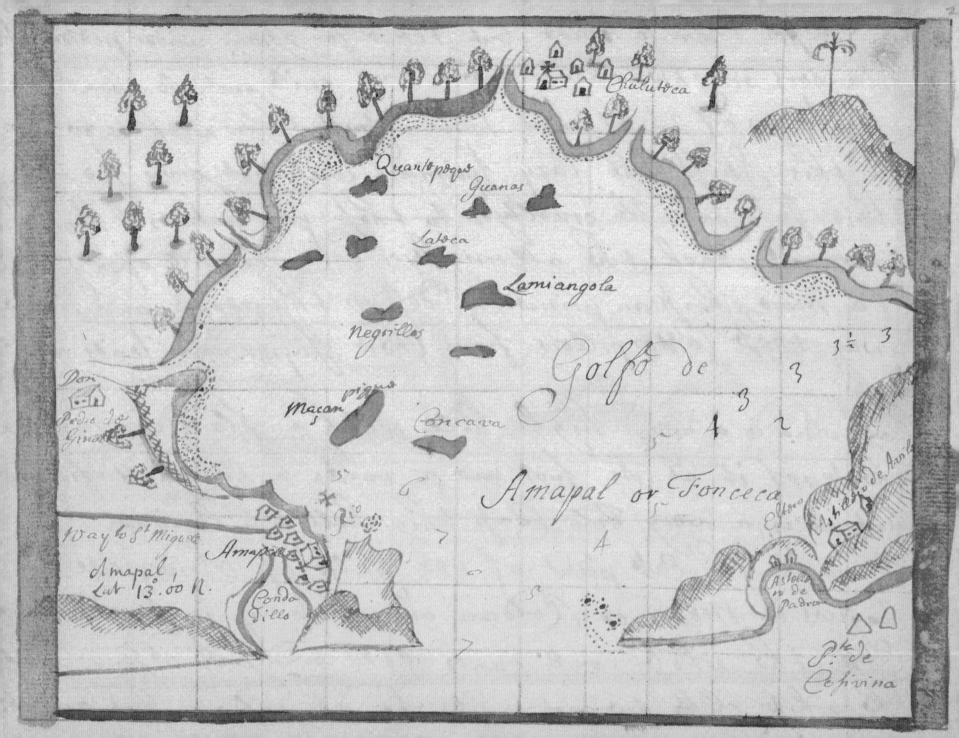

Chulutoca

Quantepoges
Guanas

Latoca

Lamiangola

Negrillos

Don
Pedro de
Ginova

Macan
pigno

Concava

Golfo de

Amapal or Fonceca

Way to St Miguel

Amapal

Amapal
Lat 13.00 N.

Condo
dillo

Eftero

Astefo de Aula

Astello
n de
Padro

Pta de
Cefivina

$3\frac{1}{2}$ 3
3
3
4   2

The Sea Journal

SEAFARERS' SKETCHBOOKS

⚓

Huw Lewis-Jones

FOREWORD BY Don Walsh

with over 450 illustrations

CHRONICLE BOOKS

SAN FRANCISCO

First published in the United Kingdom in 2019 by Thames & Hudson Ltd.

First published in the United States in 2020 by Chronicle Books LLC.

Library of Congress Cataloging-in-Publication Data is available.
ISBN: 978-1-4521-8115-8
Manufactured in China.

10 9 8 7 6 5 4 3 2 1
Chronicle Books LLC
680 Second Street
San Francisco, CA 94107
www.chroniclebooks.com

Chronicle books and gifts are available at special quantity discounts to corporations, professional associations, literacy programs, and other organizations. For details and discount information, please contact our premiums department at *corporatesales@chroniclebooks.com* or at 1-800-759-0190.

CONTENTS

FOREWORD

WE ARE ALL CREW

Don Walsh

Down, down, down we went into the abyssal dark. It was a voyage like no other: to the deepest point in the world's oceans. Seven miles down in the Mariana Trench east of the Philippines, further than anyone had ever been. After a five-hour dive in the US Navy's bathyscaphe *Trieste* we landed on the seafloor at 35,840 ft (almost 11,000 m) below the surface and what did we see? Well, to be perfectly honest, not much at all. The major find was a small, singular flatfish rather like a halibut, but it was proof that there was life at this greatest depth. But we neither made sketches nor took photographs. Through the toughened windows of our craft all we could see was a thick cloud of white sediment, stirred up from the bottom when we touched down. It was like being inside a bowl of milk.

My co-pilot on this voyage in 1960 was Swiss ocean engineer Jacques Piccard, whose father Auguste had invented the submersible and piloted a balloon to a record altitude in the early 1930s – not for fame, but to gather data on cosmic radiation. For Jacques and I, our job was as test pilots of a new research platform for ocean science. At about 31,000 ft (9,500 m) we heard a bang, but couldn't identify the cause. Once at the seafloor we found the answer: a curved acrylic window at the back of our entrance tube had a huge crack. So we were only twenty minutes on the bottom before we began our trip back up to the surface. It wasn't until 1995 that a Japanese remotely operated vehicle descended to record the very first images of the deepest place, and only one other person has reached it since. On our voyage, we were topside again after three hours. Ten days later we were in Washington, meeting the President at the White House.

Almost sixty years on, I write this on a ship rounding Madagascar. A few days later I tap on my laptop off the Cape of Good Hope and then send these thoughts off as we cross the South Atlantic. It's remarkable that emails from my cabin using the ship's satellite system receive near immediate replies. How much things have changed over the decades I've been afloat. On my first voyages with the Navy, communication with the outside world meant Morse transmission and radio, as well as good old letters and stamps.

My first bluewater voyage was in 1951 as a midshipman at the US Naval Academy. Our summer cruise was on the battleship *Wisconsin*, crossing the North Atlantic to Edinburgh, down to Lisbon, then onwards to Cuba for target practice with our 16-inch guns. Since then I've gone to sea regularly, including two ship commands. In all, that's sixty-seven years a sailor. So when I'm asked what does the sea mean to me, I think this says it all: it is where I want to be. Samuel Johnson said that 'when men come to like a sea life, they are not fit to live on land'. That was in the 1770s, but there is still some truth in it.

I have huge admiration for seafarers from all ages. There are many whose stories are lost to history, for they left no trace, no journals or letters – whether the intrepid Vikings, Chinese traders in junks larger than any vessel afloat at the time, or Polynesian wayfinders travelling thousands of miles in their ocean canoes, long before the Europeans crossed to North America. Magellan is a hero to some; I prefer Francis Drake – he was second to circumnavigate the world, but at least he survived the trip. Many are the definitions of what makes a voyage great, but my own feeling is simple. Exploration is curiosity acted upon. We humans all have the 'curiosity gene', though few of us act on it.

To be a true explorer means being at the frontier of new knowledge, and being part of that discovery process. There are no bad voyages, just interesting ones. Everything adds to your experience, and at sea – whether on the surface or thousands of feet below – both experience and imagination count. True explorers want to see what's over the next hill; in the oceans, it's what's over that far horizon, or what might lurk deep down in the dark.

Serving on ships of all kinds I kept logbooks and journals, but nowadays most of my notes are in my head. Lest you think that is too casual, remember that seagoing thrives in the realm of oral history. Facts always get lost or improved in the retelling, so who is to say? In Brazilian Portuguese there's an expression *história de pescador*, or in English 'a fisherman's tale'. Since the very first voyages, sailors have spun stories about the giant creatures they almost caught or some fantastic monster they saw out on the ocean. And there are still things today that are hard to explain.

Inside sea journals we can glimpse marvels. This book dives deeply into collections all round the world to bring to the surface wondrous things. It is a treasure chest of maritime art. With only about fifteen per cent of our oceans explored today, there is still much we can do, and yet we want to return to the Moon and land people on Mars. For now, we're confined to this one planet. I'd say it's more important to understand how it works and try to repair the damage we're doing. We must. As the late Marshall McLuhan once wrote, 'there are no passengers on Spaceship Earth. We are all crew'.

INTRODUCTION

UNKNOWN WATERS

Huw Lewis-Jones

There's a magic in the distance,
where the sea-line meets the sky.
ALFRED NOYES, 1930

You know it's getting rough when there's tea in your boots. But things could be much worse. Safely down from the outer deck, I'm now in my cabin trying to write the log. My tin mug is on the floor, wedged between my rubber boots, and my back is braced against the bunk. The porthole above me is bolted shut and covered in a layer of ice half an inch thick. With each heave and roll, waves block out the sun hanging low in the sky. Up on the bridge, the view is of unending ocean. Storm clouds steel grey and bruised purple are gathering. Icebergs are on the horizon and are scattered further still across the radar screen.

A few days ago we crossed the Antarctic Circle and have made good progress. But last night the waves rose and bitter winds came on from the south. Now as we punch our way through the swell, our ship strains and groans. I think of the mariners who sailed these seas before us in their wooden ships. In conditions like these they would have had to run before the wind, or reef sails to weather the storm under bare masts. It would have been a long and weary night indeed. No electronic charts to guide them. No hope of rescue should they need it.

The sea is a broad canvas for imagining. And whether sailor or artist, a passenger or simply a holidaymaker on the beach enjoying the view, our eyes – and our minds – continue to be drawn to the sea. Ships have been part of the human story from early on and our efforts to overcome the challenges of the oceans began long before written accounts. Craft of all kinds have set out to sea, and people and ideas moved around the world with them. Men and women, families and nations, all have dared the impossible when setting out on their journeys. Some of the earliest stories that survive are accounts of sea voyages.

So much has changed for seafarers since then, however. The world's coastlines are known, and its hazards mostly charted. A century ago, ships' bridges were open and there were no self-steering systems as we have now to keep a safe course. Sailors couldn't always take shelter when things got rough – they had to be out there, in the open, at the helm, up on the yards. Nor were there winches to help muscles control the sheets and halyards. The seafaring life created a tough, uncompromising breed, experienced in nature's frequently vicious moods. The prayer of Elizabethan captain John Davis says it all. A veteran of the Arctic, he had hoped to circumnavigate the world, but the odds were against him. In 1592 his crew was down to just five fit men. 'Oh Lord, if we are bound to die,' Davis wrote in his journal, 'then I would rather have it in proceeding than retreating.'

In the end, most ships are wrecked, sunk, scrapped or sold. Only a few survive. That is the way of history. As I write my journal, braced against my bunk, I remember the ships that have come south into these waters. *Erebus* and *Terror* were the first to penetrate the Ross Sea in 1841 and were later assigned to an Arctic expedition, disappearing off the map. The first men to overwinter on the Antarctic mainland, in 1899, came on *Southern Cross,* but by 1914 she was sealing, hit ice and sank near Newfoundland. Douglas Mawson's steam yacht *Aurora* was lost at sea in 1917 returning to New Zealand, having hit a mine laid by the German merchant raider *Wolf.* The only trace of *Aurora* was a lifebuoy picked up near Australia, covered in barnacles.

It is clear therefore that seasickness is the least of a sailor's worries. In these pages we encounter scurvy and shark attack, pirates, poisoning, starvation, dysentery, hurricanes, even cannibalism. We might wonder why anyone would join a ship at all. When adrift in an open boat, or caught in the doldrums with no breath of wind, parts of the Pacific are surely more like a desert than an ocean. The sun beating down, fierce, merciless; nowhere to shelter; unable to move; not

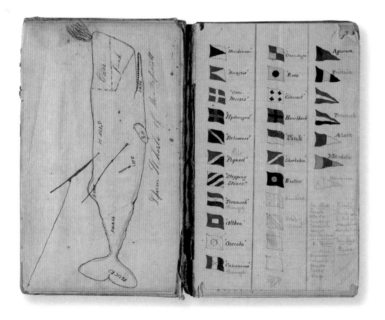

a drop of fresh water to drink. Of course, through the centuries a life at sea also gave sailors exactly that: a living. The sea offered opportunities – the promise, if not the reality, of freedom, the chance of employment, the means to escape, the idea of new lands beyond the horizon. Though for many seafarers this was not to be, their lives cut short.

⚓

To sail the oceans takes skill as well as experience. Sea charts, often with a coastal view, were the tool by which ships of trade and transport completed their course, and sea journals of all kinds were their natural companion. The Italian merchant venturers of the thirteenth century developed the earliest portolan pilot charts of the Mediterranean. The extraordinary voyages of European mariners across the Atlantic to a New World, and to the east to India and the Spice Islands, were both a result of the development of new charts and technologies, as well as an aid to it. By the eighteenth century the discovery and charting of the world's coasts and oceans had become a focus of commerce and political strategy.

Navigators followed Magellan into the Pacific through the strait that bears his name, and later pushed south, searching for the coast of an unknown continent, or north towards an Arctic maze of ice and islands. James Cook, an astronaut of the Enlightenment, chose his officers and sailors well, and many of his men were also talented with brush and pen. Often official artists, such as William Hodges, joined ships, and the sketchbooks that survive speak of their achievements afloat and ashore. Their journals allow us to feel something of the sea breeze on our faces; they send us back in time, and also send us out on journeys of our own.

The voyages that set out from many nations gradually redefined the limits of what was fearful and unknown, but peril was always close at hand. Writing a journal was often a routine for mariners, or perhaps a way to overcome boredom as much as danger, when locked in ice floes, adrift, becalmed, awaiting the whale,

Frank Hurley kept a detailed journal on Ernest Shackleton's *Endurance* voyage (above left), recounting their ordeal 'on the drifting sea ice' until rescued in 1916. Pages from the journal of Solomon Barstow (left), during a four-year voyage to the South Pacific, show a sperm whale and ships' flags. Whaler Joseph Ray decorated his sea journal on the *Edward Cary* with this watercolour title-page (opposite); Perry Winslow was the master, as they sailed from Nantucket in 1854.

or homeward bound, but it was also an act of hope: the wish for something of worth to survive them. Consider James Teer, who was wrecked in *General Grant* on the Auckland Islands, and despite impossible hardship still felt the need to keep a journal. We know from other survivors that he made one from sealskin, writing with pieces of charcoal from the edge of the fire they dreaded might go out. In the brutal wet and cold of the remote sub-Antarctic, their lives depended upon that fire. For a castaway like Teer, the journal provided comfort, a semblance of order in dire circumstances. While Teer's journal is lost, in this book there are many others, including that of the remarkable Frank Hurley. Shipwrecked with Shackleton in Antarctica and left for many months with others on an island in the heart of a hostile southern sea, sheltering under a boat walled round with stones, Hurley kept a journal. It helped him to survive; it offered him a future.

For many seafarers, therefore, keeping a log or writing a journal was not just a case of navigational necessity – to work out where they were, and where they were headed – but a way of locating themselves emotionally in a world turned upside down. A journal could combat loneliness, fear, frustration, even mutiny. For William Bligh of the *Bounty*, cast adrift in an open boat, keeping an accurate logbook was important testimony. As he navigated his way to safety through little-known Australian reefs, he took care to describe the men who had abandoned him; his pencil notes of the marks on their skin might identify them in a future manhunt. And despite all the hardships he suffered, he also took time to describe the new shores they touched on. Always exploring, he was an immense mariner and a deft artist, not the sea-monster Hollywood films might suggest. A small journal helped to keep Bligh and his companions alive.

⚓

From the earliest voyages, ships' officers were encouraged to make careful records. 'Take with you paper and ynke', instructed a well-educated mariner in the 1580s, 'and keepe a continuall journal … that it may be shewed and read at your returne.' And not just on ship, but on forays ashore too: 'An inquisitive traveller should never be without paper, pen and ink in his pocket', wrote another. Keeping a journal fostered a mindset of regular observation and careful recording, and offered the means to share that information with others when safely home.

Ship William Baker of Warren — In the South Atlantic Ocean. 1838.

Wednesday Nov 21st 1838.

Commences with light winds from the N. W. heading to the Southward saw right whales and chased starboard boat struck waist boat killed and about sunset took him alongside and took in sail, and shortly after the wind shifted to the S. W. middle and latter part fresh breezes at daylight commenced cutting and after we got through stood to the N. W.

So ends these 24 hours.   Lat. by obs. 36. 11.
     Long. by ch. 23. 30.

Thursday Nov 22d 1838.

Begins with fine breezes from the Westward at about 5 P. M. saw a large sperm whale lowered and chased but did not strike, whale bound to the West middle part light breezes latter part nearly calm saw a right whale. All hands employed in boiling.

So ends these 24 hours.   Lat. by obs. 35. 55.
     Long. by ch. 23. 40.

Friday Nov 23d 1838.

Commences with moderate winds from the Northward standing to the Westward spoke the Ship Hannibal of Sag-Harbor with 90 bbls. sperm oil and about the same time we caught a porpoise, middle part fresh breeze latter part moderate employed in stowing down.

So ends these 24 hours.   Lat. by obs. 36. 16.
     Long. by ch. 24. 19
     By Lunar.

Saturday Nov 24th 1838.

Begins with light winds heading to the N. E. saw a right whale and chased and spoke the Ship Condor of New Bedford with 1650 bbls. of oil, middle and latter part light breezes saw right whales starboard boat struck larboard boat killed and sunk.

So ends these 24 hours.   Lat. by D. R. 36. 08.

Sunday Nov 25th 1838.

Commences with light winds from the Northward saw plenty of whales lowered and chased starboard boat struck and he stove the boat and were obliged to cut the line and let him go, middle and latter part light breezes saw whales and chased waist boat struck and drawed.

So ends these 24 hours.   Lat. 36. 08.
     Long. 23. 59.

Monday Nov 26th 1838.

Begins with very light breezes and chased a right whale, middle part nearly calm latter part fine breezes from the Northward saw whales and chased without success, and caught two porpoises.

So ends these 24 hours.   Lat. by obs. 36. 34.
     Long. by ch. 24. 25.

Tuesday Nov 27th 1838.

Commences with fresh breezes from the Northward saw plenty of whales and chased middle part fresh breezes latter part strong breezes saw right whales and chased.

So ends these 24 hours. Lat. by D. R. 36. 30.

Wednesday Nov 28th 1838.

Begins with light breezes from the Westward and fine weather saw right whales and chased but did not strike, middle part much the same latter part fresh breezes saw a right whale and chased.

So ends these 24 hours.   Lat. by obs. 36. 43.
     Long. by ch. 24. 07.

Thursday Nov 29th 1838.

Commences with light breezes from the Westward, middle part light breezes latter part fresh gales from the Northward and rainy. So ends these 24 hours.   No obs.

All the sketches in this book have survived journeys. They are eyewitness to great explorations and intimate personal histories. James Cook was fond of using the phrase 'voyages of discovery' to describe his endeavours. A brilliant mapmaker even before he entered the Pacific, he journeyed emotionally and intellectually into unknown waters, yet encountered people who had their own histories of voyaging. Māori, Tahitians and Hawaiians would place this enigmatic visitor on their own maps, in ways Cook could neither understand nor control. The knowledge of the Pacific's sea of islands accumulated by the navigator Tupaia greatly assisted Cook. For generations of Polynesian voyagers the sea was not so much an obstacle as a *way*.

So what does it mean to make a voyage? Of course, in the simplest sense, it's a long journey at sea, from one point on land to another. As for discovery, it's a word that comes from the Old French *descovrir*, 'to uncover, unroof, unveil or reveal'. At first it was used with a sense of betrayal or malicious exposure ('discoverer' originally meant 'informant'), but the positive modern sense of 'obtaining sight of the unknown' finds wide usage from the 1550s. Sea journals are filled with discoveries and unknown sights of all kinds.

Voyages of discovery, like Cook's, were true explorations. The word explore comes from the Latin *explorare*, 'to investigate, search out, examine', obvious enough, but is also said to have origins as a hunter's term meaning to 'cry out'. In this sense, explorers set out to find and tell the world of their new discoveries. Another favourite word found so often in seafarers' journals is adventure, which comes from the Old French *aventure*, 'to happen by chance', and from a form of Latin, *adventura*, a thing 'about to happen'. This mix of spontaneity and future, with the addition of risk and danger, is its truest meaning. For adventure in the fifteenth century you might read 'perilous undertaking', and then in the sixteenth 'a novel or exciting incident'. For thirteenth-century readers it is said to have meant 'a wonder, a miracle; an account of marvellous things'. Today we might think of adventure as many things too: a risky undertaking of unknown outcome, an exciting sequence of events, a commercial speculation. Historic voyages were frequently all of these things. Seafarers set forth to venture, to hazard, and they also brought back proofs of marvels. Within sea journals may be found the wonders of the deep. As Petrarch put it we go 'forth to behold the mighty surge of the sea, the inexhaustible ocean, and the paths of the stars', and in so doing 'lose ourselves in wonderment'.

Opposite: The log of George Bliss of the whaling ship *William Baker*, which sailed from Warren, Rhode Island, bound for the South Atlantic in 1838.

Above: James Cook's journal from *Endeavour* on his epic first voyage. He set out in 1768 bound for Tahiti to observe the transit of Venus, but also carried secret instructions from the Admiralty to find the mythical southern continent.

From ships' logs to online blogs, for many centuries mariners have taken journals to sea to report, record, observe. They are filled with personal discoveries and insights that help us appreciate the perils and the pleasures of the seafaring life. In sea journals we can see people thinking and discovering. In exploring them we can share their experiences. What follows here is a gathering of superlative original artworks, which I hope manages to capture the spirit of the ocean, and of the men and women who met the call of the sea in their ships: in travel and trade, in sunset, storm and silence, amid the trials of trade and war, disaster and endeavour. From endless Arctic ice to the sultry South Pacific, from seashore to seafloor, artists and pioneers have captured something of their observations in pencil, paint and ink. And all of this can be found within the pages of small tattered journals, notebooks, sea-logs, diaries and cloth-bound sketchbooks. This is the fear and fascination of the ocean at first-hand, the edges of the world at first sight.

The process of creating this book has been a continued exploration, a treasure hunt, tracking down these rare objects in obscure libraries, private collections, dusty attics and deep sea chests, passed down through families perhaps, often presumed lost. Journals go on many journeys after returning from a voyage and may have curious histories themselves. Surviving shipwreck, tempest, mutiny, war or simple neglect, and now bearing signs of their lives at sea, they are all the more remarkable for this.

This is also an opportunity to bring forward seafarers whose lives deserve to be revisited – it requires digging more deeply in scattered archives, but rich histories are there if time is taken to find them. In these pages are famous mariners of course – including da Gama, Drake, Nelson, Bligh – and more recent yachtsmen too – Francis Chichester and Peter Blake – but also a whaler's wife, a ship's cook, a cartographer, a cabin-boy, sailors and surgeons, travellers and traders, celebrated artists, and a pirate or two. Equally, the crew includes a German alchemist, a Turkish admiral, a French botanist, a Dutch fisherman, a Tahitian priest and many more. Beyond the leaders of every celebrated voyage, there was always a range of talents on a ship to ensure success.

Representing Magellan's great voyage, for example, is not the captain himself, but Antonio Pigafetta, the Venetian scholar who sailed with Magellan round the world and who, unlike him, survived to tell his tale. Without his chronicle, and his journal jewelled with some of the very first Pacific island charts, much of Magellan's story would have been lost to history. One twentieth-century voyage that grabbed global headlines was the drift of the balsa-wood raft *Kon-Tiki*. But instead of its leader Thor Heyerdahl, the navigator Erik Hesselberg is profiled. Instead of James Cook here is his sailing master Joseph Gilbert. And instead of French navigator Bougainville, whose famous name is given to various places and flora, is another plant collector, the remarkable Jeanne Baret, the first woman to circumnavigate the globe, a stowaway, who suffered greatly for her science. 'Such risks', Cook would write, 'are the unavoidable companions of the man who goes on Discoveries.' True of course, but it was not just men who braved voyages worth remembering. For famous oceanographer William Beebe, who enraptured the world with radio commentary diving half a mile deep, two of the many women who joined his expeditions and made his discoveries accessible are included: the German Else Bostelmann and American Gloria Hollister.

This collection begins with the pioneering circumnavigator Commodore Anson, and he is followed by others from many countries, who recorded all manner of depictions of new creatures, coastlines and the peoples they encountered. Some modern mariners too reflect on voyages of their own. Don Walsh takes us to the deepest point of the ocean; Roz Savage battles the Atlantic; Rodney Russ reaches the farthest south; while other explorers and artists offer glimpses of their seafaring lives. And we end with William Wyllie, who once lived a few doors along from Robin Knox-Johnston's home in Portsmouth today. Like so many mariners included here, Wyllie just loved the sea: for its beauties as much as for its challenges, and for the enjoyment of seeing different ships making their way upon it. Wyllie did most of his sketching out on the water, often in craft that he built himself, but he painted on dry land too. Well, *dry-ish*. On a spring tide, or when gales blew from the Solent, waves broke in at his teak doors and his studio was awash, no matter how watertight he tried to make the jambs. He'd stand at his canvas painting bare-footed, with his trousers and long-johns rolled half way up his shins, while his children bailed with buckets.

In April 1832 Augustus Earle joined the *Beagle* as artist. His sketch shows the crew presenting specimens to a figure in a top hat - Charles Darwin. This is the only known image of him on arguably the most important scientific voyage in history.

Page 18: Detail of a chart of the 'Society Islands' drawn by Tupaia for James Cook in August 1769 - essentially a transcription of his multi-layered knowledge, informed by oral history, of the patterns of ocean swell, wind and currents, and the stars.

Page 19: Dutch pastor Jan Brandes sailed for Java in 1778. In later years he travelled to Ceylon and South Africa and filled his journals with colourful eyewitness sketches ashore and afloat.

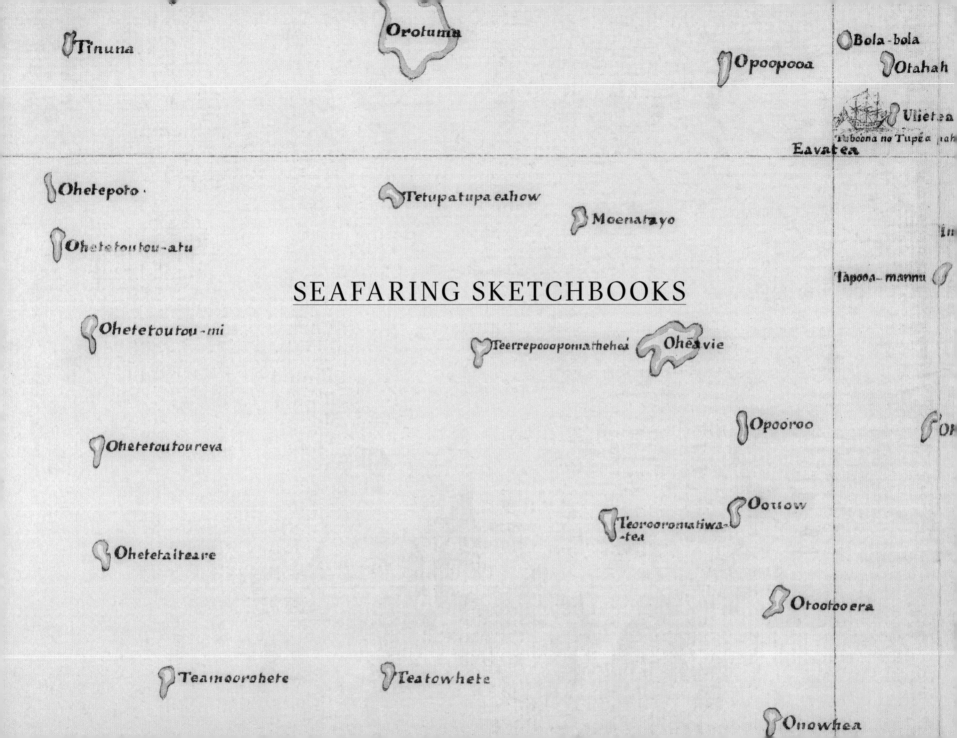

SEAFARING SKETCHBOOKS

GEORGE ANSON 1697–1762

Patience and Perseverance are two of the
Vertues most remarkable.

As the corners of the globe were explored and opened up to trade, seafarers in the service of the state were increasingly required to record their journeys accurately – keeping a journal or sea-log was an essential activity. Reports of travels were often top secret because of their value in detailing new territories and potential new markets, but many others were published and captured a keen readership. James Cook's account of his first voyage was one of the most widely read books of the age. Earlier, George Anson's retelling of his eventful circumnavigation had also been a bestseller, despite his aversion to putting pen to paper himself.

Anson came from wealth and joined the navy in 1712, rising quickly through family connections. By 1722 he was master and commander of the sloop *Weasel* cruising in the North Sea against Dutch smugglers. As captain of the frigate *Scarborough* he was off South Carolina for six years, protecting trade and suppressing piracy. In 1740, with Britain at war with Spain, he was appointed to lead a squadron of eight ships to raid and plunder the Pacific coast of South America and harass the Spanish gold galleons. In beating westward round Cape Horn in terrible conditions, some of the ships were forced home and one was wrecked. Only three sailed on, and scurvy, cold, starvation and disease took a further catastrophic toll, killing all but 335 of 961 surviving men, leaving barely enough to work the ships.

Yet Anson persisted. He crossed the Pacific, losing more men to scurvy, and was reduced to just one ship, *Centurion*. On 20 June 1743 he achieved a life-defining victory. Off the coast of the Philippines he intercepted the *Nuestra Señora de Covadonga* which was carrying 1,313,843 pieces of eight and 35,862 ounces of silver. Anson sailed to Canton and then returned to England in 1744, having completed a voyage round the world. Despite the losses and disasters, he and his treasure were paraded through the streets of London to huge crowds. An account of the voyage was published in 1748, compiled from Anson's notes and papers and the journals of others, and including useful charts; it was a great success. Charles Darwin read it when he was exploring on the *Beagle*, almost a hundred years later.

Anson was promoted to admiral, dabbled in politics, and took control of squadrons in the Channel. A naval commander turned statesman, and later Admiralty First Lord, he always preferred to be at sea. A new generation of seafarers were inspired by his calm leadership, perseverance and his concern for the practicalities of a sailor's life, but he would never quite forget the horrors of his world voyage.

A manuscript journal of Anson's voyage (opposite), illustrated with some of the birds and creatures the crew met along the way, was probably made by Lawrence Millechamp. A 'picture strip' souvenir print sold later in London (right) shows the main events of the voyage: in the middle, *Centurion* takes the Spanish galleon, and at the bottom is Anson, looking towards his camp on Juan Fernández and flanked by sea lions.

A
Narrative of
Comodore Anson's Voyage
into the
Great South Sea
and
Round the World.

Perform'd between the 18th September 1740

and the 15th of June 1744.

LOUIS APOL 1850–1936

To sketch at sea is not too much a problem; to get home safely, well, that is the most important thing.

In 1871 a Norwegian walrus hunter was working his way along the coast of a remote Russian archipelago. The season was coming to a close and it was almost time to turn for home when he discovered the ruins of a hut entombed by ice. Within it were the relics of a famed expedition led by Dutch navigator Willem Barentsz, which had overwintered there in 1596. Still preserved were the ship's clock, copper cooking pans, candlesticks, muskets, a flute, some goblets, and the small shoes of the ship's boy who had died there. There was also a final letter written by Barentsz, folded into a gunpowder horn and tucked in the chimney.

Back in the Netherlands, this was a stimulus for a new generation to learn about the seafarers of their celebrated past, but there was also a geopolitical edge. To protect their Arctic heritage in the face of increased activity by Scandinavian and British mariners, the Dutch set up a 'Committee for Navigation', which ordered the construction of a research vessel fit for polar seas. Lacking funds it was not the steamship hoped for, but it was, nonetheless, a 28-m (92-ft) schooner with space for fourteen crew and marine scientists, and was named *Willem Barents*. The ship embarked on its maiden voyage in 1878, placing memorials along its route at old whaling sites in Spitsbergen, and then sailed for Novaya Zemlya before heavy ice stopped progress (see also p. 286).

In 1880, to raise the profile of their efforts, the crew were joined by a Dutch artist renowned for his dramatic winterscapes. His name was Lodewijk Franciscus Hendrik Apol, known as Louis; he relished the chance to head north. A prominent member of the Hague School, he had his first exhibition aged nineteen, winning a scholarship from King Willem III. His work was displayed at the 1876 World's Fair in Philadelphia as part of the Dutch stand. For Apol, the Arctic voyage was tough, but also an experience that fuelled much of his later life as an inspirational resource: his sketchbooks are filled with studies and motifs for later paintings. The expedition made a number of landings – including spending time in a Samoyed settlement and a Russian refuge hut – but damage to the ship meant they sailed for home before winter set in.

Apol's Arctic visions made their way into private collections, and graced the walls of genteel parlours, but his ambitions were larger. In 1896, he proudly opened his vast 'Panorama Nova-Zembla' in the heart of Amsterdam's fashionable Plantage district, over 100 m (300 ft) long and perhaps 40 m (130 ft) tall. An immersive experience, it allowed audiences to imagine what a northern voyage might feel like long before motion pictures. It was here that some of the Barentsz relics were also displayed before being transferred to the recently opened Rijksmuseum. Sadly, Apol's polar panorama was destroyed in Haarlem in 1943, in a fire caused by an air raid, though a small canvas he painted when Princess Wilhelmina visited survives in Amsterdam's Maritime Museum.

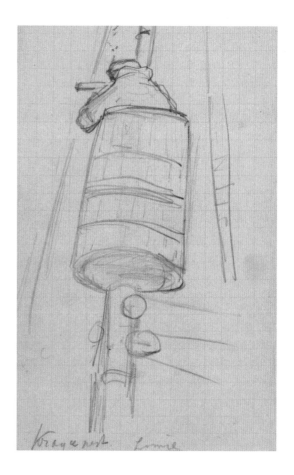

A crewman searches for a safe passage from the crow's nest as the schooner *Willem Barents* works its way through the ice. Opposite, a slow approach is needed when hunting for seal and walrus on the ice.

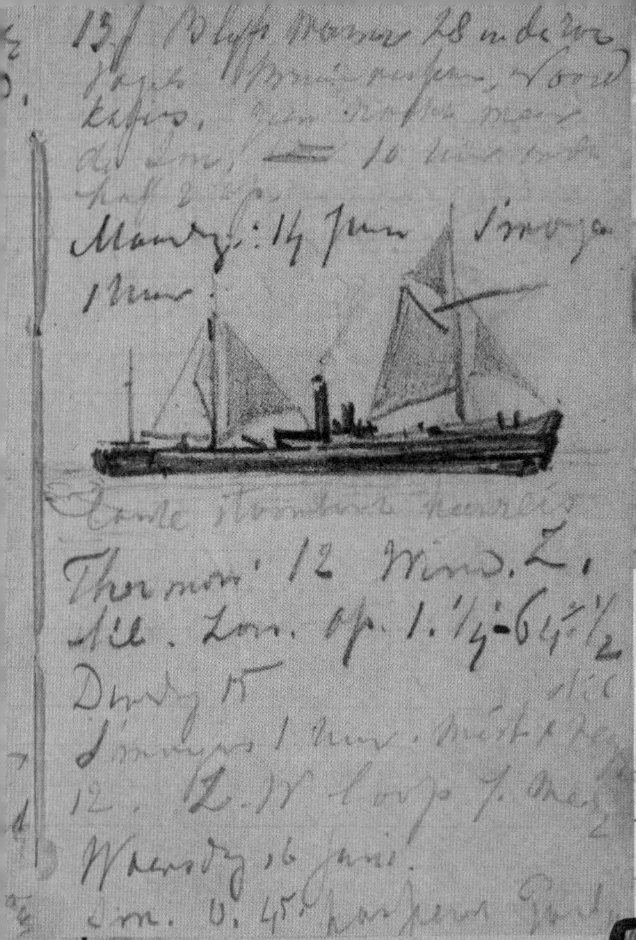

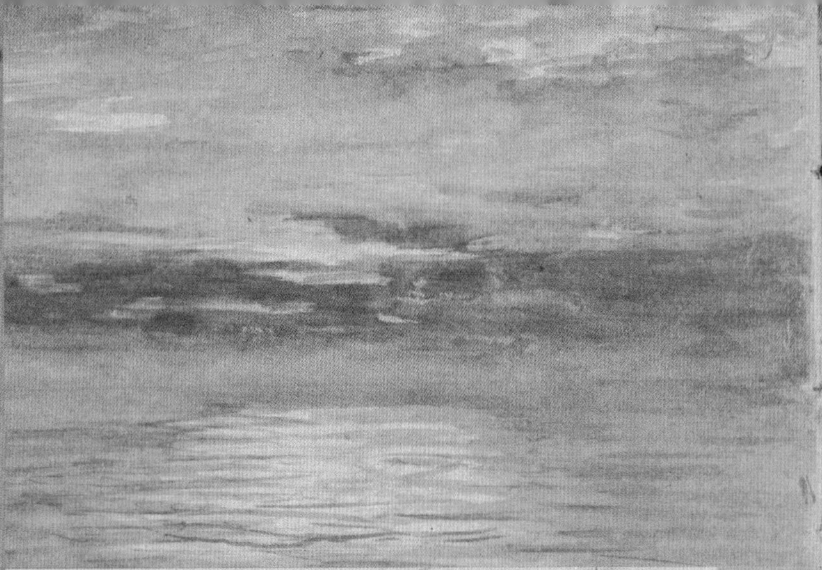

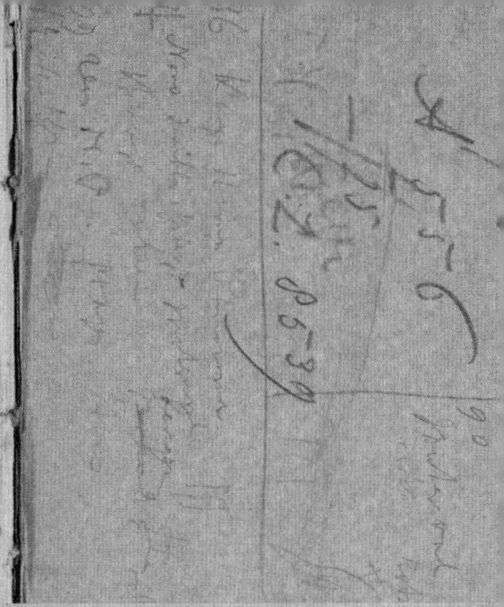

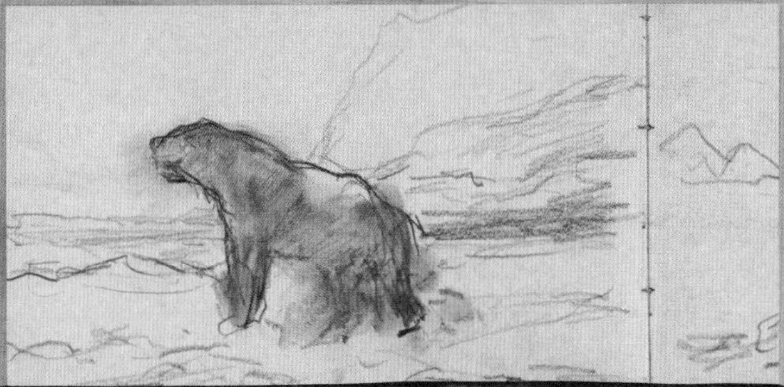

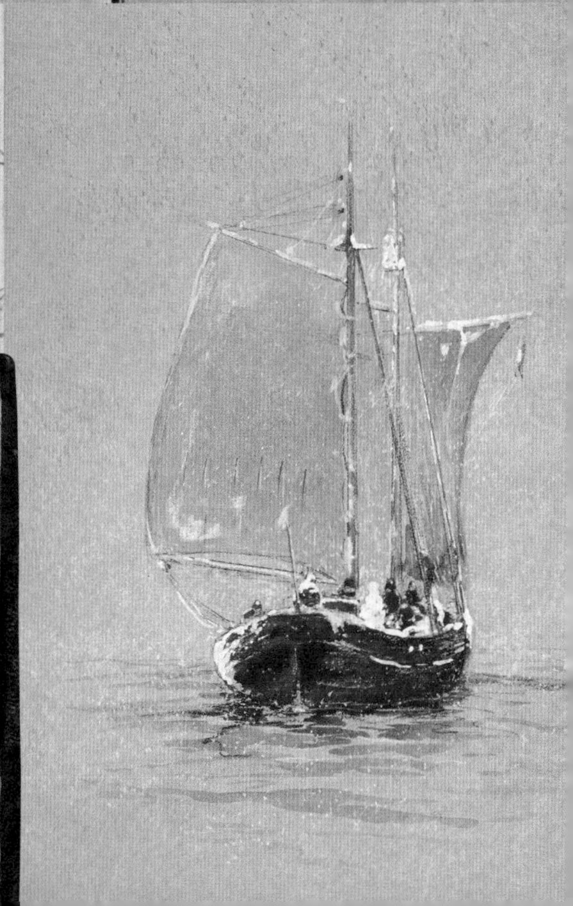

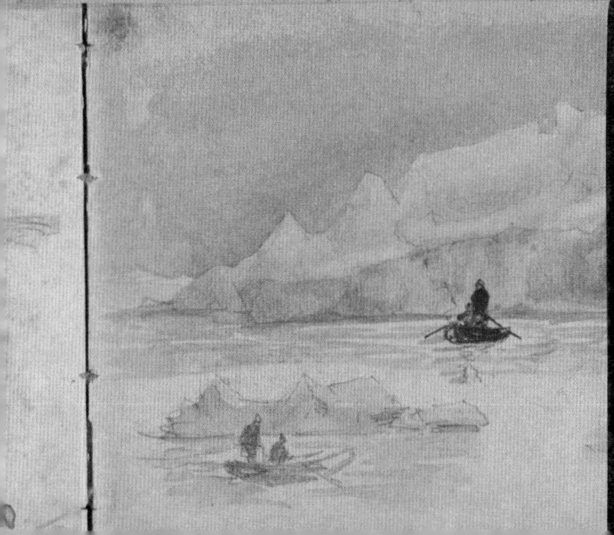

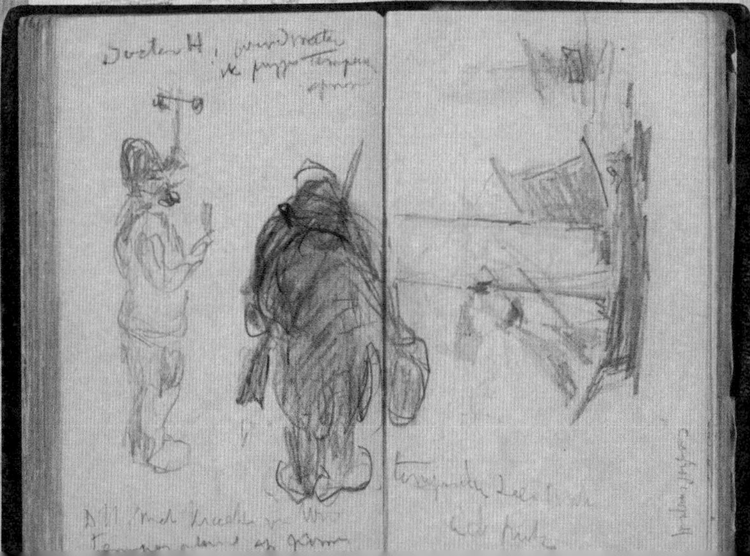

Many of Apol's paintings, engravings and studies
are held in the Rijksmuseum, Amsterdam. On these
and previous pages sketches from the 1880 voyage to
Novaya Zemlya give a glimpse of activities on board
ship, including testing wind speeds, 'our zoologist
Dr Hamaker doing his work' and a walrus hunter, as
well as numerous studies of ice and skies, which
formed the basis of later finished paintings.

SIGISMUND BACSTROM 1750–1808

A storm in high latitudes is so intensely cold …
as literally to tear the skin off the face.

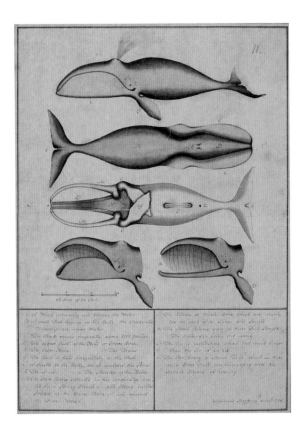

One of the earliest images of a whale in the archive of the Natural History Museum in London is a sketch by a little-known German surgeon, who later developed a passion for alchemy, translating hieroglyphics and trying to distil light from the Moon.

Sigismund Bacstrom lived most of his adult life either on a ship or in London. He first appears in the archival record in letters to the celebrated botanist Joseph Banks, offering him his services. Banks was planning to join James Cook's second Pacific voyage, but disagreements meant this did not happen. Having gathered equipment and personnel for a grand mission, Banks decided to make a trip northwards instead. He chartered the brig *Sir Lawrence* and sailed on 12 July 1772, the same day that Cook took his ships out of Plymouth Sound. With Banks came Bacstrom, now his personal secretary, as well as Swedish botanist Daniel Solander, Bavarian brothers James and John Müller as draughtsmen, a French cook, a gardener and a retinue of servants.

After leaving the service of Banks in 1775, Bacstrom attached himself for a few years to William Kent, ship's captain and part-time plant collector. Between 1780 and 1786 he then made four northern voyages to the fisheries as a merchant surgeon, and two expeditions to the West African coast and Jamaica on slave traders. He considered heading to Australia to gather specimens for botanical collectors, but instead helped Edward Shute to set up a 'Chymical' laboratory, where he was to make medicines. By 1789, however, Bacstrom's patron was dead, and he and his wife were reduced to selling their own clothes to pay the rent.

Bacstrom was eventually invited to join a commercial expedition to the Pacific, tasked with discovering 'valuable druggs and natural products'. The flotilla of three merchant ships sailed in 1791, with the unstated but obvious aim of challenging Spanish territorial claims to the fur-trading area around Nootka Sound on the northwest coast of North America. Banks also offered to pay Bacstrom for specimens: 'sixpence for each species of which there is either flowers or fruits & a shilling when there are both'.

The expedition began to unravel when it reached Nootka Sound, where its commander, William Brown, allowed his men to rob and kill some indigenous Nuu-chah-nulth. Bacstrom jumped ship, seeking asylum at the Spanish military camp. His efforts to get home proved an ordeal of epic proportions, first sailing on a Newcastle brig to Alaska, then an American fur trader to China, where he was stranded in Canton when the ship was seized as a war prize by the British. He found a bunk on an ex-East Indiaman, but the French crew mutinied near the Cape of Good Hope and Bacstrom was left for six months in a Mauritian jail.

It was here, it is believed, that he came to learn some secrets of the alchemic arts and joined a Masonic fraternity. He bought passage on an American ship bound for New York, but was again captured by the British Royal Navy and put ashore at the British Virgin Islands. He eventually returned to London in 1795, four years and eight months after he left, and supported himself for a while by selling sketches and prints from his rather eventful voyage around the globe.

Grove and
Hillocks
with Reeds
behind them.

here is a Wood.

ese Slaty Stones are
gularly shaped by
ature, as it is more
ccurately delineated
n the finished Drawing
f this Same View.
herefore this should
be condemned.

a large Rock
here.

Drawing
The finished ~~Sketch~~ is the most accurate
this should be condemned.

a View of Staaten Island with a Herd of Seals

Drawn on ☿ 22 March 1793

a double Canoe from the Sandwich Islands.

Even the greatest abilities will not exempt a man from the common lot of mortals, Death, and the casualties, perils, and disagreeable occurrences that may happen in the course of so long a Voyage.

Original Sketches after nature   £, 85,, 11,, 6
not framed.

1/ View of Cape Hoorn and Tierra del Fuego .   „ „ 5„
2/ Magdalena, one of the Marquesas Islands .   „ „ 5„
3/ 4/ Two new discovered Islands in the South Seas,
        situate under the Æquator, discovered by
        Capt. Marchal from Marseilles in 1796 .   „ 1„ 1„
5/ View of Oahoo, one of the Sandwich Islands,
        a finished Sketch .   „ „ 10„ 6
6/ Witlity Bay in the Island Oahoo .   „ „ 10„ 6
7/ 8/ 9/ Three views of the Island Oonehow .   „ „ 10„ 6
10/ View in Bocarelli Sound, an accurate Sketch
        in black lead pencil .   „ „ 5„
11/ View in Tattesko, or Hains's Cove .   „ „ 5„
12/ View of Two Indian Villages .   „ „ 5„
13/ View of an Indian Village in Norfolk Sound . „ „ 10„ 6
14/ Two Canoes of the Marquesas Islands .   „ „ 10„ 6
15/ a double Canoe of the Sandwich Islands .   „ „ 10„ 6
16/ a Nootka Canoe .   „ „ 5„
17/ Two Canoes of Juan de Fuca Straits .   „ „ 5„
18/ Bow and Arrow from Norfolk Sound .   „ „ 5„
19/ View of the Island Onrust near Batavia;
        an accurate Sketch in black lead pencil, .   „ „ 10„ 6
20/ a Chinese Jonk of 500 Ton ; in pencil .   „ „ 5„
21/ The American Sea plant in Colours .   „ „ 5„
22/ a Chinese Jonk of War of 600 Ton ;
        a finished drawing in Colours .   „ „ 10„ 6
23/ a Jonk or Chinese Craft which carries
        the Teas from Canton to Wampoo, to load
        the English East India men .   „ „ 10„ 6

                                            £, 93,, 17„ —

Page 28: Bacstrom's pioneering studies of a 'Greenland Right Whale', the bowhead or *Balaena mysticetus*, drawn in 1786.

Page 29: 'A View of Staaten Island with a Herd of Seals' - the Isla de los Estados, off the eastern extremity of Tierra del Fuego. Seal hunters had a short-lived factory camp here in 1787, which they abandoned after their ship was wrecked bringing in supplies. Bacstrom's voyage camped here in March 1792, clubbing seals and boiling their oil.

When finally back in England, Bacstrom made a list of some of his artworks (left), hoping to sell more paintings. Opposite is 'a double Canoe from the Sandwich Islands' sketched during his Pacific expedition in 1792. From Cape Horn north into the Pacific all went well, but off the northwest coast of modern-day Vancouver things started to fall apart. It would take Bacstrom over four years to get home.

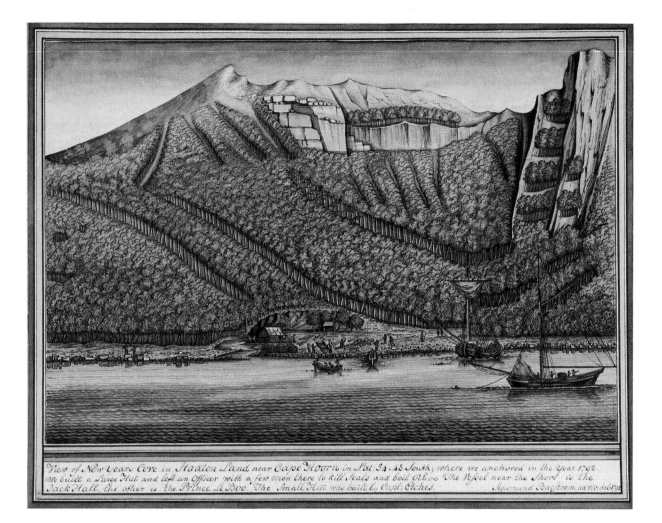

View of New Years Cove in Staaten Land near Cape Hoorn in Lat: 54.43 South; where we anchored in the Year 1792. We built a Large Hut and left an Officer with a few men there to kill Seals and boil Oil.— The Vessel near the Shore is the Jack Hall, the other is the Prince Le Boo. The Small Hut was built by Capt: Etches.   *Sigismund Bacstrom ad vid: del 1793*

The view of the Spanish fort at Friendly Cove, or Santa Cruz de Nuca, as it appeared to Bacstrom from the deck of the *Three Brothers* on 20 February 1793.

Opposite: sketches include a 'Chief of Nootka Sitting on the Ground'; 'A view of Cape St James, the 'southernmost part of the Q. Charlotte's Islands' and Magdalena Island, the 'Southermost of the Marquesas'. Bacstrom sketched the wife of Hatzia, a Haida chief, and her young son in Port Rose on 1 March 1793.

a Chief at Nootka sitting on the ground

N. 39.

those sides of the battlement a little darker

Highly finished Portraits of Indians
done after nature, not in frames.

1) Closa- Nanulth an Indian Chief at Nootka
2) Tchua a Chief of Queen Charlotte's Island
3) Tzachey a Chief in Norfolk Sound
4) Cunny-Ha a Chief on the North Side of
    Queen Charlotte's Island
5) Hatzia a Chief in Port-Rose, South-End
    of Queen Charlotte's Island and his Wife
6) The Wife of Hatzia at Port-Rose
7) Keels-Rist a Well known Indian Woman

Dark blue green

yellow green jade

JEANNE BARET 1740-1807

She dared confront the stress, the dangers, and everything that happened that one could realistically expect on such a voyage.

In April 1768, two French Navy ships lay at anchor off the coast of Tahiti. On the beach stood a lone woman, surrounded by Tahitian men. In fear she cried out for help. To the amazement of the officers, the woman was one of their own crew. 'They have discovered that the servant of Mr Commerson was a girl,' an observer remarked, 'who until now has been taken for a boy.' If this account is to be believed, Jeanne Baret had managed to keep her true identity concealed for nearly a year and a half, despite being in close-quarters with 115 officers and men aboard *Étoile*, the supply ship for Louis-Antoine de Bougainville's celebrated expedition – the first French scientific voyage around the world.

Baret had joined the expedition disguised as valet to her lover, botanist Philibert Commerson. She shared his cabin, an unusual practice for a servant, but the couple cited the crowded conditions on the ship. Suspicions soon arose, however. Baret was never seen to relieve 'himself' at the heads like other men. Vivès, the surgeon, noted the special care which Baret took of his master, which 'did not seem natural for a male servant'. Rumours circulated further when the expedition sailed on to the Equator and the crew stripped for the usual rituals of 'Crossing the Line', but Baret remained fully clothed. When confronted, she declared that she was a eunuch, which provoked such surprise and revulsion that she was not pressed further.

As the ships progressed to Brazil and through the Strait of Magellan, Commerson and Baret went ashore to collect specimens. Hindered with a leg injury, the naturalist had to rely on Baret to climb the steep and slippery escarpments to bring back plants for his collection, such as the vibrant tropical vine that would be named for the expedition's commander: *Bougainvillea*. Some of the crew referred to her as Commerson's 'beast of burden'.

Bougainville's crews suffered greatly from scurvy and malnutrition. By the time they reached New Guinea, the men were struggling to climb the rigging. The sick lay on makeshift beds of sailcloth and sacks; the stench below decks was unbearable; rats over-ran the ship. Baret endured every challenge and maintained her disguise. But eventually, her secret unravelled.

Though Bougainville wrote that her sex was revealed in Tahiti, four other narratives insist she was cornered and stripped by crew members in the New Hebrides, now Vanuatu. Bougainville allowed Baret to remain on board, despite this contravening his naval regulations. As luck would have it, Commerson was offered a position at the botanic garden of Pamplemousses in Île de France, now Mauritius. Baret, seven months pregnant, stayed with him. Commerson died four years later and Baret eventually secured a passage home. Arriving in La Rochelle in 1775, nine years after first setting sail, she became the first woman to have completed a circumnavigation of the globe. Her story revealed, Bougainville petitioned the Ministry of Marine for an annual pension for 'this extraordinary woman'.

The only known image of Baret is an engraving of 1816, in an Italian edition of Cook's voyages. Bougainville's expedition reached Tahiti, 'Nouvelle Cythere', in April 1768, and it was on the beach there that Baret's secret was revealed.

Navig. di Cook - Bougainville T. II. pag. 204.

Dall'Acqua inc.

MAD.^LLA BARÉ.

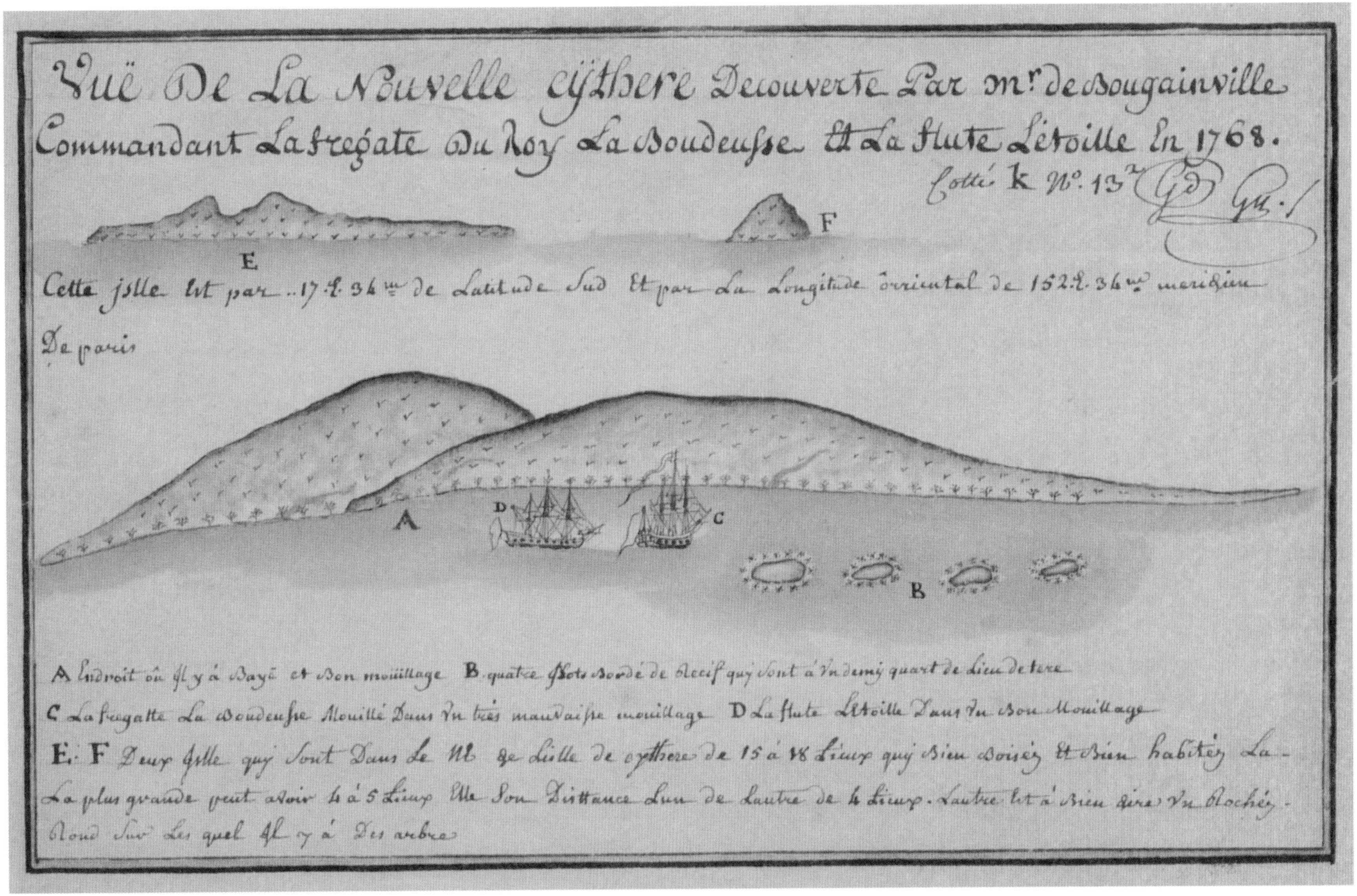

Vüe De La Nouvelle cijthere Decouverte Par Mr de Bougainville Commandant La Fregate Du Roy La Boudeusse Et La Flute L'etoille En 1768.

Cotté K No. 13

E

F

Cette jslle Lit par 17d 36m de Latitude Sud Et par La Longitude orriental de 152d 36m meridien De paris

A   D   C   B

A L'endroit ou jl y à Bayë et Bon mouillage   B. quatre jslots bordé de Recif quy Sont à Vn demj quart de Lieu de tere

C La fregatte La Boudeusse Mouillé Dans Vn très mauvaise mouillage   D La flute L'etoille Dans Vn bon Mouillage

E. F Deux jslle quy Sont Dans Le No de l'islle de cijthere de 15 à 18 Lieux quy Bien Boisé et Bien habité La La plus grande peut avoir 4 à 5 Lieux Vle Son Distance Lun de Lautre de 4 Lieux. Lautre Lit à Bien dire Vn Rochér Rond Sur Les quel jl y à Des arbres

EDWARD BARLOW 1642-1706

One of our men died as soon as he came aboard,
and another the next day, so that we had then
lost forty men since our coming from England.

Between 1550 and 1650 one in five ships was lost between Portugal and India, and it is estimated that sailors had a one in ten chance of dying on a voyage. Shipwrecks happened for many reasons, including the weather, but accurate logs and experience mattered a great deal. The Dutch and English trading route into the Indian Ocean led east from the Cape of Good Hope until reaching the correct longitude to turn north towards Indonesia. If ships sailed too far the reefs of Australia's western coast awaited them.

Edward Barlow was a mariner who faced many perils. His long career at sea began as apprentice to the master's mate on the warship *Naseby* in 1659, and he was aboard when Charles II was carried back from the Netherlands at the Restoration of the monarchy after the English Civil War. Barlow's first merchant voyage was to Barcelona, followed by Brazil in 1662, and he served as a seaman through the Second Anglo-Dutch War on *Monck*, surviving all the major engagements. In 1670 he made his first trip to the East Indies, sailing on the *Experiment*, but on a second voyage was captured by the Dutch. It was during his time imprisoned in Batavia (Jakarta) that he taught himself to write and began his journal, a narrative of his life which he updated on later voyages. It is probably the most important first-hand account of seafaring in the seventeenth century.

Barlow was transported back to Europe as a prisoner of war in 1674, and when in the Netherlands signed on the *Florentine* as a gunner for a voyage to Bergen. The ship was wrecked on the Goodwin Sands in August 1675 and Barlow,

who like most sailors was rather superstitious, claimed the disaster was caused by Norwegian witches with whom the crew had quarrelled. But he managed to swim ashore. Undeterred, he continued to serve on other merchantmen, voyaging to the Mediterranean and across to Jamaica, eventually becoming chief mate.

In a rare period ashore in 1678 Barlow got married, but was soon at sea again. First to the East Indies in *Delight*, followed by another decade's worth of trading voyages in many ships, and also volunteering in the English navy aboard *Royal Sovereign*. He later returned to England in the frigate *Kingfisher* from St Helena. In June 1705 he finally achieved his life's ambition of becoming a captain, gaining command of the East Indiaman *Liampo* for a voyage to Mocha in the Red Sea. The ship sailed from Portsmouth on 7 January 1706, but was lost off Mozambique, Barlow with it. This time he had left his journal with his wife, which is how it survived to tell his remarkable story.

Barlow began writing and decorating his journal
when taken prisoner in the Dutch East Indies,
and continued it when safely back in England.
The pages here show *Experiment* losing its mast in
a storm, a view of Dutch Batavia and an array of
sea 'foules', bonito, flying fish and a hammerhead
shark. Elsewhere, Barlow detailed a shark attack,
'the Most Ravenous fish that Swimes in the Sea'.

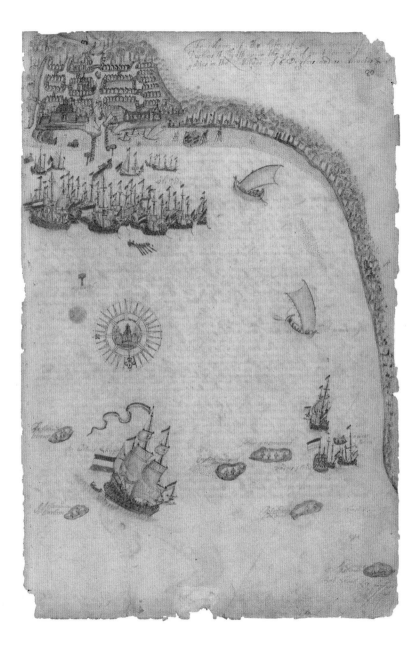

FRANCIS BEAUFORT 1774–1857

Hereafter I shall estimate the force of the wind
according to the following scale …

Mention the name Beaufort today and many people, in Britain at least, think of his wind scale. Among sailors, and hydrographers in particular, it is revered with an admiration that borders on awe. More than a thousand new charts were issued during Beaufort's time at the Admiralty, opening fresh areas of the world to settlement and trade, and saving an infinite number of lives and ships.

Born in County Meath, Ireland, Beaufort was the son of a wealthy heiress and a Protestant clergyman with a passion for cartography. Rejected by a school in England on the grounds that his Irish accent would corrupt the speech of the other boys, he was sent instead to a marine academy in Dublin. In 1789 he joined the East Indiaman *Vansittart*, bound for Indonesia, as an officer in training. Surveying the Gaspar Strait, the ship was wrecked but Beaufort survived. Returning to England he was mobilized for war against France, and was wounded in the Mediterranean while storming the Spanish ship *San Josef*. Having received sixteen musket shots and three sabre wounds to head and arms, he was lucky to be alive, and deserved his promotion to commander.

Returning to active service, Beaufort became captain in 1810. When at leisure, he spent his days taking soundings and bearings and measuring shorelines. At night he perfected methods of astronomical observation to better determine longitude and latitude. It was during these years that Beaufort developed the first versions of his 'Wind Force Scale', which he was to use in his journals throughout his life.

In 1829, on the brink of retirement, Beaufort became the Hydrographer of the Admiralty and held the post for the next twenty-six years. Considering he still carried a lead ball in his chest, had been knocked down by a runaway post office van, was deaf and survived a heart attack at his desk, he was still surprisingly active. He transformed what was essentially a storage depot into the finest surveying institution in the world, encouraging his surveyors to excellence and publishing their charts. Many are still used today, over 150 years after they were created.

Beaufort also took over the administration of the observatories at Greenwich and the Cape of Good Hope, and helped found the Royal Geographical Society. He established weather recording as a science and encouraged the development of the first tide tables. Numerous pioneering maritime endeavours benefited from his support, including James Clark Ross' expedition to Antarctica and Robert FitzRoy's circumnavigation in *Beagle*, on which the young Charles Darwin followed Beaufort's mantra to keep his eyes open to the world. Beaufort's name has been inked on the chart too: the Beaufort Sea in the Arctic, inlets in Western Australia and North Carolina, and a remote island in the Antarctic, home to a colony of penguins.

Beaufort kept weather diaries for much of his
career and created the Beaufort Scale in 1806 while
in command of HMS *Woolwich*. He revised his scale
in 1807 to the more familiar 12 forces, with the
strongest described as 'hurricane'. By the 1830s
he was still keeping an intricately detailed weather
log, here with marbled papers and a printed key.

… as nothing can convey a more uncertain idea of wind and weather than the old expression of moderate and cloudy etc.

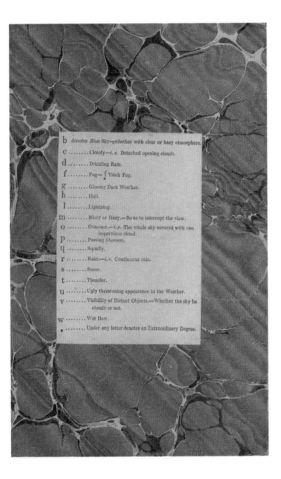

Scale of Wind.

1. Light air — Or that which will enable a Man of War to Steer.
2. Light breeze — Or that which will carry a Man of War with all Sail set 3 or 4 knots
3. Gentle breeze — d°. . . d°. . . . d°. . . . 4 or 5
4. Moderate breeze — d°. . . d°. . . . d°. . . . 5 or 6
5. Fresh breeze — Or that to which whole T. G⁴. Royals, Fly. jib, & Stay. May be carried full & by.
6. Stiff breeze — Or that, when 1 reef T. G⁴. Jib & Driver would be carried by a wholesome frigate, when fairly pressed in chase by the wind.
7. Moderate Gale — Or that to which the same Ship would carry 2 reefs T. & Jib.
8. Fresh Gale — Or that when same Ship could barely carry Courses & Treble reefd T.
9. Strong Gale — Or that when a well conditioned frigate would beat off a lee shore with reefd Courses, & close reefd T.⁵ & M.⁵ Sails.
10. Whole Gale — Or that, in which a Man of War could shew no other canvas than Storm Stay Sails
11. Storm — Or that which would blow away any Sail made in the usual way
12. Hurricane — — Hurricane!

Key to Weather Column.

b. Blue Sky	h. Hazy.	t. Thunder
f. Fair	l. Lightning.	w. Watery Sky
c. Clear horizon, objects visible afar	p. Passing clouds	thr. Threatening appearance
cl. Cloudy	r. Rain	
da. Damp atmosphere	sr. Small rain	
dk. Dark weather	hr. Heavy rain	
dr. Drizzling rain	sh. Showery	
fg. Fog	sq. Squally	
gl. Gloomy dark weather	hsq. Hard Squalls	
gr. Greasy	hsh. Heavy Showers	

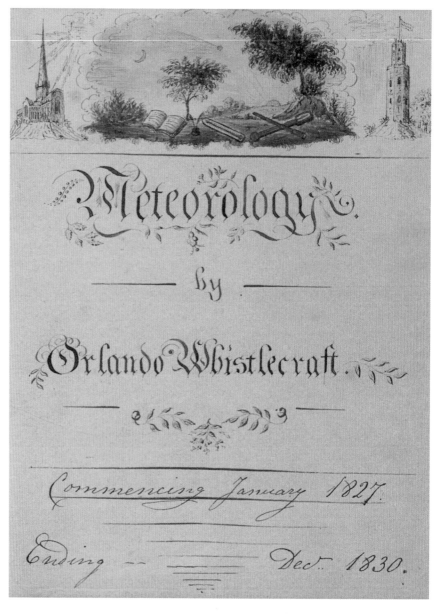

'The Beaufort Scale Revised, 1906' (opposite left), by George Simpson. A meteorologist and explorer, Simpson extended the observations from sea to land. He later set up one of the first meteorological stations in Antarctica during Captain Scott's ill-fated expedition. Another notable early meteorologist was Orlando Whistlecraft, who kept regular journals and produced annual weather almanacs (opposite right).

Beaufort was a talented artist and some of his journals are filled with meticulous sketches of natural specimens. He drew this scorpionfly (*Panorpa coa*) while exploring the classical ruins of southern Anatolia in 1812, before being shot in the hip by a 'mob of fanatical Turks'. It was published as an engraving in his book *Karamania*.

CHARLES BENSON 1830–1881

The sea is like glass, birds are flying all around us,
it seems as though we & the birds were all alone
in the world, every thing is so still and lonely.

'What a miserable life a Sea fareing life is', lamented Charles Benson in his journal in 1862, 'I will stop it if I live.' Yet, despite this, he worked on merchant ships for more than two decades, determined to make a better life for his loved ones. Sometimes he was away at sea for fifty weeks of a year. But Benson faced challenges beyond homesickness and heartache, storm or shipwreck, especially when it came to his status with officers and crew. In nineteenth-century America thousands of black men served on ships, but their stories are little told and their contributions to maritime life rarely acknowledged.

Raised in rural Massachusetts, Benson was the great-great-grandson of slaves. Though his grandfather was a veteran of the American Revolution, even as a free black man in the North, Benson's prospects were limited. He had hoped for a career as a shoemaker, but after his first marriage failed he moved to the port city of Salem resolving to become a mariner and a good Christian. His career at sea began some-time in the 1850s, first as a cook and later as ship's steward.

As steward, Benson was spared the dangerous duties of a regular sailor – such as going aloft in fierce weather to reef the sails or loading cargo in blistering tropical heat – but his work was still demanding. He was in constant contact with the officers, serving their meals and tending to their needs, mostly helping the captain dress and shave each morning, scrubbing his quarters and dealing with laundry. As such, he was cut off from the sailors, but neither did he share the rank of the officers. As keeper of the ship's stores, he also had to bear daily grumbles about the food. Benson spent most

evenings alone in his cabin, or perhaps smoking a pipe in the galley with the cook, often the only other black man aboard. On occasion he baked apple pies or his favourite 'Sugar Cakes', also the pet name he gave his new wife, Jennie, whom he adored and missed greatly. The pictures of pretty girls pasted into the pages of his journals were meagre comfort.

In 1879 he was steward on *Glide*, which left Boston in March for Tamatave, now Toamasina, on Madagascar's eastern coast, with a hold laden with bales of brown cotton. Benson wrote in his diary each night before falling asleep, noting co-ordinates and the day's weather, sometimes describing shipboard tasks or the ailments of the crew, to whom he administered medicines. He is by turns upbeat, downcast, hopeful and lonely. *Glide* was back in Boston in time for Christmas, but shipped out once more before the year was through. 'Here I am again upon the Wild Ocean', Benson inked in his diary the night they left. 'Well it is for the best I think.' When he passed away at sea a couple of years later, his darling Jennie did as countless sailors' wives did: she carried on alone, even as their children died one by one. She was a widow for forty years.

Benson left Boston on the bark *Glide*, bound for the Indian Ocean in 1879. 'Comfort was there any comfort any time, or anywhere at sea? I cannot really say I ever did see any. It is the excitement, danger and money that a sea life brings that keeps me at sea, nothing else.' The pages of his journal are filled with images of saucy women and actresses in their stage-show fashions, clipped from illustrated periodicals.

... everything is quiet, the captain & mates are reading, the sailors are either reading, sewing, or asleep, and you can hear nothing but the rush of water past the vessel & the snapping & creaking of ropes & timbers.

Wednesday Aug 20th   Current East
          Latt 4°17 Long 46°21' Ther 75° Barom 30°12
          Wind S. SSE.   Course S W½ W. WSW. ENE.
   Came in with a moderate breeze & partialy, cloudy,
squally weather. There is a heavy sea running.
People overhauling Blocks, rigging, &c. Opened a
BBl of flour. 2d Mate found a leak in the deck rott-
ing the hides. Captain set the Mate at work putting
peices in the deck. 8 Pm brisk breeze & heavy sea
I am home sick, & want to get home. 159 days out

Thursday Aug 21   Current N W 19 miles
          Latt 5°03 Long 47°00 Ther 75° Barom 30.10
          Wind S. SSE   Course 2NE. SW. SW½W.
   Came in with a brisk breeze, & partialy cloudy
weather. 7 Am looks, squally all around. Noon
pleasant. 1½ Pm rain squall, with stiff breeze.
3 Pm 2d mate caught a porpoise. Captain came
near falling down fore hatch. The Boy Wallace's
eyes dont seem to gain much. All our men are
very dirty in their habits. they wash but seldom.
& then mostly about the head and neck. they have
plenty lice & Bedbugs in the forecastle. 160 days from
                              home

owards Magunga

20 miles
Barom 30°10'
rse S W½. S W ¼ W
tialy cloudy weather
ote trying to stop a
to scrub ship.
running sails. Mate
partition between
t has been long
t into execution
y through the car
61 days from home

N W 40 miles
75° Barom 30°10
Course S W. SSE. E ¼ S.
breeze & passing.
p. Mate at work
wind very light.
ny like fun. hens
most every day.
els "polar." I dont
2 days from home

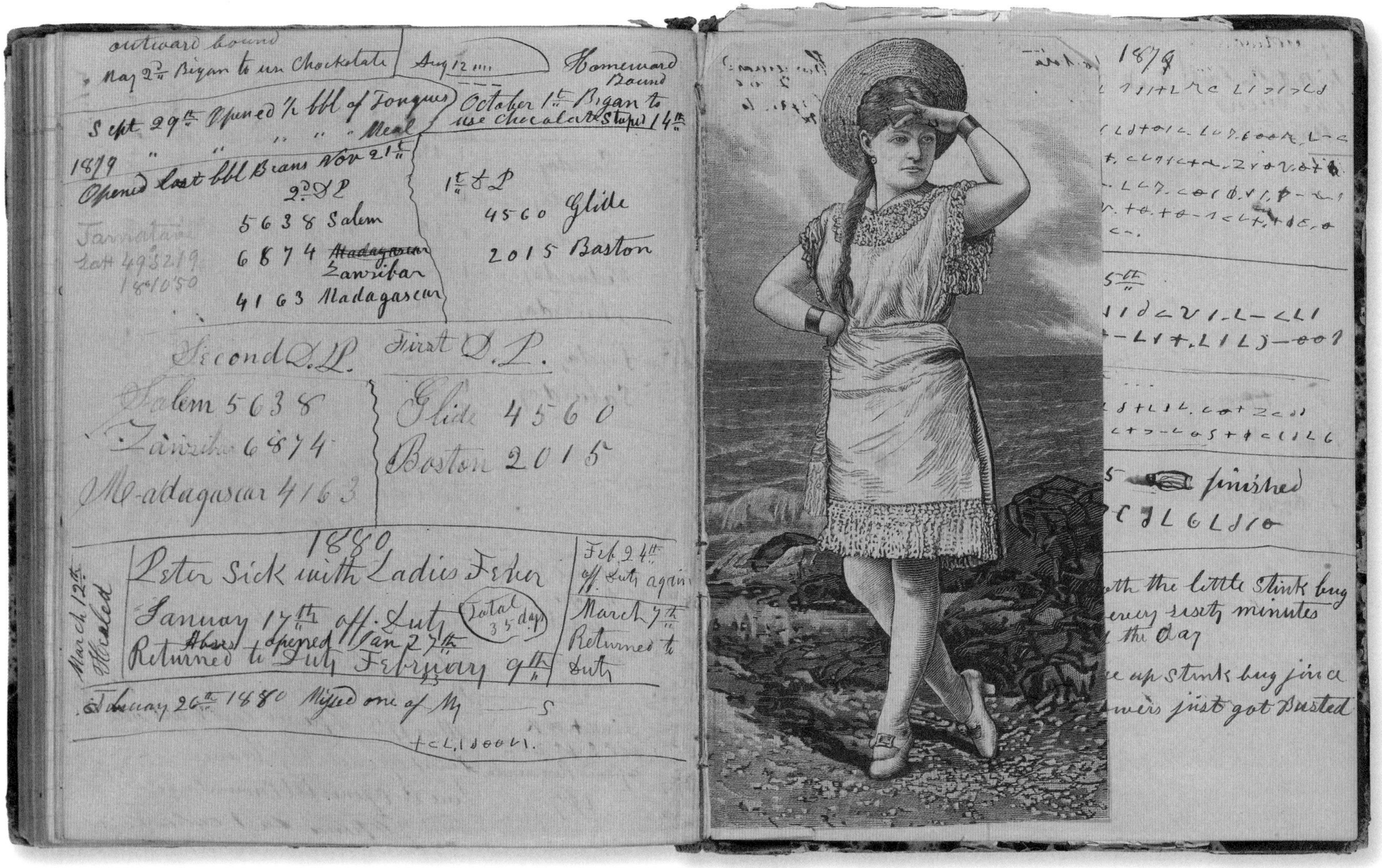

outward bound
May 2nd Began to use Chocolate | Aug 12 ... | Homeward Bound
Sept 29th Opened ½ bbl of Tongues | October 1st Began to use chocolate Stop 14th
1879 " " " Meal
Opened last bbl Beans Nov 21st

2d & P | 1st & P
5 6 3 8 Salem | 4 5 6 0 Glide
Tamatave 6 8 7 4 Zanzibar | 2 0 1 5 Baston
Lat 49°32'19 4 1 6 3 Madagascar
16°10'50

Second S.P. | First S.P.
Salem 5 6 3 8 | Glide 4 5 6 0
Zanzibar 6 8 7 4 | Boston 2 0 1 5
Madagascar 4 1 6 3

1880
Peter Sick with Ladies Fever | Feb 24th off Duty again
January 17th off Duty Total 35 day | March 7th Returned to Duty
March 12th Healed Absent opened Jan 27th Returned to Duty February 9th
February 26th 1880 Missed one of My ___ S

1879

5th finished

with the little stink bug every sixty minutes the day
up stink bug since wiers just got Busted

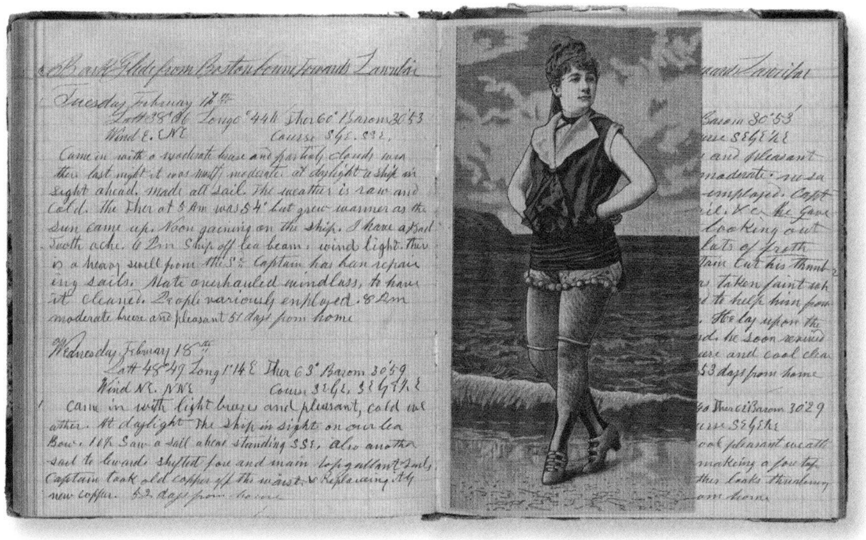

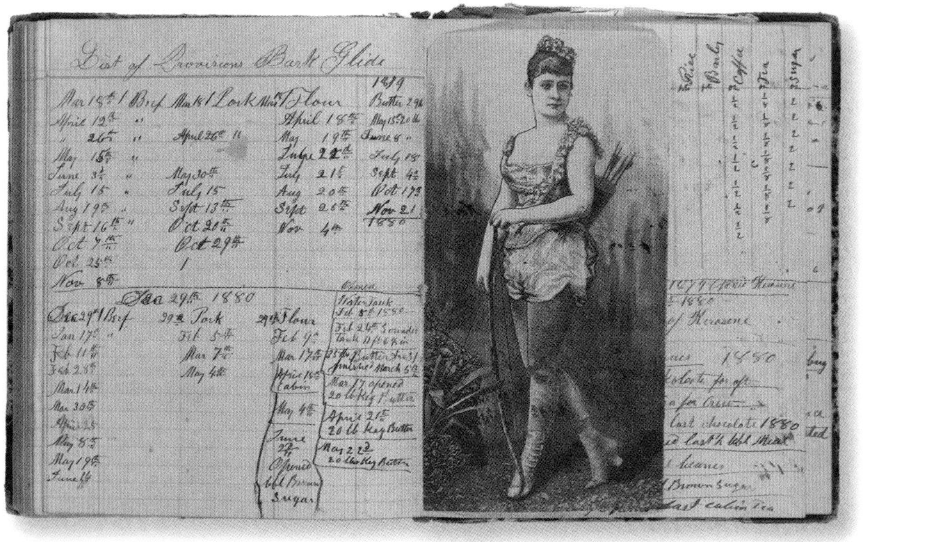

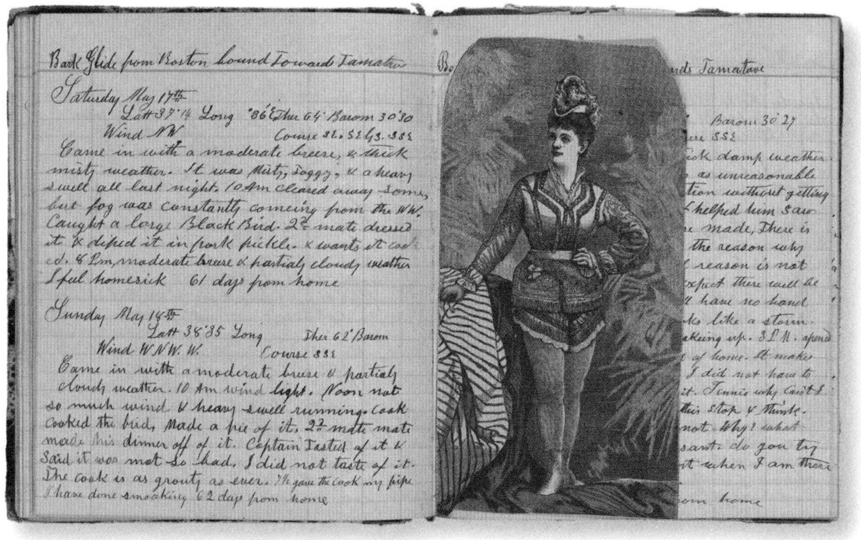

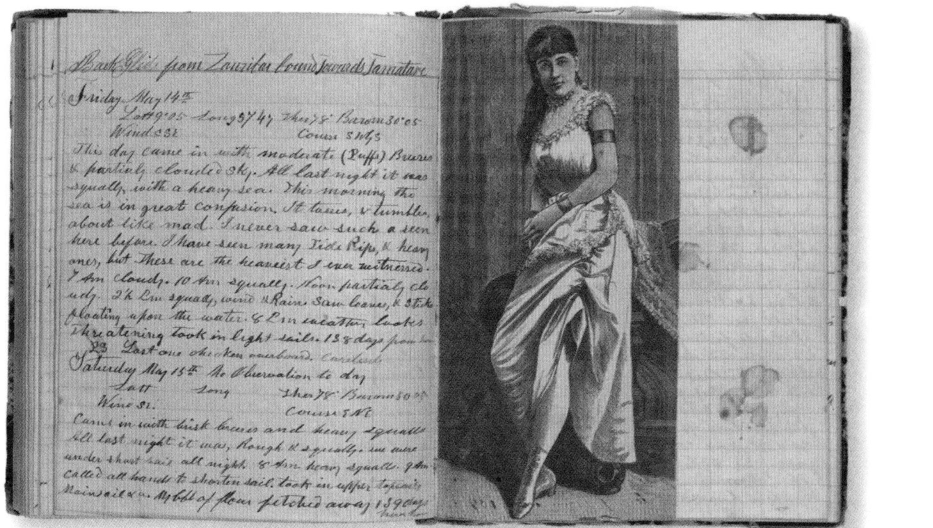

PETER BLAKE 1948–2001

I think everyone really needs to understand that
we are a part of the environment, not apart from it.

Blake's log for the Whitbread Round the World Race
on maxi-yacht *Lion*. Leg 3 became a race against
time after they hit a whale.

On 1 April 1994 thousands lined the quayside in Brest, northwestern France, to cheer as a yacht came in. Peter Blake, skipper of *Enza*, has just circumnavigated the world with his friend Robin Knox-Johnston. In 74 days and 22 hours they had also become the fastest men to do it, winning the coveted Jules Verne Trophy. Charismatic New Zealander Blake was a man born for the sea and his achievements are without equal. In a thirty-year career he won every significant bluewater race and then turned his attention to the cause of conservation with characteristic tenacity, integrity and passion.

Blake grew up on the northern flanks of Auckland's Waitemata Harbour. His father was a gunboat captain in the Royal Navy during the Second World War, who encouraged his children to grow up with the sea as their playground. When Blake was eight his father built him a single-handed wooden dinghy: *Pee Bee* was launched with due ceremony, lemonade instead of champagne. Other boats soon followed, each larger and faster, including *Bandit*, a boat he built himself.

Blake's horizons widened. He competed in five Whitbread round the world races, and in his last, in 1990, he skippered the ketch *Steinlager 2* to an unprecedented clean sweep, with overall honours on each of the six legs. He led New Zealand to successive victories in the America's Cup, the first non-American team successfully to defend this most prestigious sailing prize. Before every big event, his wife Pippa would give him a new pair of socks for luck. On Christmas Eve in 1994 it was a red pair. He wore them for the first race, which they won, and after that red socks were worn

throughout. Later in the campaign, Blake's personal talisman became a national obsession. As the black boats swept to victory in San Diego, New Zealanders were buying red socks by the thousands.

In 1997, Blake became the Cousteau Society's head of expeditions and skipper of the schooner *Antarctic Explorer*, which he later bought and renamed *Seamaster*. Soon afterwards he was made special envoy for the UN Environment Programme and began planning voyages to monitor ocean pollution. On 6 December 2001, *Seamaster* was anchored at the mouth of the Amazon when she was boarded at night by a gang of pirates. Blake was shot in the back as he rushed to help his crew and died shortly afterwards. He is buried at Warblington churchyard, near Emsworth on the south coast of England. His headstone bears the words of John Masefield's poem *Sea Fever*: 'I must down to the sea again, to the lonely sea and the sky, and all I ask is a tall ship and a star to steer her by.'

Opposite: On his voyage in *Seamaster* from Auckland
to South America in 2001, Blake was tragically killed
by pirates; this is his final logbook.

DATE	TUESDAY 28ᵗʰ Nov		NOON POS'N	49°52S 117°20W		DAY'S RUN 195

TIME	COURSE		GPS		BARO	WIND		SEA	EXT	SEA
	REQ'D	STR'D	LAT	LONG		SPD TRUE	DIR TRUE	STATE	AIR C°	C°
0200	100/110	105	49°31'S	119°25W	1007	12	270°	SLIGHT	7°C	
0300		105	49°35'S	119°13'W	1005	15	270	"		
0400		105	49°35'S	118°59W	1005	14	250	SLIGHT	7°C	
0500		106	49°37'S	118°47W	1005	8	250	SLIGHT	6°C	
0600		102	49°39'	118°34W	1006	8	250	"	6°C	4°C
0700		108	49°41'S	118°23W	1006	12	250	"	7°C	
0800		104	49°45'	118°07	1005	15	300	"	"	
0900		103	49°46'S	117°59W	1005	12	270	"	7°C	
1000										
1100		110	49°50S	117°31	1004	14	W	"	8°C	
1200		110	49°52S	117°20'	1003	18	W	"	6°C	
1300		073	49°50S	117°10W	1002	18	W	SLIGHT	9°C	
1400		060	49°48'S	117°01W	1002	20	W	SLIGHT	9°C	
1500		065	49°45'S	116°51W	1002	25	W	SLIGHT		
1600		065	49°41'S	116°39W	1002	19	W	SLIGHT	8°C	
1700		087	49°38'S	116°28W	1001	20	NW	"	8°C	
1800		070	49°35'S	116°16W	1002	15/20	300	"	9°C	
1900		060	49°33'S	116°07W	1002	15/20	270	"	7°C	
2000		059	49°27'S	115°59W	1002	20	270	"	"	
2100		140	49°30S	115°51W	1003	13	240	"	7°C	
2200		093	49°31'S	115°58	1003	19	260	"	7°C	
2300		085	49°30S	115°35	1003	20	250	"	6°C	
2400		105	49°52'S	115°34	1003	20	260	"	6°C	

Engines / Generators A02

ENGINES		GENERATORS		REMARKS
ON	OFF	ON	OFF	
✓			✓	STARRY NIGHT — LITTLE WIND — GLOW IN SOUTH AS SUN TRAVELS JUST BELOW HORIZON.
✓			✓	
✓			✓	COOL, CRISP, CLEAR MORNING. IT IS A HARD LIFE
✓			✓	PASTEL ORANGE SKY. ALL IS WELL
✓		#2 0700	✓	Looks like Engines today
✓		✓		Large Wandering Albatross. 50 degree sth is Elusive. Generator started — Watermaker on — bunkering in progress
✓		✓		All go this shift.
✓				→ Wind swinging NW with approaching rain
✓		✓		Michael takes a sextant shot at 10AM — Like the Canadian election — still waiting for results.
✓		✓		
✓		✓		1330 Sails up. Single reef in main + foresail
off	✓	✓		Headsail rolled out. Engine stopped. Bliss.
	✓	✓		Janet Dangling around in the rigging
	✓	✓		
	✓	✓		
	✓	✓		This 50° line is elusive. On watch end it appears we have bounced off + heading NE. Will try again soon. The wind is failing us 19:40hrs
	✓	✓		
	✓	✓		17:45 Guest Chef dinner in progress Michael/Sean
✓		✓	2115	Jibe/Jibe Adjust sails — Start M/E Motor Sail — Poor Winds
✓		✓		Rain squall — increase in wind speed w/squall.
✓		✓		
✓		✓		More Rain Wind up + down w/the squalls.

TOTAL ENGINE HOURS THIS PAGE

WILLIAM BLIGH 1754–1817

The little rum I had was of great service to us; when our nights were particularly distressing, I generally served a teaspoonful.

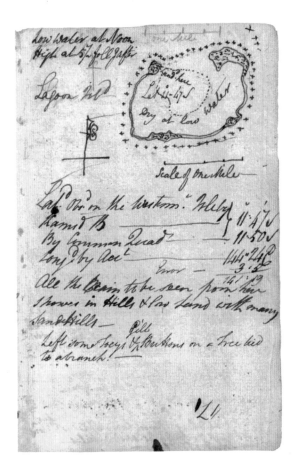

As day broke it was done. The ship's commander was dragged from his bunk at the point of a cutlass, his hands bound behind his back. In the early light the mutineers gathered on the *Bounty*'s deck and there he stood in his nightshirt, held captive in a circle of bayonets. The ship's launch was hoisted and nineteen men were forced into the open boat. Soon they were cast adrift on the wide ocean, with a small amount of bread, water and rum; no charts to guide their course; no firearms should they manage a landfall on hostile shores. It was 28 April 1789, a day that would haunt William Bligh for the rest of his life.

His name has become a byword of maritime villainy, shorthand for severity of command at sea and a sadistic bully of monstrous proportions. The lead mutineer – and his former friend – Fletcher Christian, in contrast, is the romantic hero standing up for a long-suffering crew, a rebel resisting injustice, since rewritten in novels and re-enacted by Hollywood heart-throbs including Clark Gable and Marlon Brando.

And yet, seek the truth more carefully and an able, decent and admirable man emerges, rather than the tyrannous, cruel Bligh. Though his people skills were surely lacking – his 'bad language' and 'violent tornados of temper' aroused opposition – his navigational expertise is indisputable and he showed great courage at sea and in battle. In leading that open boat on its 5,800-km (3,600-mile) journey to safety in the Dutch East Indies, and in finding justice for his loyal companions, Bligh deserves more praise than the caricature would allow.

Bligh was an experienced sailor, having joined the navy at just seven years old as cabin boy on the battleship *Monmouth*.

He rose through the ranks and at the age of twenty-three was selected by James Cook on his third voyage to explore the northern Pacific to be the master of *Resolution*. Bligh was also tasked with 'constructing charts ... and drawing plans of bays and harbours'. When Cook was killed by Hawaiian islanders, it was Bligh who navigated the expedition home.

During the American War of Independence and the Anglo-Dutch conflicts, Bligh fought in several major sea battles. In peacetime he returned on other ships to his original *Bounty* mission of transporting breadfruit plants from Tahiti to the West Indies, where it was hoped the crop could be grown to feed the slaves cultivating cotton that would help increase British trade with Asia (see also p. 256).

Bligh continued his naval career, fighting bravely at the Battle of Camperdown in 1797, capturing a Dutch flag vessel and one of their admirals. Horatio Nelson praised Bligh's actions during the Battle of Copenhagen in 1801. His reputation for strength secured him the role of Governor of New South Wales in turbulent times, and though he was later deposed in a rebellion, he continued to advance in rank, becoming Vice Admiral of the Blue. And yet, for all this, it is likely that the notorious mutiny, one fateful morning, will forever define him.

The original notebook from the epic survival voyage in the *Bounty*'s launch. Despite all the hardships, Bligh still found time to chart part of the coast of Australia. The little notebook had previously belonged to midshipman Hayward, who had it in his pocket when they were forced into the open boat.

Right: Bligh compiled a list of 'Pirates', describing each mutineer's physical appearance in detail, including 'Fletcher Christian. Aged 24 years, 5 feet 9 in. high. Dark swarthy complexion.' Copies were later forwarded from Batavia to Lord Cornwallis, then Governor-General of India, at Calcutta, and to Governor Philips, at New South Wales, to provide evidence when tracking the outlaws down.

Above: Bligh transposed entries from the notebook 'into my fair Journal every day when the weather would admit' and, incredibly, also sketched profiles of the coasts they encountered, here 'Restoration Island'.

Cannoe of Whytootackee – discovered by H.M.S. Bounty

In 1791 Bligh returned to the Pacific in command of the ships *Providence* and *Assistant*, and this time succeeded in bringing breadfruit to the West Indies. On these and the following pages are some of his beautiful sketches from this second voyage: 'Cannoe of Whytootackee'; 'Oeeree of Otaheite'; 'Mow Tommattah or Bonnet Shark of Maheite 4 feet long'; 'The small blue Paroquet of Otaheite called Aiwinnee' and other birds from Van Diemen's Land (Tasmania), and 'A Dolphin six feet long' and 'A Pilot fish the size of life'.

Oeeree of Otaheite

More Tommattah – or Bonnet Shark of Otahiete 4 feet long.

The small blue Paroquet of Otahite called Aivinnee

J H

Male

Female

Van Diemans Land

A Dolphin six feet long.

A Pilot Fish the size of Life

Large Parraquet of Van Diemans Land

A Gull of Van Diemans Land

ELSE BOSTELMANN 1882–1961

Hesitantly, step by step, I went downward,
thrilled with the expectancy of the vast unknown.

Wearing her favourite red bathing suit, artist Else Bostelmann stepped on to the long metal ladder suspended from the expedition launch anchored off Bermuda, and climbed down into the sea, gripping the iron chains as she swayed back and forth. A copper diving helmet rested heavily on her shoulders before she was submerged, and through its glass window she could see the coastline of her island home. Beneath her was a valley of white sand, swaying sea-plumes and purple sea-fans. 'I had descended to fairyland,' she later wrote, 'six fathoms below the surface.'

Spellbound, she drew the life forms around her, using a steel pin on a zinc engraver's plate. Trying to capture everything underwater was tricky and she had to be careful not to tip her head in case her helmet tumbled off and with it her oxygen supply, but again and again she returned to the sea-floor. On subsequent dives an iron music stand was lowered to the seabed, on which she tied a canvas and a lead-weighted palette daubed with oil paint. Her brushes floated with their wooden handles upright, tugging lightly at their strings.

German-born, Bostelmann had immigrated to America shortly after her marriage to the concert cellist Monroe Bostelmann. With Monroe's career failing, the couple moved to Texas where he became a cotton grower, but later died of exhaustion. Devastated, Else moved to New York and supported herself and her daughter as a freelance illustrator. Her fortunes changed in 1929 when she showed some of her pen and ink sketches to William Beebe, the director of tropical research at the New York Zoological Society. She was hired on the spot for his expeditions, and for several seasons her home would be Nonsuch Island, Bermuda. Her primary task would be to record in detail the underwater specimens Beebe hoped to discover.

A pioneer in exploration, William Beebe became internationally famous for deep-sea dives with his colleague, engineer Otis Barton, in the 'Bathysphere'. Caught in the bathysphere's spotlight, a strange undersea world was revealed. Connected to the ship via a telephone line, Beebe described his observations to ichthyologist Gloria Hollister above, who methodically transcribed every word (p. 146). Wherever possible, specimens were taken up to the surface for further study. In her paintings, Bostelmann skilfully brought them back to life.

Hundreds of scientific illustrations, sketches and paintings were created in Bermuda, many of which were featured in magazines such as *National Geographic*. A prolific artist, Bostelmann later also illustrated children's books and created textile designs and wallpaper, as well as murals for private yachts. But her fantastical depictions of 'otherworldly chimeras' and bioluminescence would be her best – images that helped open the eyes of a generation to the wonders of the deep.

Opposite left: Bostelmann entitled this watercolour she painted off Bermuda in 1934 'Big Bad Wolves of an Abyssal Chamber of Horrors'. Her arresting depictions of marine life ranged from delicate corals to what can only be described as sea monsters.

Opposite right: In the quiet darkness of the depths of the ocean, two massive fish encircle Beebe's bathysphere. Bostelmann painted this scene from his dramatic descriptions and gave it the title 'Bathysphaera intacta'.

Overleaf: The specimens on Bostelmann's table 'vary from one foot in length to the dimensions of a pea - or less', from tiny fish to nudibranch sea slugs. She also wrote that 'The first time I was confronted by the scaleless, silvery or jet black fish, my curiosity quickly gave way to enthusiasm.' *Saccopharynx harrisoni* was drawn off Bermuda in 1931.

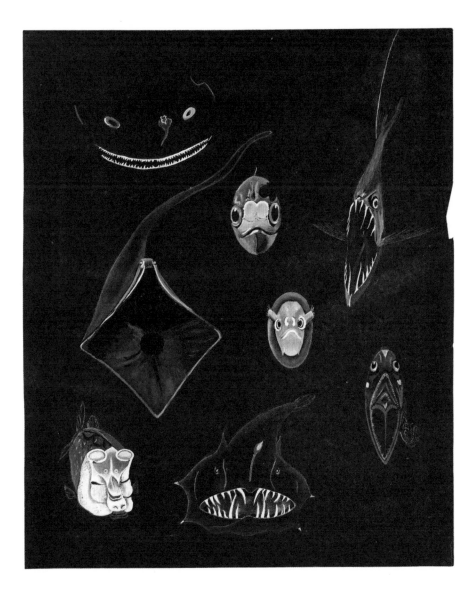

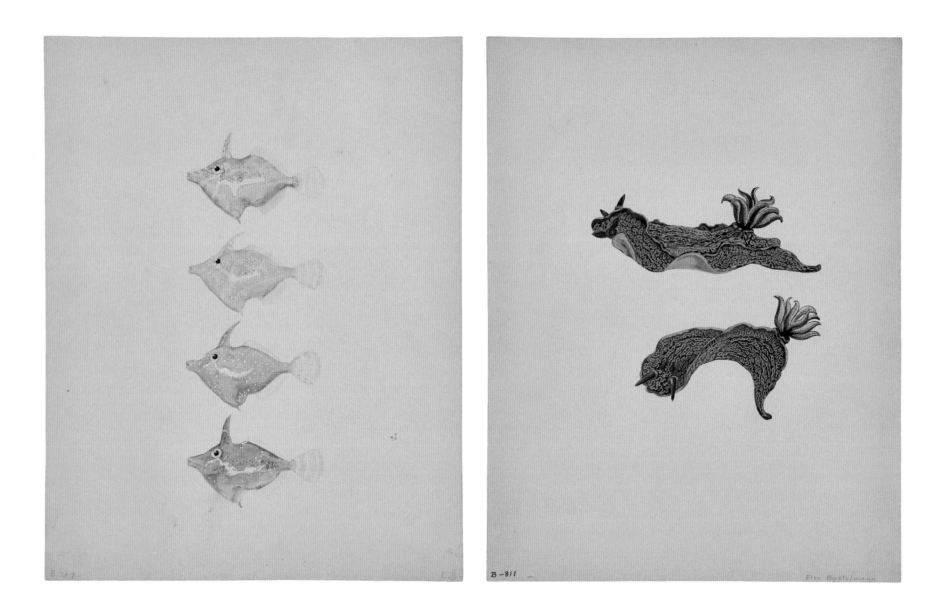

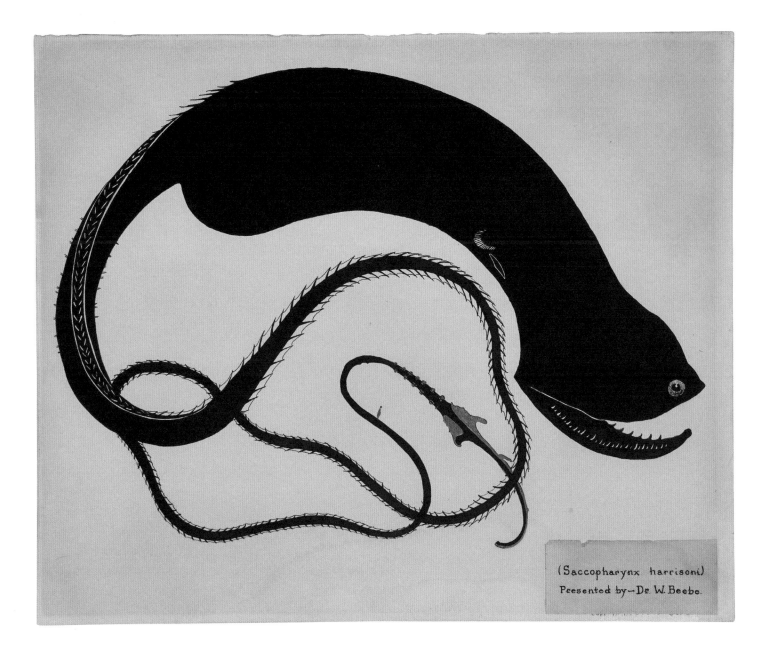

(Saccopharynx harrisoni)
Presented by—Dr. W. Beebe.

JUST DIVE IN

Robin Knox-Johnston

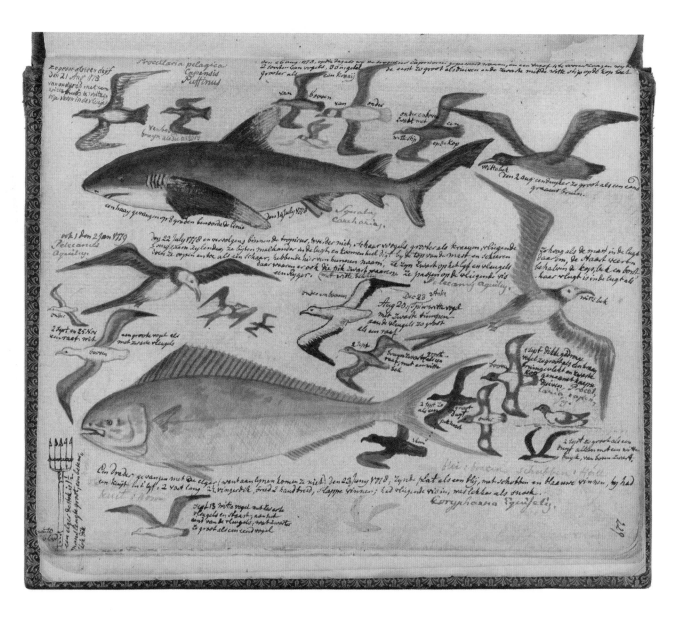

We shall go, always a little further: it may be,
Beyond that last blue mountain barred with snow,
Across that angry or that glimmering sea.
JAMES ELROY FLECKER, 1922

Opposite: All manner of sea creatures - a great white shark, pompano dolphinfish, and countless birds - are found in the journal of intrepid Dutch clergyman Jan Brandes. He left Europe for the East Indies in 1778.

Overleaf: Knox-Johnston kept his first sea journal when a marine cadet. Many years later, shown here on his table at home in Portsmouth, are the diary and log from his celebrated voyage in Suhaili. It was the first time anyone had sailed single-handed and non-stop around the world.

I had no one to look out for sharks. It's a problem when you're sailing solo. It was July 1968. I was one of a handful of yachtsmen spread out over the Atlantic, each racing to be the first to sail round the world, alone, without stopping. Down past the Cape Verde Islands, more than 480 km (300 miles) off the African coast, and water begins to leak into the hold of my boat. You know immediately you've got to jump overboard to find the hole and patch it. Among the jumble of stores, spare sails and sodden kit you try to find your mask and snorkel. And that's when you start worrying about sharks.

There's no use in over-thinking. You've just got to dive in. I found the gap, along a seam by the keel, and as the boat pitched and rolled I could see it opening and closing. Caulking was the answer; easier said than done when you have to do it underwater. Normally, dry twisted cotton is worked into the seam, stopped with filler, and then painted over, as has been done on wooden hulls for hundreds of years.

With a knife strapped to my leg, I jumped in many times, hammering away and glancing nervously over my shoulder for an unwanted visitor. I eventually managed to patch the leak, having sewed the cotton into a line of canvas, coated in Stockholm Tar and held in place with tacks. I covered it with a copper strip that had been left on board by the Marconi engineers when they fitted my new radio. The finished job looked a bit ragged, but necessity is the mother of invention.

Halfway through the mend, I came up on deck for a coffee and a smoke and it was then I noticed a lean grey shape moving sinuously past the boat. The sharks had found me at last. I watched this one for ten minutes, hoping it would go away as I didn't want to have to kill it. I wasn't just being nice: I didn't want to get blood in the water, attracting other sharks, and not be able to get the job finished. But the shark just kept circling, so I got out my rifle and put a hole in

its head. I took a deep breath and went over the side again and in an hour or so finally sorted the port side. A light wind was getting up, which forced me to leave the starboard for another time.

Dive in, that's what you have to do. It's the same with a voyage. At some point you just have to get going. Stop worrying, stop planning, just go. And it's the same with life. You can always play it safe, but where's the adventure in that? Whatever you do there are always people who delight in telling you you're wrong, who raise a difficulty for every solution. Of course I had my doubts. Bar a major mishap, like the leak returning, or losing a mast, or running aground, I knew the boat could make it. But would I?

I'd never been alone for more than 24 hours! In the 1960s I had served in the merchant navy in India and it was there I had built my ketch *Suhaili*, which means 'southeast wind' in Arabic. My brother and I sailed her back to London. Based on Norwegian lifeboat designs, and solidly built in Indian teak, *Suhaili* was a tough little cruiser. But could I do it? Would I cope on my own for months on end, or would I go round the bend? I kept myself busy. When not on the helm there were always jobs to do. Hundreds of little things – fixing, rearranging, adjusting the sails, charging the batteries, inspecting the rigging, plugging more holes, walking round with a marlinspike and checking each of the pins was tight. Food was usually a moment to look forward to: eggs with something for breakfast, cheese with something for lunch. Maybe a few luxuries like sardines or a pickled onion. And then variations of bully beef stew and tinned peas for dinner for some 30,000 nautical miles.

I had music to listen to including cassette tapes of Gilbert and Sullivan, or some classical music, or I'd find myself shaking to Little Richard or whatever else came on the radio if I managed to get a signal. I had 120 cans of Tennant's Lager and 3,000 cigarettes and slowly made my way through them. But apart from the occasional radio message, which usually left me feeling even more miserable, I was out of touch with the world.

When I really felt the loneliness of my situation I sought comfort in books. I took the usual Admiralty pilots and almanacs, but also had classics such as *War and Peace* and Melville's *Billy Budd*, a complete works of Shakespeare and, appropriately enough, Darwin's *The Voyage of the Beagle*. I had a guide for improving my chess (playing myself), and a Bible bought just before leaving port. I once spent a whole day in full foul-weather gear reading *Vanity Fair*.

But the mainstay of my existence was my journal. I'd usually down tools at 5 p.m. for a beer, and while I enjoyed that I would write. It became a comforting routine, a ritual. Besides which, I'd managed to land a book deal before I left, which paid for most of my supplies and the boat's refitting, and so I needed to write something every day. I started with my logbook and then soon filled up a diary too, scribbling details down before they could escape.

Back then I had no electronic navigational equipment. In some respects, I had much the same gear as Captain Cook – a sextant and chronometer. I plotted my course by the stars and the sun. I even used strands of wool fastened to the rigging to give some idea of where the breeze was coming from. My fresh water came from the clouds. Conditions were not much different from those for sailors on square-riggers a century earlier, and once my radio broke I was as isolated as they had been. From then on I had no contact at all apart from sighting a few ships, most of which did not notice me. I was just a tiny speck on a vast ocean.

So, from a navigational point of view an accurate logbook is essential. If it all goes wrong, it's important to know where you are – or at least where you were. A good logbook could save your life. Plus, I consoled myself that if I never made it home at least there might be a record of what I'd done. As my publisher said before I left: 'I'll be working with you on the book when you get back, and with your logbooks if you don't.'

Writing each day helped keep me sane. It's something that I was trained to do in the merchant navy. Of course there are always days when it's just too rough to write for long. But even when water is pouring in through the skylights, you just have to do it, if only the barest of descriptions. Sometimes what you

experience at sea is indescribable: intense storms, waves rearing like mountains in the Southern Ocean, even the mirrored calms of the tropics. Flying fish weave across the surface and sunsets fill the sky with vermilion.

A few days after I'd shot the shark, I managed to stop the leak and finally dried out. *Suhaili* was then struck by a large squall. I recorded it my journal: 'I handed the spinnaker and set the jib at 1730 as I could see it coming, then, just before it arrived I struck the staysail and reefed the main and mizzen and put buckets beneath the goosenecks. It was glorious. I had a bath and it was all I could do to stop myself dancing – beautiful cold water.'

When you've been sailing for nigh on seven decades, some days tend to merge into others, but I remember that one so clearly, out there alone in the Atlantic. There was a wonderful sunset too. 'The clouds were all tinted blue ... except for one which was golden', continues the scrawl in my journal. 'A beautiful sight – I wish I could paint.'

ANNIE BRASSEY 1839-1887

A good deal of water came on board, and it was impossible to sit anywhere in comfort, unless lashed or firmly wedged in.

From hidden creeks and hollows they came: a flotilla of canoes, brimming with Fuegians dressed in sea-otter skins and armed with bows and spears. Fires burned in the bottom of their boats as they paddled furiously towards the *Sunbeam*. Annie Brassey grabbed some beads and looking-glasses in the hope that this might appease the locals, but the current was strong and the yacht was carried quickly away. 'I was quite sorry for their disappointment at losing their hoped-for luxuries,' Brassey wrote mildly.

Had *Sunbeam* been surrounded, the story might have been very different. Tierra del Fuego, the 'Land of Fire', was said to be populated by giants and cannibals. It was October 1876, and the Brassey family were three months into their voyage around the world on their yacht *Sunbeam*. They had encountered challenges from the start: storms with tremendous waves that almost swept the captain and their eldest daughter overboard; near shipwreck; and a volcanic dust-storm far out at sea, which pelted the deck with black dust and ashes. 'Happily,' Brassey observed, as the yacht lurched and the cabins filled yet again with water, 'the children don't know what fear is.'

Annie Allnutt was twenty-one when she married Thomas Brassey, soon to be Member of Parliament, and later a Lord of the Admiralty. Thomas was a keen yachtsman, and before long they were embarking on daring voyages. Their children always accompanied them, as did the family's pets: their two pugs were joined by several monkeys and exotic birds, a tiny anteater given by the Sultan of Johor, which clung to Annie's arm like a bracelet, and a pig presented to her by a Pacific Island chief. The gift of a young puma in Cordova, however, was shipped directly to London. With children on board Annie thought it prudent to send it to the zoo.

Daily she wrote long letters home, describing the exotic places they visited and the people they met. Her family urged her to publish them, and the result was *A Voyage in the 'Sunbeam'*. Annie's keen eye for detail, her charm, humour and curiosity, as well as her vivid descriptions of distant lands, won her a huge audience; the book became a bestseller.

Despite episodic, debilitating attacks of malaria, Annie Brassey entered into each experience with enormous enthusiasm. In particular, she made it her mission to try to establish branches all over the world of the St John Ambulance, a charity devoted to providing and teaching first aid. Her extensive travels, however, eventually took their toll. Weakened by a bout of bronchitis, Annie died of malaria off the coast of Australia in September 1887. Her body was committed to the Indian Ocean. Her final diary was published posthumously as *The Last Voyage*. Devastated by the loss of his wife, Thomas dedicated it to their children: 'How we shall miss her in everything! ... We have seen how she used her opportunities to make the world a little better than she found it.'

Creating photographs, and collecting those from professional photographers, was a means of sketching the places Brassey visited, and she fitted out the *Sunbeam* with a darkroom. Her account of the family's circumnavigation was published in nine editions and seventeen languages.

A VOYAGE IN THE 'SUNBEAM'

OUR HOME ON THE OCEAN FOR ELEVEN MONTHS

BY

MRS. BRASSEY

CAPE BRASSEY : SMYTH'S SOUND

ILLUSTRATED

CHICAGO:
BELFORD, CLARKE & CO.
1881.

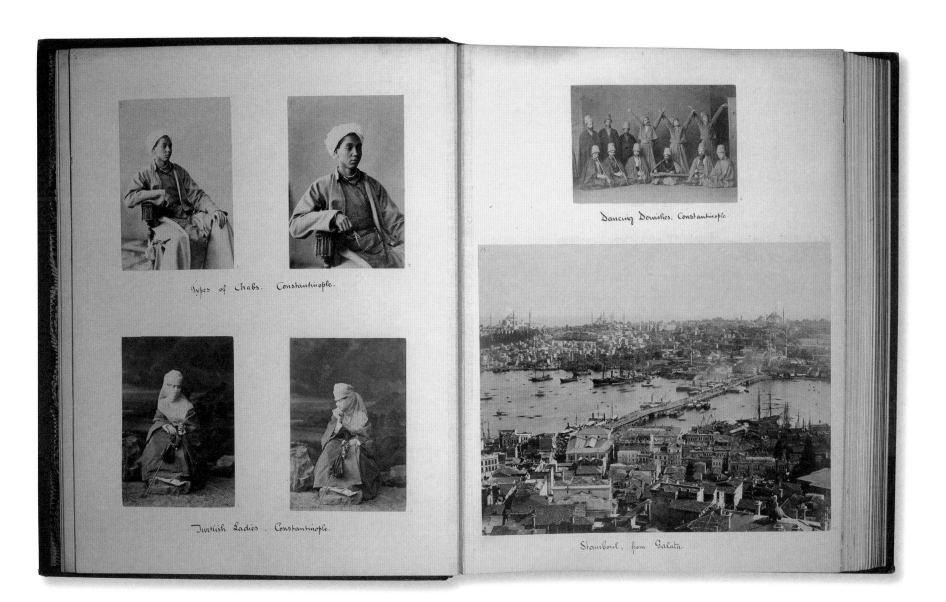

Types of Arabs. Constantinople.

Turkish Ladies. Constantinople.

Dancing Dervishes. Constantinople

Stamboul, from Galata.

GABRIEL BRAY 1750–1823

The whole population are smugglers.
Here are fisherman who never fish,
but always have pockets of money.

Draughtsmanship was long considered to be one of the valued skills of a good sailor as a means to record unfamiliar coastlines, and it became an important aspect of a sea officer's formal education. Though improved mapping methods and later the development of photography gradually reduced the need for these skills, officers and men continued to draw for their own pleasure, and to describe their travels to family and friends. Sketches were often included with letters sent home, and these were sometimes pasted into albums for posterity.

The son of a mariner, Gabriel Bray joined the navy at fifteen as a captain's servant. In the first six years of his sea career he served on six different ships and managed to pass his lieutenant exams in 1770, but no ships were available for a posting. His lucky break came in 1773, when assisting on the royal yacht *Augusta* at the fleet review in Spithead. He secretly sketched the scene and, having sat up all night to finish the painting, then managed to have it presented as a surprise gift for King George III the following day; the king apparently liked it so much he promoted Bray on the spot.

As a keen artist, Bray made numerous watercolours on his voyages to West Africa and Jamaica when lieutenant on the frigate *Pallas*. His commander was Sir William Cornwallis, later the well-known admiral 'Billy Blue', a friend of Nelson and commander of the Channel Fleet during the war with France. Lacking the right family connections, Bray never advanced beyond the rank of lieutenant, so settled instead for commands of the revenue cutters *Sprightly, Enterprise, Nimble* and *Scourge*, defending the English coast against smugglers.

High taxes on a wide range of luxury goods, as well as basic commodities including salt, imposed to finance the wars with America and France between 1775 and 1815, encouraged enterprising fishermen on both sides of the Channel to boost their incomes in the 'trade', as smuggling was known. Much of the spirits and tobacco shipped to England came through Guernsey, which Cornish fishermen could visit in their luggers and then later land their stash at secluded coves. It has been estimated that at one point import duty had been paid on only 20 per cent of the tea drunk in England, and there was so much illegally imported gin in Kent that people were using it to clean their windows. Bray's task was to intercept the contraband, policing the seas and sometimes making raids ashore. On one notable occasion it is said he even fought off a Frenchman wielding a blunderbuss. After all this drama, he spent his final years in Dorset, a happy churchwarden.

Bray was lieutenant on the voyages of *Pallas* to Africa and the Caribbean, inspecting and protecting coastal trading forts. He painted this self-portrait using a mirror in his cabin. Opposite, one sketch is of 'a sailor bringing up his hammock', and the other shows a friend later admiring the drawing in his journal.

JOHNNY BROCHMANN 1901-1957

And so, a well-known coast
came up behind the horizon...

Sailor Johannes, 'Johnny', Brochmann is little known today, but the sketches he created are an important record of momentous world events and great changes in ocean travel. Born in Christiana, Norway, in 1901, he was a cadet in the Royal Norwegian Navy in the 1920s and sketched throughout his time afloat, right up to the Second World War. His father Diderik was a skipper and renowned shanty singer, who also edited a shipping newspaper, so it's no surprise that Johnny followed a long family tradition by going to sea.

At sixteen, his first major voyage was on the steamship *Lygenfjord,* which had been built in Glasgow for a Greek tycoon then sold into service carrying mail and cargo for the Norwegian America Line during the First World War. Brochmann was the 'youngest fellow on board', a line he inked proudly on the front of his sketchbook. His service took him back and forth to America in dangerous times, as German U-boats started sinking American merchant ships in the North Atlantic. The US Navy finally joined the war effort in 1917.

When Brunel's oak-hulled steamer *Great Western* had first crossed the Atlantic in 1838 it took fifteen days and was considered a major innovation. In a new century, liners like the *Mauretania,* with turbine steam engines and quadruple screws, would reduce the crossing to under five days. The Norwegian America Line ran regular transatlantic passenger services from Europe to New York, and soon to East Africa too, and in its heyday owned a fleet of more than twenty ships. In peacetime, competition from air travel would eventually see Norwegian's operations shift to container shipping, as passenger expectations for Atlantic crossings became hours instead of days. The last of its two cruise ships were finally sold to Cunard in 1984. As for *Lygenfjord,* she was inevitably replaced by faster ships, was captured by the Germans in the 1940s and was later torpedoed by a British submarine.

In 1919 Brochmann was on the ocean liner *Bergensfjord,* assisting its quartermaster. She was the pride of a new fleet, with Marconi wireless and electric light, and space for 1,200 passengers, most of whom were emigrating from Europe looking for a new life after the horrors of the war. In 1920 he joined the naval academy in Horten and later sketched on voyages up Norway's northern coast, or south to warmer waters in Spain and the Canary Islands.

Nine of Brochmann's sketchbooks were donated to the Vancouver Maritime Museum in the 1970s by his son Harold. Brochmann's teaching career had taken him from Ghana and the West Indies to Nova Scotia, but he settled on Salt Spring, in the Gulf Islands, taking his yacht *Whisper* out into local waters. He was Commodore of the Salt Spring Island Sailing Club, where his old sextant is still awarded each year as a trophy for seamanship through adversity.

Brochmann's sketchbooks take us across the Atlantic and up to Arctic Norway, 'Nordenfor Nordkap', in 1921. He also created an incredible inventory of sketches of different ships from many nations - cruise and cargo ships, clipper ships, battleships, paddle-steamers, tankers, tug-boats and whalers - together with pasted pin-ups and all sorts of cartoons.

NORDENFOR NORDKAP
1921

...EVESER OG
...TAGELSER
...KADET-BROCHMANN

...ERNE

TØFTOP

BRANDBAAT

SHIPPING BOARDS FLOATE

DONK
PONK

ELFSBORG
(blevsterklædt, jordenrundet her)

TASKERE

GÖTEBORG

ARGENTINSK SKOLESKIB

ATRAS

ARMADA ARGENTINA

NIELS JUELL

...AV KONG HAAKONS
...OER OMFORD PAA NIELS JUELL"

"YANKEEN"

STYRMANDS-
ELEVEN

DEN
FASTE

FAMILIEFORSØR-
GEREN (MASKINIS...

MEDECINEREN

VIKAGUTTEN

SKIPPEREN

DEN NORSKE SJOMAND
I KONGENS KLER

SKOLESKIBE
CIVILE

DANMARK

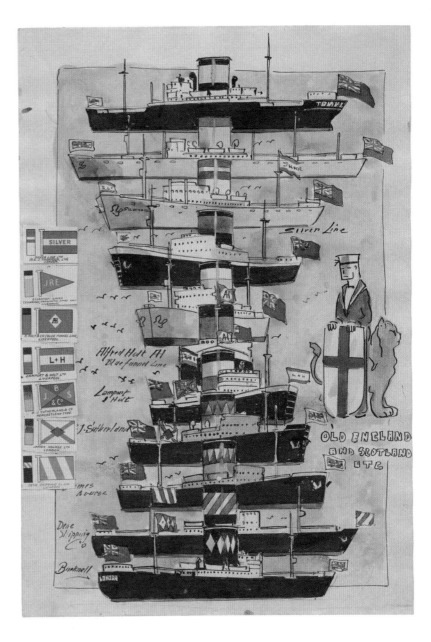

NORSKE HVALBAATER
FORSØKER AT
STYRE UT FRA
LAS PALMAS

FRANCIS CHICHESTER 1901–1972

I think I was awake when the boat began to roll
over … perhaps when the wave hit her I woke.
It was pitch dark.

Asked many times why he took such risks at sea and in the sky, Francis Chichester's answer was simple: 'because it intensifies life'. He was born in Devon, southwest England, but after an unhappy childhood left for New Zealand. Aged eighteen at the time, he had just ten sovereigns in his pocket. Eventually he found success in forestry and as a property developer, and became wealthy. He bought a plane, a de Havilland Gipsy Moth, and learnt to fly. Back in England visiting his family in 1929, he determined to fly to Australia, so having acquired a plane, after nineteen days' solo flying he landed in Sydney to a rapturous welcome. He was the second person ever to complete this dangerous trip.

In 1931 his next goal was to become the first to fly solo across the Tasman Sea, starting in New Zealand. He navigated in his small cockpit with just a sextant, logarithmic tables and a scribbling pad strapped to his knee. He made two landings en route, Norfolk Island and the tiny Lord Howe Island, where his plane sank and had to be rebuilt before he could fly to safety. After reaching Australia he made the first solo flight to Japan on what he hoped would be the beginning of an epic round-the-world expedition, but he later crashed into telephone wires. He was seriously injured and his plane was damaged beyond repair.

On leaving hospital, Chichester vowed to take up ocean racing instead, which he began after the Second World War, first as a navigator and later, in 1953, with his own boat, *Gipsy Moth II*. In the following year he was diagnosed with lung cancer and told he had just six months to live, but he recovered sufficiently to win the first single-handed transatlantic race in 1960. He achieved worldwide fame when at the age of 65 he sailed solo around the world. He left Plymouth in 1966 in his new ketch *Gipsy Moth IV*, stopping only once in Australia and completing the journey after 226 days of sailing. His hero, Joshua Slocum, had accomplished the first solo circumnavigation in 1898, but it had taken him three years and numerous stops.

A crowd of more than 250,000 people were waiting at the harbour to welcome Chichester home. He would soon be celebrated at gala dinners all over the world. When he was honoured by Queen Elizabeth II in 1967 she took up the same sword that Elizabeth I had used when knighting Francis Drake, the first Englishman to complete a circumnavigation.

Chichester finally succumbed to cancer in 1972. *Gipsy Moth IV* was for some time on display in Greenwich, London, land-locked in dry dock next to the famous clipper *Cutty Sark*. Rescued from neglect and restored, she is now owned by a charitable trust and used as a training yacht to inspire a new generation.

One of several precious logbooks from Chichester's pioneering circumnavigation. The entry for 26 March 1967 at 21.05 tells the story: 'Hot news! Passed half way today…' With this voyage, Chichester didn't just break records, he set the new yardstick. Of the yacht itself he said: '*Gipsy Moth IV* is cantankerous and difficult and needs a crew of three - a man to navigate, an elephant to move the tiller and a chimpanzee with arms 8-feet long to get about below and work the gear.'

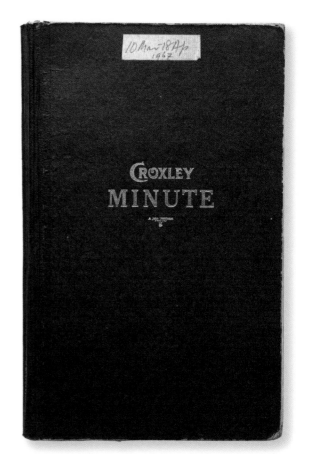

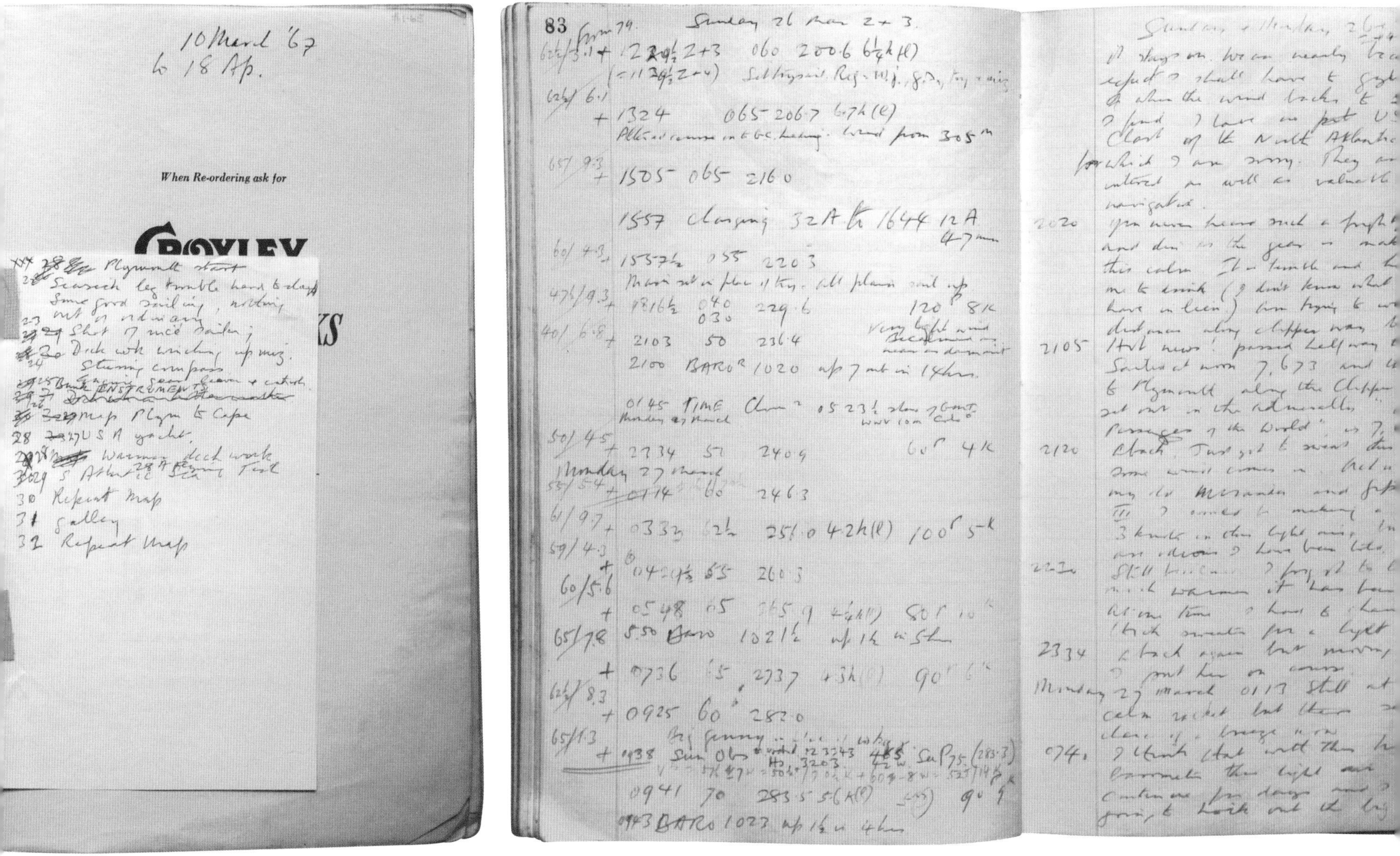

When Re-ordering ask for

CROSLEY

[handwritten note card, partly legible:]

28 Plymouth start
Seasick leg trouble hand to chafe
Some good sailing, nothing
out of ordinary
Shot 7 mice sailing;
Dick wk winching up mizzen
Steering compass
Map Plym to Cape
USA yacht.
Warming deck work
S Atlantic Sea Trial
30 Repeat Map
31 Galley
32 Repeat Map

---

83 (from 74.   Sunday 26 Mar 2+3.
1224½ 2+3   060   2006 6¾H(l)
(=1129½ 2+4)
1324   065 206·7 6·7H(l)

1505   065 2160

1557 Charging 32A to 1644 12A
                                    47 min
1557½ 055 2203

1816½ 040 229·6   120 8K
       030
2103   50   236·4   Very light
2100 BARO 1020 up 7 at in 1½ hrs

0145 TIME Chm² 0523½
2734   57   240·9   60 4K
Monday 27 March
0114 60   246·3
0332 62½ 251·0 42H(l) 100 5·K
0420½ 65   260·3
0548   65   265·9 4½H(l) 80 10K
5·50 BARO 1021½ up 1½ in 5 hrs
0736   65   273·7 +3h(l) 90 6K
0925   60   282·0
1138 Sun Obs   Sū β75 (283·3)
0941   70   283·5 5(A(l) −45) 90 9
0943 BARO 1023 up 1½ in 4 hrs

[right page, handwritten prose, largely illegible]
2020
2105
2120
2230
2334
Monday 27 March 0113 still at
074.

LOUIS CHORIS 1795–1828

May Heaven defend a ship from
being wrecked on this coast!

A Ukrainian of German stock, Louis Choris was born in Ekaterinoslav (now Dnipro), and was a young artist living in St Petersburg when in 1815 he was chosen for a great adventure. He joined the expedition ship *Rurik*, under the command of Otto von Kotzebue, as official artist on a voyage financed by the statesman Count Rumyantsev. As a teenager Choris had already served as the botanical sketcher on an expedition to the Caucasus and his reputation was on the rise in Moscow artistic circles. The expedition's aim was to search the Alaskan coast for a passage through the Bering Strait, so that the Russians could supply their trading posts between California and Alaska without having to sail all the way round Cape Horn. The *Rurik* carried twenty-seven people, including Captain von Kotzebue and a small scientific team headed by German poet and botanist Adelbert von Chamisso.

Setting out from St Petersburg in July, the *Rurik* rounded the tip of South America and touched at Chile before crossing the Pacific to winter in Kamchatka. During the summer of 1816 the expedition explored the Bering Strait and the Aleutian island of Unalaska, heading to California in the autumn to stock up on fresh meat and vegetables, and spending most of October anchored in San Francisco Bay. This gave Choris plenty of time to sketch its inhabitants and the wildlife. 'The rocks are commonly covered with sea-lions', he wrote. 'Bears are very plentiful on land. When the Spaniards wish to amuse themselves, they catch them alive and make them fight with bulls.'

Hawaii, then called the Sandwich Islands, was the next stop, where the voyagers spent several months from November 1816 to March 1817, cruising, mapping and sketching. A second visit the following autumn gave Choris another chance to make drawings and observations in his journal. The ship finally reached the Arctic again in the summer of 1817, but illness and unexpected ice cover forced von Kotzebue to head home in July. After visiting Guam, the Philippines, South Africa and London, the expedition returned to St Petersburg in August 1818, having circumnavigated the globe.

Choris went to Paris in 1819 and arranged for one of the most talented printers in France to reproduce his drawings from the voyage using the relatively new technique of lithography. He sold the sumptuous folio volume of more than one hundred plates by subscription, with the Russian tsar and the kings of France and Prussia among his customers.

Still fired by an irresistible craving for adventure, and with money burning a hole in his pocket, Choris left France in 1827 for South America, hoping to study and sketch indigenous peoples. He would never return. Riding from Veracruz on the Gulf Coast towards Mexico City, he was killed when robbers attacked his party.

The Choris sketchbooks contain some of the earliest known depictions of the native Iñupiat, in the area now named for Kotzebue along the coasts of the southern Chukchi Sea, as well as other peoples on the shores of the Bering Strait.

Opposite: 'Vue de l'île de St Paul dans la mer de Kamtchatka' shows a Yupik hunting sea lions in his distinctive semi-conical bentwood hat, waterproof seal-gut parka and short-stern kayak.

Choris del.

Imp. Lith. de Bove dirigée par Noël ainé & Cᵉ

Vue de l'île de Sᵗ Paul dans la mer de Kamtchatka (avec des lions marins)

Many of the indigenous groups in coastal Alaska, such as Aleut and Eskimo, wore labrets, an ornamental plug piercing below the lower lip. Different decorations indicated territorial boundaries and social rank and they were traditionally made of bone or marine ivory. As contact with the outside world increased, they were even decorated with blue glass trade beads.

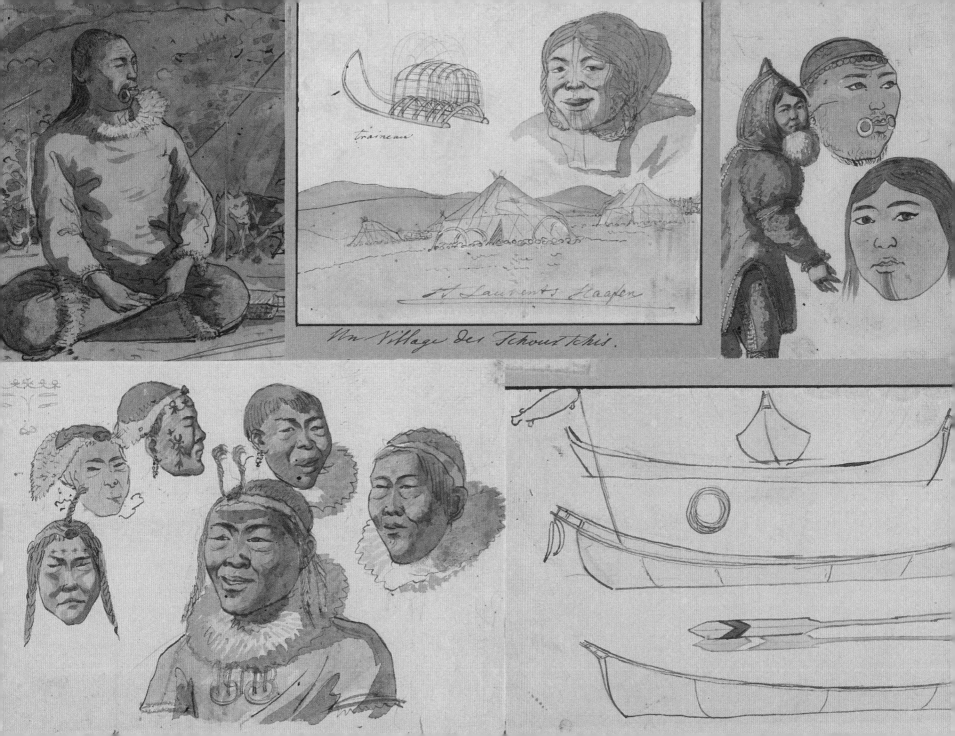

traineau

St Laurents Haafen

Un Village des Tchouktchis.

Opposite: A closely observed herd of sea lions by
Choris. It has been said of him that he 'painted
nature as he found it. The essence of his art
is truth; a fresh, vigorous view of life, and
an originality in portrayal'.

Below: Kotzebue's narrative of the voyage included
many illustrations based on sketches by Choris,
including further to the south, the 'dance hairstyles
of the Californians' admired near present-day
San Francisco.

dess et Lith par Choris

XII

Lith. de Langlumé.

Coiffures de danse des habitans de la Californie.

FREDERIC CHURCH 1826–1900

An iceberg, in itself alone, is a miracle
of beauty and grandeur.

Over the centuries, seafarers were drawn to the far north for many reasons. Early explorers attempted to penetrate the myriad northwest passages, but fishermen and whalers were the true pioneers. Later, artists also found these high latitudes appealing. Just as the whaling trade was in decline, the American painter Frederic Church was helping to shape the public imagining of the Arctic as a sublime wilderness – harsh and dangerous, but also enthralling in its romantic possibilities. When his luminous canvas *The Icebergs* was unveiled in New York in 1861 one newspaper described it as 'the most splendid work of art that has yet been produced in this country'.

Church had already travelled far and had captured the wonders of South America in blockbuster landscapes and, in 1857, the magnificent Niagara Falls. In 1859, with his fame growing and a London exhibition beckoning, he booked a passage north on the steamer *Merlin* for a month-long voyage cruising through the North Atlantic to Newfoundland and Labrador, and from there he chartered the schooner *Integrity* so he could get closer to the ice. Overcoming seasickness, he even used a little rowing boat to get among the icebergs to sketch.

His friend, the clergyman Louis Noble, joined him and wrote a book about the voyage, *After Icebergs with a Painter*, which helped arouse even more interest in the art: 'Our game, for once, is the wandering alp of the waves; our wilderness, the ocean; our steed, the winged vessel; our arms, the pencil and the pen; our gamebags, the portfolio, painting-box, and note-book.'

Interestingly, between the American unveiling of *The Icebergs* and its subsequent exhibition in England, Church added a broken ship's mast at the bottom of his canvas, both for scale and as an echo of the doomed sailors of the missing Franklin expedition. Church's art reminds us even now of the precariousness of human efforts in so vast, yet fragile, an environment.

Louis Noble accompanied Church on his voyage north in 1859, and described their experiences in a book. 'Lights and shadows, hues and tints, shower the scene, and are thrown in all ways, and multiplied by reflection.'

Opposite: Church voyaged from Boston to Nova Scotia and Newfoundland, and then further north still to Labrador. He used his sketchbooks as an inspirational resource for later paintings, including his masterwork *The Icebergs*. Church made this oil study on 4 July 1859.

WILLIAM COATES 1865–1917

Mercy me; wee live in fearsome tymes.

He sketched to escape the horrors of the war. The threat of destruction was constant, whether by being bombed from above by biplanes, blown to bits by floating mines or torpedoed by submarines from below. Each day, the lives of those on the small British ship hung in the balance, and each day the captain took his mind off their troubles by sketching into the night. Alone in his cabin, he re-imagined their perils in the First World War in ink and paint as if voyaging on an eighteenth-century brig. His sketchbook remains unfinished as his luck eventually ran out.

Not much is known of Commander William Herbert Coates of the Royal Naval Reserve. Like thousands of men, he was called up in 1914 and was willing to join an effort that would surely be over by Christmas. And like thousands of men, Coates would never return home. His ship *Clacton* was a channel mail packet owned by the Great Eastern Railway, one of hundreds of ships requisitioned by the Admiralty as the war began. Converted for use as a minesweeper, *Clacton* left Portsmouth in December on a training voyage up to the Orkney Islands, made her rendezvous with the fleet to head for Malta, and then sailed onward to the Greek island of Lemnos. It was here that the Allied forces gathered, following plans conceived by Winston Churchill, to force their way through the Dardanelles and push on to Constantinople.

The first attempt, launched on 18 March 1915, was a disaster. An unsuspected Turkish minefield laid waste to five Allied warships. *Clacton* ended up ferrying troops into the battle zone and returning with wounded to the hospital ships. She also landed soldiers at Cape Helles on the barren Gallipoli peninsula on that fateful day, 25 April 1915. It was a bloodbath, with thousands killed as Ottoman bullets rained down on them from the castle above, and though a small foothold was eventually won, the men who remained had to be evacuated.

On 3 August 1916 in the Aegean Sea *Clacton* was torpedoed and sunk by a German U-boat. There were five casualties – two officers and three crew – but Coates lived to fight another day and was awarded the DSO for his 'gallant conduct'. He even saved his sketchbooks. Having survived the sinking, he was given command of steamer *Redbreast*, a fleet messenger and Q-ship, a 'mystery ship', sent out on perilous runs as a decoy to lure U-boats into making surface attacks. On 15 July 1917 she was duly hunted down and sunk by submarine UC-38. Commander Coates and forty-three of his men died that day. The few corpses that were eventually recovered were buried on a nearby island.

Created in the heat of conflict during the First World War, Coates' drawing books fortunately survived. Opposite, he re-imagines the ship *Rowan* under attack, being bombed by a German aircraft or 'monstrous bird'. Overleaf are Coates' visions of the interior of the captain's cabin on the *Clacton*, and of himself and his shipmates as buccaneers, once the war is over, hiding their treasure in Tortuga.

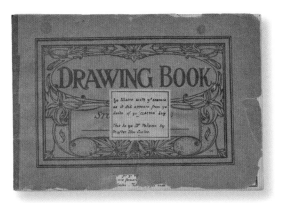

Mercy me! wee live in fearsome tymes.

For ye Huns, by meanes of Blacke and Magick Arts, hath devised a monstrous Bird, ye which, it is said spits fyres & arrowes. This Beaste attacked ye hired armed brig, ye "ROWAN", dropping bombes & lances, & retired. She retourned an houre later with more bombes, — but ye "ROWAN" plied ye beaste soe diligentlie with musquet shotte that ye bird fled. About ye same tyme ye fine brig, ye "SNAEFELL", was fired on by ye gunne, commonlie knowne as "Bulgar Bill", & hitte alle ye sterne.

It is said that ye above foule birds hath even attacked ye large frigate "ENDYMION", ye "MONITOURE", & ye "SNAEFELL", H.M. armed brig, but were soone driven off.

QUARTER
GALLERY.

Ye Cabbin
of ye Captayne.
in ye Olde Brig, ye "Clacton"
Anno Domini 1915.

And when ye Warre be over
I warrant Coales once more
will seeke hys Treasure-trove
on Cernes golden shore.

1789.
Ye societie of Ye Tortoise.

And often-time he thinketh
of ye flurring days of olde
when ye treasure so ill-gotten
was hid by pyrates bolde.
Olde Songe.

ADRIAEN COENEN 1514–1587

Its skin had no scales and was like leather, as grey as lead ... his tongue lay in the throat like a liver and was the size of a barrel of beer.

In 1577 Adriaen Coenen began his *Visboek* – the 'Book of Fish' – which grew into an epic 800-page tome. He lived in the Dutch fishing port of Scheveningen, and over a period of three years he created an intriguing masterwork informed by a life beside the sea, pouring his knowledge of the coasts and coastal waters, fishing grounds and marine animals into its pages.

Although he had little formal education – he was a fisher-man and, in later life, a wreck master and fish auctioneer – as news of his ambitious project spread, he attracted a host of new acquaintances, from professors to Dutch nobility. Before long he was on personal terms with William, Prince of Orange. Fishermen and sailors began bringing him strange specimens from distant waters, many of which he dried and displayed about his home. Academics gave him access to rare books, which provided a rich source of material. Patrons such as Cornelis Suys, President of the Court of Holland in The Hague, provided him with pamphlets describing unusual species.

Coenen studied learned works on the sea, such as Olaus Magnus' *Historia de Gentibus Septentrionalibus*, then copied extracts and illustrated them in his own style. He related how some fish were spellbound by sound, and described the process of fishing with bells. In one of his scenes, dolphins circle a boat as a fisherman plays the harp. After the perfor-mance, the dolphins apparently beat their tails hard against the water as a token of their appreciation.

Part maritime sketchbook, part almanac, part fairy story, Coenen's *Visboek* is a cabinet of curiosities: as much a celebration of fishermen's tales as it was a catalogue of the maritime world he had himself experienced. Sirens and cyclops, mermaids and mermen frequent the pages, though Coenen remained sceptical as to their existence: 'I cannot find a man to this day who with his own eye in 1579 has seen one.' He recounted stories of strange fish-people too, such as the woman found in 1403 in the Dutch town of Purmer, who searched for food in the sea, slept in the water and was dressed in moss and slime.

A canny businessman, Coenen saw his project not only as a means of sharing knowledge, but also as a commercial enterprise. He periodically put his journal on display in The Hague town hall, charging visitors. Some of his more unusual specimens, such as a giant squid, were also exhibited, before being sold to wealthy collectors. Today, Coenen's *Visboek* is regarded as a remarkable contemporary record, providing detailed insight into sixteenth-century marine life, as well as fishing techniques and vessels used at the time. But it is also a homage to the weird and the wonderful. In the depths of the ocean, there are marvels beyond imagination.

On 21 October 1546, Coenen bought a large squid at the local fish auction. He studied other squid caught by fishermen, and drew on a French text by Pierre Belon. On the left and far right, he presents an array of fish.

Overleaf: One of the most beautiful pictures in the *Visboek* is a flying fish. Found in tropical seas, its nickname was 'sea swallow'. Another of the marvels to be admired was 'The true Portrait and size of a Whale', which had been captured in July 1577.

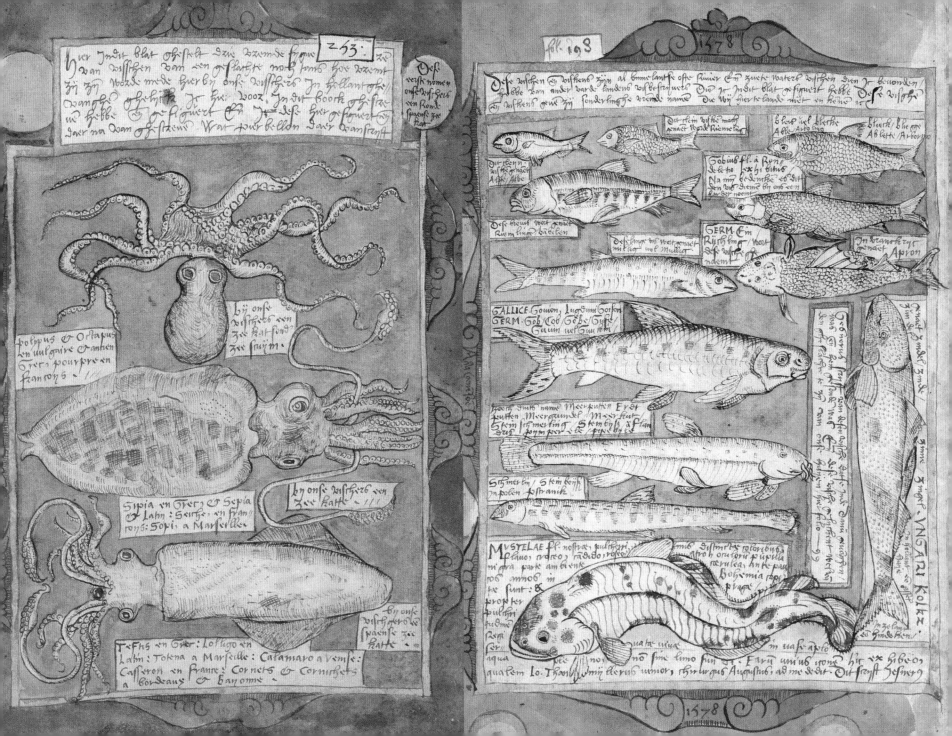

Von de muraals onderscheit
ende zwart ... fisch ... murael vermischt sich mit den Schlangen van die murael ...

Marer vil / es ~~sollen~~ seien unter den Murähn nur Rögner / vnnd die selbigen sollen sich mit den Schlangen vermischen / weil dem solches die Fischer wissen / pfeifen sie am vfer gleich den Schlangen / locken also die Muräl offtermals mit hauffen auffs tröckne / vnnd fangents da sie kömens aber mit keinem stecken ~~auff trucken~~ vmbbringen / aber mit dem kraut ferula, werden sie leichtlich hingericht.

Das leben haben sie fürnemlich im Schwantz / vnnd so man sie dar an trifft / sterben sie zu stund / am kopff kan man sie schwerlich so hart schlagen dasz sie dauon abtrucken. Vom Melch werden sie gar feist.

Von etlichen fischen die Ihre farb endern.

Maeris, Mæna

Desen meer baersch dat is onsen zeebaers en dese wort bij onse visschers genaemt de knoff

Den houtinck es hier bij ons een ~~Ende~~ wareschi vissche hij en wort niet voor lecker gehouden alser ander meer visschen zijn

Möne houtinck Meerschleisz linck.

Den zeebaers ofte knof gefigureert folio ... En ook daer van gescreven ... vissche

Den houtinck ghefigureert folio —— En ook daer van gescreven

Phycis Streinling Ein art der meer bersiche. Meergle. Trüschegle

Die Moene sind des Winters schnee weisz Im Sommer aber verendern sie Ihre farb / vnnd zucken etwas auffs schwartze.

Die Trüschegle bleibt auch nicht auff einer farbe denn im Früling wirt sie bundt / zu anderer zeit aber ist sie weisz. Diser fisch hat sonderlich die art an Ihm / dasz er Ihm ein Nest von den Meerblumen macht / vnnd darinn leichet.

Al meest alle vissche bij ons vergaen haer oder inder doot hoe schoone kolcer dat die vissche hebben die schoonheyt vergaet int sterven ... men ... tijt ende zee ... die als hij levendich es een zeer schoone ... die noch tans niet al ...

HIRVNDO

Fliegender Rotfisch

Ein meer schwalb.

Ein zee swalwe

Dese dus gen woord ... ghevangen ... die hoeck ... zee ...

Dese zee swalwe ... kennen wel onsen zee haen ... de haer ... groote vinnen

Als dese vissen door ... vliegen ... gevallen ... so brengen die schippers ...

Alter ... menschen als ... zijn ...

Meerschwalb oder Schwalbfisch von den alten nach der spraach bedeüttung genennet. Ist der geweltigest auch aller fliegenden fischen vnnd der schönest.

Auf den schönsten fischen / so vn / der allen ~~...~~ wasserthiere sein mögend ist diser gäntzen wir tiger fliegender Schwalmen fisch: Dann die natur / das ist der ewig Gott hat auch etlichen der vischen sölliche schöpfung mitgeteilt dz sij fliegen könnend ausserthalb vnd auff dem wasser: wirdt von seiner gestalt / färbe / fliegen rc.

Noch folio 364 ende folio 374 van al ... gefigureert ... in ... zee hanen folio 137 ende 139

Ende vande Rotbert folio 338 mede een ... zee haen

hier nv ...

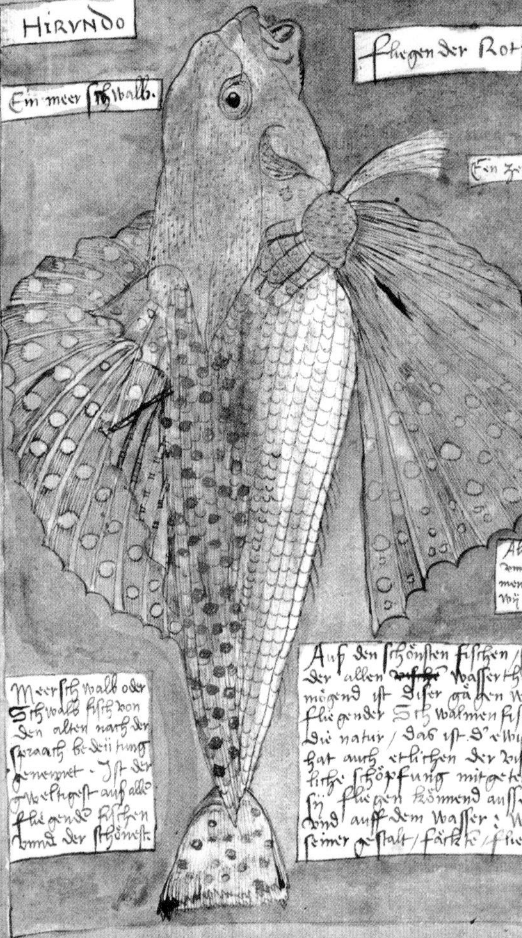

Het warachtich Conterfeytsel ende afmetinghe van desen Walvisch die ghe-
vanghen is gheweest den ij Julij Anno M·D·lxxvij

FLOATING ALONG

Roz Savage

> Courage is resistance to fear, mastery
> of fear, not absence of fear.
> MARK TWAIN, 1894

A Saturday night, 2005. Latitude 25°39'N. Longitude 24°24'W. If I were a normal person I might be having a drink with friends. But I'm not really normal, not anymore. I have thrown in my job and invested everything in a new way of living. I'm lying alone in a small ocean rowing boat about 800 km (500 miles) off the west coast of Africa. Over 3,200 km (2,000 miles) in the other direction is my goal: Antigua in the West Indies.

The wind is against me, so the sea anchor is out to stop me being blown backwards. I'm in my cabin, lying on my bunk. The cabin is about the width and length of a double bed, tapering to about 45 cm (18 inches) wide at the aft end, where my head is. At its highest point the cabin roof is just shy of a metre. It's cosy but not quite comfortable. Lying is easier than sitting.

It's sticky and stuffy in here. I've got the hatch and ventilation holes closed in case the wind blows up while I'm asleep – this cabin is a buoyancy chamber that will help the boat self-right if it capsizes – so the only air comes through a ventilator installed above my head. Some nights I can see the moon and stars through the hatch, seeming to dance around in my little window as the boat pitches and yaws. But not tonight – it is overcast and dark out there.

There's a faint smell of chocolate and crystallized ginger from my snack packs, stowed in the lockers beneath the floor of the cabin. At first the smell made me feel hungry, but now I'm rather sick of it. My mouth is dry – I deliberately let myself dehydrate when I know I'll be confined for a while, as it's a nuisance having to go out to the cockpit to use the bedpan. It's noisy in the cabin, but in a soothing kind of way. The boat creaks. Water laps against the hull and swirls gurgling around the rudder, which is just behind my head. When there is a gap in the sound I can hear the sigh of the ocean, and the breath of the wind.

The movement of the boat is different when she is on the sea anchor. She twitches and strains like a terrier at its leash. We rock from left to right and occasionally in a circular motion – up and over and around and down. Sometimes part way through one of these manoeuvres, when the line to the anchor brings us up short, we're jerked back. And once in a while one of those express train waves will steam in and sideswipe us, and the whole boat is knocked through sixty degrees.

I'm not scared. The sea is rough, but *Sedna* has proved her seaworthiness in worse conditions than this. But I'm not relaxed either – even while I sleep my ears are pricked for any unfamiliar sound, any signal that an oar or the rudder or the anchor has come to grief. Another long night. I read for a while, then doze, dreaming of Jonah and the whale, then wake up, and it's still only 10.30 p.m. It doesn't get light until 8 a.m. So I'm here, whiling away the time by writing a journal, tapping out these thoughts on my iPAQ handset, with its little screen the only light in my darkened cabin. It has just started to rain, pattering down on the aft hatch. Thoughts blur into daydreams, which blend into night dreams.

I wrote this last night. Today I've been on the para-anchor again. The wind is 20 knots from the south so it's impossible for me to make headway rowing. The low pressure will eventually blow through, so I know I just have to spend another day riding it out. *Acceptance.* That's a word I'm learning is really helpful when you're on the sea. I've got to be patient. It's too windy for me even to stick my head out the hatch to check the instruments.

Ocean rowing? Based on the last two days it seems to involve a lot of lying around, listening to music and eating chocolate. But no doubt all too soon things will kick off again and I'll be back out in the cockpit, down in my rowing seat, at turns exhausted, hot, wet, fearful. And probably naked if the weather improves. The VHF radio occasionally crackles into life. The rest of the Atlantic Rowing Race fleet also sits and waits. It's my birthday in a few days and my mind turns to home. At an age when most of my contemporaries are settling down to a life of responsible breadwinning and parenting, I'm off mucking about on the Atlantic.

I wouldn't have it any other way. A bad day on the water is better than a good day in the office, as the saying goes. Back home I felt unhappy, just floating along in the city, commuting on the train in a suit, cruising slowly to nowhere, with real life escaping me. The sea offered me a route out. Of course I'm floating along right now, but at least I'm where I want to be. Or, at least I will be if only the wind changes and I can get back on the oars.

Have I fallen in love with the ocean? It's a question many people asked when they found out I was going to try to row the Atlantic. I've met so many who genuinely love the sea and can't wait for their next opportunity to go sailing, cruising or just playing on the water. I can see why. People love the ocean they know. I have had some magic moments – rowing quietly on a calm, moonlit sea, surfing along on rolling blue waves, watching the setting sun sink into golden waters. But I've seen the other side too – the big scary stormy waves, the spiteful little breaker that comes along and soaks me just before the end of a shift, the occasional hit-and-run wave that knocks me for six.

I haven't yet reached the level of ocean rage experienced by John Fairfax, an early ocean rower. He got so angry that in a magnificently futile gesture he fired his harpoon into the waves. Despite the downsides, do I love the ocean? I love the solitude, the wildness, the beauty. But the ocean and I would get along much better if only it would stop trying to get in the boat with me. And if it weren't quite so dauntingly, occasionally overwhelmingly, big.

My small boat is my world for the next few months. I tap away at my journal some more. The satellite tells me I have overtaken two pairs, so I'm no longer coming last. I'm not really here for the race, but for an adventure: to prove to myself that I can do it. It will also be Christmas in a few days and I've got freeze-dried chicken with cranberries to look forward to. But what I really want for Christmas is a nice steady northeasterly.

Ocean-rowing is very much what you make it. Rowing technique is pretty irrelevant on the ocean. It's the psychology that's important.

JOHN KINGSLEY COOK 1911–1994

We were so tightly packed that our limbs
and bodies seemed all mixed up.

Having trained as an artist at the Royal Academy schools in London in the 1930s, John Kingsley Cook had just been appointed lecturer at the Edinburgh College of Art when war broke out. After a spell in the St John Ambulance brigade, he enrolled in the merchant navy and became a wireless radio officer. He joined the Atlantic convoys in December 1940 and was also part of a covert operation to bring relief to Malta, then under siege from German and Italian bombing. On the return voyage to Gibraltar, on 24 October 1941, his ship *Empire Guillemot* was sunk by an Italian torpedo bomber. The survivors washed ashore on the coast of Algeria, then part of occupied France, and were taken captive. Cook and the other sailors were held as prisoners of war until liberated by the Allied landing in North Africa in 1942.

After a few months recuperating following his return home, Cook resumed service in the merchant navy and was posted to the Mediterranean, refuelling tankers. He was discharged in August 1945 and was finally able to take up his post in Edinburgh. For many years he taught engraving and graphic design, and was appointed Head of Design in 1960. Throughout the war, Cook had made drawings of his life aboard ship, often using scraps he found on the bridge, such as envelopes, packing paper and old navigational charts. He later often cast his mind back to the shipwreck, creating a number of retrospective drawings, and working on his wartime memoirs, which are yet to be published.

Left: During his service in the merchant navy, Cook regularly sketched portraits of his crewmates, and a few self-portraits also survive. Shortly before he made this one on 25 March 1941, on a day's leave on shore, an unfortunate tennis accident gave him a black eye. Perhaps this is why half his face is in shadow.

Opposite: Many of Cook's sketches were made on the back of carefully cut up fragments of old navigational charts; here are 'Northbound Convoy off the coast of Ireland' and 'The Mate on the Bridge 6am. March 28th 1941'.

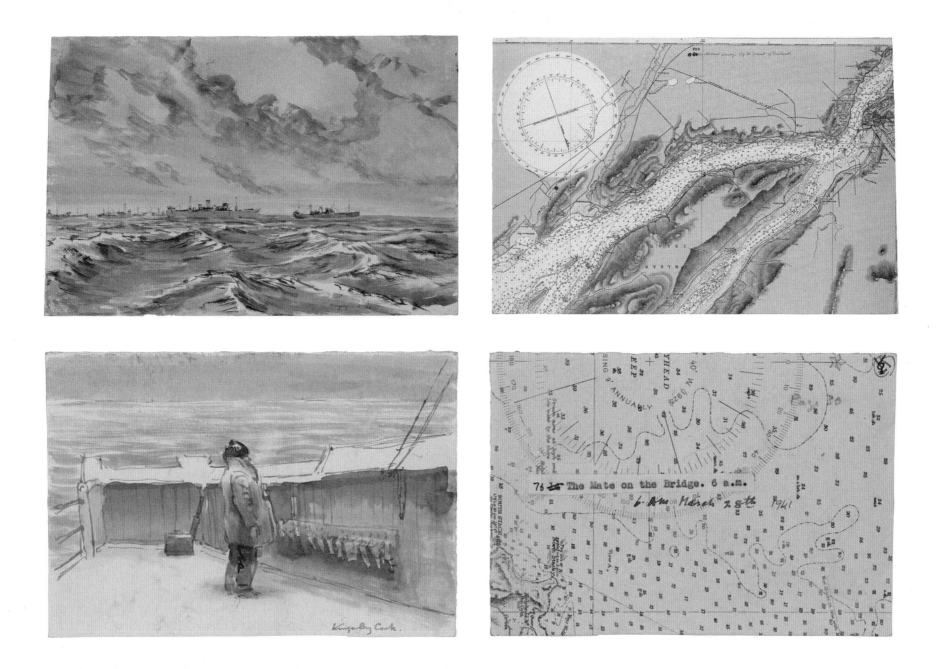

Kingsley Cook.

76 ~~76~~ The Mate on the Bridge. 6 a.m.

6. A.m. March 28th 1941

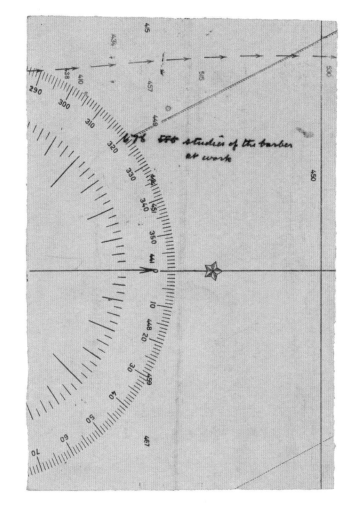

Opposite: Cook later worked on a manuscript of his experiences, from his enrolment to his liberation from captivity in Algeria. The memoirs were to be illustrated with on-the-spot drawings as well as retrospective sketches, such as this evocative scene of his ship *Empire Guillemot* sinking on 24 October 1941.

Above: '4th Engineer cutting the Chief's hair ... studies of the barber at work' - another sketch made on the back of a navigational chart.

'Searchlights at Gibraltar, 7 June 1944.' It was
when the *Empire Guillemot* was sailing for Gibraltar
in October 1941 that it was attacked by an Italian
torpedo bomber and sank. Cook and his surviving
shipmates made it to shore in Algeria, where
they were imprisoned for a year.

Opposite: An unnamed coastal view, and an 'Informal
pose in the Wheelhouse, 1941'.

EDWARD CREE 1814–1901

The typhoon moderated somewhat,
but no breakfast to be had except
some cold meat and a bottle of beer.

On 29 April 1841, Dr Edward Cree sat sketching near the walls of Canton. For eleven months he had been stationed in Chinese waters aboard the British naval troopship *Rattlesnake* and had taken every opportunity to explore. But with Britain engaged in military action against Qing Dynasty China, a pleasurable excursion could turn into something more dangerous. As Cree sketched, a sharp 'whip' of a shot rang out. After retreating quickly to the safety of the ship, he noticed a bullet hole in the brim of his straw hat. It was rather 'too close to be pleasant', he noted dryly.

An Englishman of Scottish heritage, twenty-three-year-old Cree had received his appointment from the Admiralty as Assistant Surgeon in 1837, a few days before Queen Victoria came to the throne. During his ten years in the Far East, he witnessed the devastating bombardments of the First Opium War, and saw action against the piratical fleets which operated along the southern coast of China and beyond, plundering and killing as they went. Cree recorded it all with empathy and candour, but there was also the grisly aftermath to deal with. As in any conflict, there were victims on both sides, and as a surgeon, Cree administered help to the wounded, whoever they were fighting for.

The climate and conditions made the experience all the more challenging. On top of fatal wounds, the troops were dying from dysentery, diarrhoea, cholera and fever. 'Death is making great havoc in the force, which is very sickly', Cree noted. 'I don't wonder at it considering the water we are drinking, stagnant from the paddy fields, all well mixed with liquid manure.'

Cree served with the Royal Navy for thirty-two years, including in the Baltic against the Russians, and he also saw the capture of Sebastopol and Kinburn during the Crimean War. Not all his shipboard life was spent in the horrors of war, and he made the most of the opportunities. He was a genial man, with a zest for life. In lighter moments, he spent his time sketching and writing, visiting friends, or taking a siesta on some far-flung island. He loved to dance, freely joined the revelries on board ship and enjoyed the company of pretty young women from Ceylon to Hong Kong. Tearful partings often followed, such as when leaving his favourite 'little fairy', Emily Pett, at Trincomalee.

'Everything one sees is so new and interesting', Cree wrote on his first voyage, and his enthusiasm for discovery never waned. During the course of his career he wrote well over a million words in his journals and completed some seventeen hundred watercolours and sketches.

Against a background of dramatic historical events, Cree's artworks record life at sea, his duties as a surgeon and his impressions of the people and places he encountered on his travels in peace and war. Here is the busy harbour at Canton in 1841.

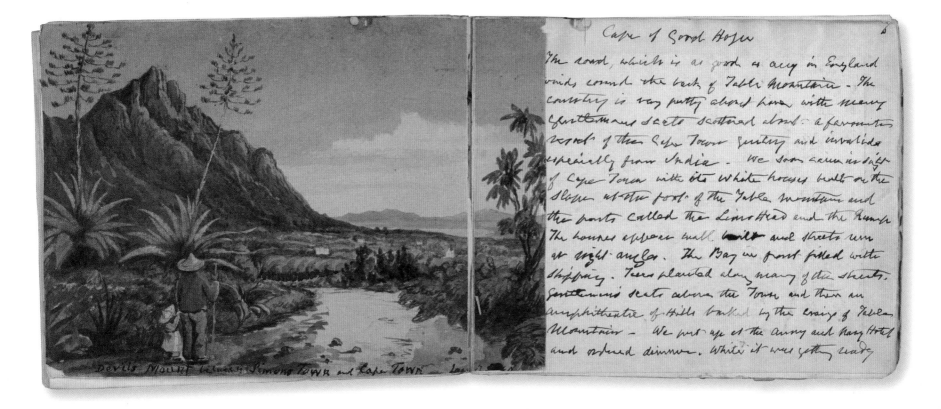

The road, which is as good as any in England winds round the back of Table Mountain. The country is very pretty about here with many Gentlemen's seats scattered about — a favourite resort of the Cape Town Gentry and invalids especially from India. We soon came in sight of Cape Town with its white houses built on the slopes at the foot of the Table mountain and the points called the Lions Head and the Rump. The houses appear well built and streets run at right angles. The Bay in front filled with shipping. Trees planted along many of the streets. Gentlemen's seats above the Town and then an amphitheatre of Hills backed by the crags of Table Mountain — We put up at the Army and Navy Hotel and ordered dinner. While it was getting ready

Devil's Mount between Simons Town and Cape Town

A keen artist and prolific diarist, Cree wrote and sketched in his journal almost every day. He spent his twenty-sixth birthday in 1840 at the Cape of Good Hope. He drew this sketch of what he calls Devil's Mount, between Simon's Town and Cape Town.

Some of the men got a lathering with pea soup and tar and scraped with a bit of iron hoop and a dab of tarbrush in the mouth if they opened it and afterwards half drowned ... by noon all was over ... the ship was put under easy sail and the sailors were allowed to get drunk on the rum which had been given by the officers.

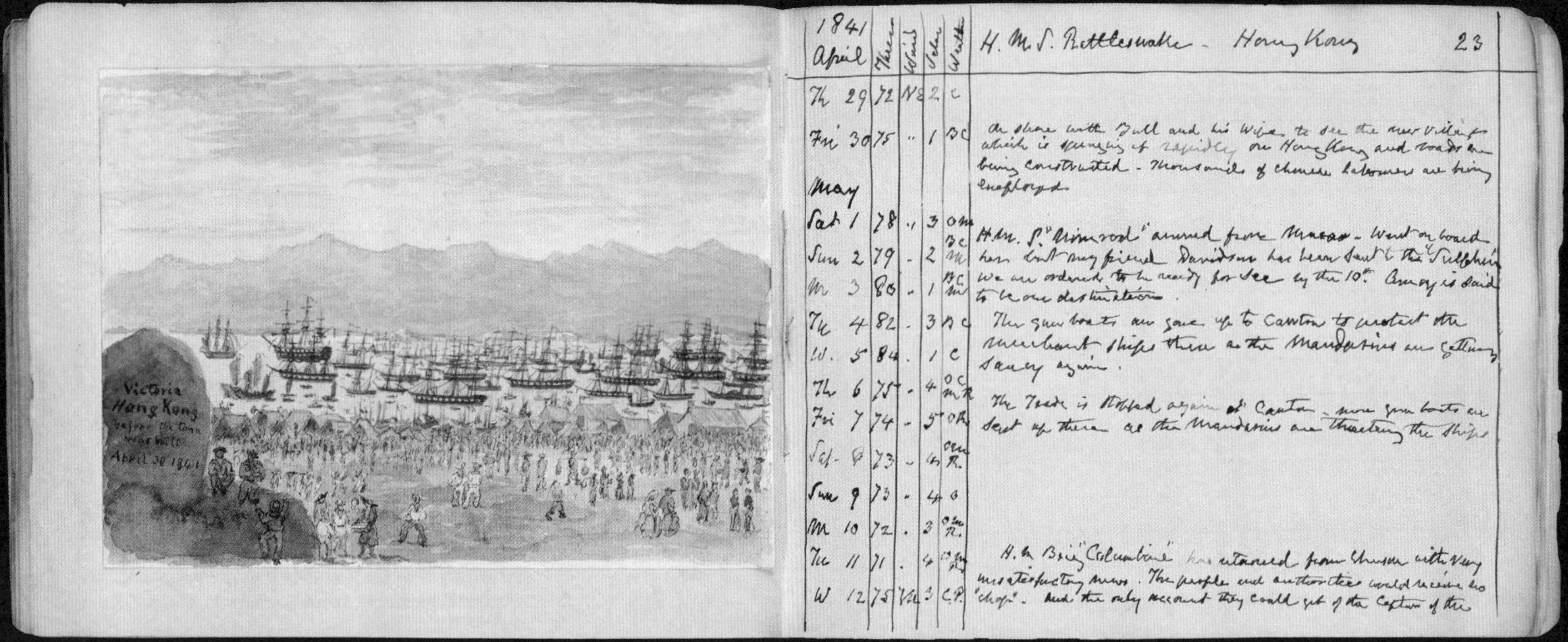

Victoria
Hong Kong
before the town
was built
April 30 1841

1841
April — H. M. S. Rattlesnake — Hong Kong — 23

19 April 1841: 'Went to Hong Kong, where the people all living under canvas.' Just two weeks later and already the village is 'springing up rapidly ... roads are being constructed. Thousands of Chinese labourers are being employed.'

Opposite: Sailing across the Equator heralded time-honoured rituals and newly invented traditions. Here is the elaborate 'Crossing the Line' ceremony on *Rattlesnake*. 'Father Neptune', Cree wrote on 2 November 1839, made his appearance at 9.30 a.m., 'attended by his rabble with drums, fifes and horns ... I had tipped old Nep with half a gallon of rum, so I was allowed on the poop.'

Crossing the Line

AARON CUSHMAN 1800-1856

Saw a large shoal of Sperm Whales ... lowered
4 boats could not strike ... at 9 lowered again
and struck one. Iron broke and lost him ...

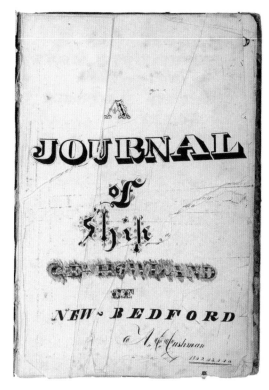

Whaling was the new frontier in the eighteenth century. In 1712 a ship was blown by a storm beyond the Nantucket fishing grounds and fell in with a school of sperm whales. The crew managed to kill one and the oil it yielded was superior to anything known before. Within a few years whaling ports had sprung up all along the eastern seaboard of America and captains were chasing sperm whales to the edges of the map, surveying new coastlines, charting the currents and opening up remote trading posts. From candles to cosmetics, from soap to street lamps, whale oil could be used in countless ways. And as a lubricant, whale oil soon kept the nation's clocks ticking and a new breed of heavy machinery moving, from locomotives to steam-powered looms. The profits were great, and so were the perils.

New Bedford, also in Massachusetts, came to rival Nantucket as a whaling centre, and with oil prices high, and demand insatiable, more ships and more men were needed. The only problem was the dwindling number of whales. With closer whaling grounds hunted to near extinction, ship owners looked further afield.

Aaron Cushman was the new captain of the *Geo Howland* when he shipped out in an easterly gale in May 1842, returning over three years later, in November 1845. He spent most of the voyage cruising up and down the west coast of South America. Like so many of the New Bedford captains, Cushman was a devout man, a Quaker, frugal, shunning ostentation; he encouraged his sailors in prayer, to think often of home, to stay sober and to avoid the temptations ashore. When supplies ran low whalers would put in at Peru or the Galapagos, but captains tried to make as few stops as possible – it was best to keep out to sea, searching and hunting, and in port there were other risks, chief of all that the crew might jump ship. Cushman's journal mentions this and that he needed to recruit replacements.

In the frenzy of the Gold Rush, San Francisco was a popular jumping off point, while others tried their luck on the larger tropical islands. Tahiti and the Marquesas became important anchorages, likewise Hawaii. Some captains were instructed to sail to the Pacific with skeleton crews and sign up extra men when there. As most whalers were only paid their wages – a tiny cut of the profits – on completion of a voyage, those who jumped usually left with their pockets empty.

Whaleship investors and merchants, on the other hand, were wealthy. The *Geo Howland* was named for its owner, a New Bedford magnate. Cushman was on his books as a captain for almost twenty years until he died at sea of a heart attack in 1856, when in command of the *Lancer*. The *Geo Howland* was back in the Galapagos in 1852 and was captured by a gang of convicts hoping to make their escape. She was retaken by a Swedish frigate, which also picked up what was left of the crew, who had survived on rainwater and turtles. The then captain of *Geo Howland*, Samuel Cromwell, had paddled to safety in an oil barrel that he'd sawn in half to make a boat.

Cushman's sea journal from his Pacific voyage in
1842-45. Many pages include whale tails - whales
sighted, but not struck - whereas whole whales appear
in the journal when caught. There are numerous other
scenes of ships, both seen and 'gamm'd', when crews
would meet with each other to smoke, dance and
trade tall tales of the hunt.

One of the sailors, a Samuel Watson, was drowned
when his small whaleboat overturned, and Cushman
has drawn a coffin floating in the sea. Once a whale
was harpooned and weakened, the men would drive their
lances repeatedly into it in the hope of striking
its 'life', a lethal jab to heart or lungs. The mortal
blow made the telltale sign: a spout of red blood.

Com'd with light winds from E.N. steering E. East in sight. Saw Blackfish. Mid' part going aback. At daylight, saw whales. At 8 lowered & 9 got. Struck & at 12 m. the one alongside. the the 4 boats in pursuit. Land in sight, East bearing S.E.

Lat in 30 P.
Long 86. 40 W.

Com'd with light winds and pleasant. Mid'dy at 1 P.M. struck 10 man whales, engaged in taking them to the ship. At 3 P.M. Took the last to the ship. a Large whale. Whose boat. 20 bbls. 9 body 24 m. & saw'd do 35. 18 & head. 9 md. Latter part engaged in Entering. Calm.

L. B. Wh B. B. 5 bls

SPERM ———— WHALING ~ Ship Geo. Howland

Thursday

Light Win...
at 4 P...
Departed...

Mid'd Par...
at 7 A.M. ...
Chewed down...
top sail to 14...
Colurs hal...
And turned...
Lat by D. R...
Long...

OIL STOWED DOWN

Date	Head		Body		Total		Brls.	Rec'd
	bbls — galls		bbls — galls		bbls — galls			
Feb. 23rd 1843	1 47	9½	154	9½				ℍℍ ℍℍ ℍℍ
" " "	64	11	2 01		5 bb 30		2	ℍℍ ℍℍ ℍℍ
"July " "	34	17	77	6½			2	30
Sep 12 "	15	17½	83	4½				
Oct 10 "	25	16	61	10½	326	24½	3	ℍℍ ℍℍ ℍℍ
do 23	22	9	50	15			1	30
do 25	33	46½	55	24½			2	ℍℍ ℍℍ ℍℍ
Nov 18	21	28½	61	29½			2	ℍℍ ℍℍ ℍℍ
Oct 5 "	10	18½	19	15½	274	1½	1	30
							4	11
							14	
Jany 6 1844	17	27½	52	18				
Feb 11½ do	86	27	166	3				
do 20 do	36	16	52	12	412	8		
June 13 do	22	26	37	22½				
July 30 do	12	16	24	8				
Aug 9 do	22	18	57	23½				
Oct 25 do	23	24½	41	11	242	23½		
Nov 11th /44	00	00	24	19½				
Jany 14 /45	31	20½	51	13½				
" 31 do	32	00	53	03½				
Feby 14 do	34	20	31	25½	256	8		
Mar 20 /45	5	27½	12	16				
July 15 3	34	12	88	03				
" 7 " 8	18	12	60	14	219	22½		
July 28 & Aug								
Feb 9 "	51	13½	94	04				
Aug 12	13	25½	54	29	214	09		

JOSEPH DESBARRES 1721-1824

There is scarcely any known shore so
much intersected with Bays, Harbours,
and Creeks as this is.

As a landlocked nation Switzerland isn't renowned for its seafarers, but it could be argued that a Swiss surveyor had an impact on the maritime world far greater than any number of pioneering explorers. Little known today, Joseph Frederick Wallet DesBarres was one of the most influential cartographers of the eighteenth century. He spent most of his life in Canada, where he lived to be over 100 years old. His charts were used on ships in times of great peril and uncertainty, through war and peace, and it was DesBarres who taught James Cook some of the finer skills of cartography.

Mariners of all nations made charts of various kinds, but after the development of printing presses, they were predominately printed in the country that held maritime supremacy: that meant the Spanish and Portuguese in the fifteenth and sixteenth centuries, the Dutch in the seventeenth, and by the eighteenth the British. The French were the first to set up a Hydrographic Office, in 1720, and the British Admiralty was then spurred on to do the same. Spain followed suit in 1800, Russia in 1827, the USA in 1830, and other nations including Germany, Japan, Italy and Chile were drawing and printing their own charts by the end of the century.

Yet it was London that became the global centre for the creation and sale of these indispensable navigational tools, and the Admiralty chart the gold standard. During the 1760s and 1770s, DesBarres surveyed the entire east coast of North America for the British, and his charts were widely used throughout the American War of Independence. The term 'Neptune' then signified a set of charts, just as the word 'Atlas'

refers to a collection of maps. DesBarres' monumental four-volume folio, the *Atlantic Neptune*, was issued in 1777 to the British fleet and contained the most accurate charts ever made.

DesBarres had emigrated to England in about 1752, studying at the Royal Military Academy at Woolwich and sailing across the Atlantic with a commission in the Royal American Regiment. He participated in the assault of Quebec, which gave control of Canada to Britain, surveying the Gulf of St Lawrence and the river approaches, and, after the fall of the citadel, he sounded the harbour and basin. DesBarres was then engaged by the Admiralty to survey the Bay of Fundy and Nova Scotia, as Cook surveyed Newfoundland.

These coastlines were intricate – 'so full of Islands, Rocks, and Shoals as are almost innumerable', DesBarres wrote – and it took him the best part of a decade. Most of the painstaking work was carried out from small open boats in the summer, and in winter DesBarres would retire to his estate, which he named 'Castle Frederick', to complete his charts and drawings. He was still making new charts long after his contemporaries has passed away, and though he was 'selfish, friendless and uncompromising', as one Admiralty report described him, 'for all his faults, he stands pre-eminent'.

James Cook was tasked with making a new survey of Newfoundland, an island bigger than Ireland. It was an enormous undertaking and occupied him for five years between 1762 and 1767. His original chart of Newfoundland survives in the Admiralty Manuscript Collection.

DesBarres was chosen to oversee the creation of a new generation of charts. The *Atlantic Neptune* began to appear in 1777, in the urgent atmosphere of the American War of Independence, and it eventually encompassed some 250 charts. Here are his 'Eight views of Nova Scotia'.

Appearance of the Land from the White Islands to St. Marys River taken two Leagues off Shore.

The Entrance of MILFORD HAVEN at the Head of Chedabucto Bay.

The Entrance of PORT BICKERTON bearing N.W.

A View taken off the Entrance of Beaver Harbor Bald Isle bearing E. 15°. S.

A View taken in the Offing of Beaver Harbor Bald Isle bearing W. by N. distant ¾ of a Mile.

Appearance of the Shore to the Westward of Cross Cranberry Isle bearing N. by E. ½ E. distant 4 Miles.

The Beaver Islands.

Appearance of the S.E. Coast of NOVA SCOTIA taken from CANSO ISLANDS shewing the distant Land of RICHMOND ISLES the BAY of CANSO &c.

THE

Atlantic Neptune,

PUBLISHED

For the use of the Royal Navy

OF

Great Britain,

By Joseph F. W. Des Barres Esqr.

Under the Directions of the

Right Honble, the Lords Commissioners of the

ADMIRALTY

Sunt ingeniorum monumenta quæ sæculis probantur. LIV.

VOL. I

LONDON.

MDCCLXXVII.

T. Tomkins Scripsit. H. Ashby Sculpsit.

1

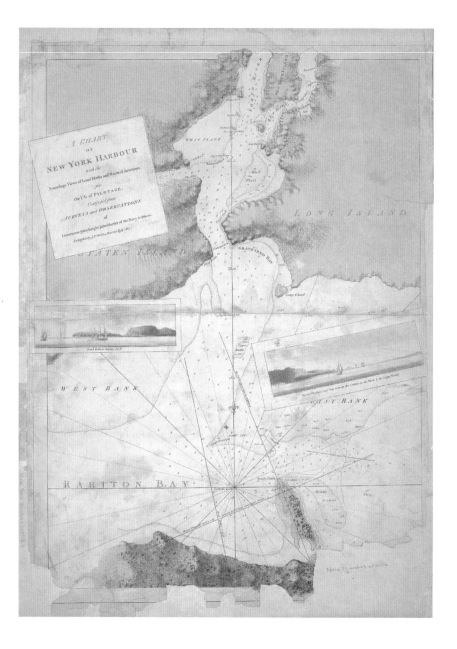

Opposite left: The title-page of the *Atlantic Neptune*, published in a folio, which extended from Nova Scotia to the Gulf of Mexico. The charts later became a priceless parting gift to the navy of the newly independent United States.

Opposite right: DesBarres was Cook's equal in surveying skill, but he lacked his exploring spirit. His chart of New York Harbour, 'with the soundings, views of land marks and nautical directions for the use of pilotage', was issued in May 1779.

Right: Not only were DesBarres' charts technically superior to anything that had come before, they were also objects of fine printing, with an 'artistry that transcended their utilitarian purpose'. DesBarres also standardized many of the symbols, such as navigational hazards, which are found on nautical charts to this day.

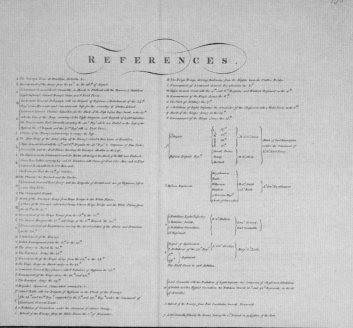

The PHOENIX and the ROSE Engaged by the ENEMY'S FIRE SHIPS and GALLEYS on the 16 Aug.st 1776.

FRANCIS DRAKE 1540-1596

Disturb us, Lord, to dare more boldly, to venture
on wider seas, where storms will show your mastery,
where losing sight of land, we shall find the stars.

To his enemies he was renowned as 'El Draque' – the dragon – a pirate and menace, the scourge of the Seven Seas. To his admirers at home, Sir Francis Drake was a dashing nautical hero, a sea captain and explorer who came to typify the buccaneering romance of an Elizabethan age that was reshaping the power balance of great nations. He took his crews to the ends of the world in search of fat foreign galleons to plunder, their bellies full of South American gold.

Born near Tavistock in Devon, a vicar's eldest son, Drake grew up surrounded by seafarers in Plymouth. He sailed first as a boy on William Hawkins' merchant ships, trading at Tenerife, the Canaries and other European ports, and later capturing ship-loads of slaves off Sierra Leone, taking them to the West Indies where both slaves and other goods were sold at huge profit. Drake spent much of the early 1570s in command of ships – often with the help of French pirate crews – raiding outposts in the Isthmus of Panama, storming forts along the coast of New Spain and amassing a small fortune. With influential backers behind him, his next great voyage would promise more of the same.

On 15 November 1577 he set out from Plymouth with five ships and 164 men on a voyage that would make him the first captain in history to circumnavigate the globe. His flagship was the 150-ton *Pelican* – lead-sheathed, double-planked and armed with eighteen guns – which he renamed *Golden Hind* mid-voyage in honour of one of his patrons, whose crest bore a red deer. In September 1580 he returned to Plymouth harbour with only 56 of his crew of 80 left, but the ship filled with more than 30 tons of silver, gold, pearls and porcelain.

Half of the treasure went to queen and country and was enough to pay off the entire national debt; Elizabeth went aboard *Golden Hind* to congratulate him with a knighthood. Drake chose as his motto *sic parvis magna*, 'thus great things from small things come'. Sadly, all first-hand records from this remarkable circumnavigation, including logs, paintings and charts, were later lost when the royal palace of Whitehall burned down in 1698.

Not content to settle down as country squire or politician, Drake went back to sea on a mission to ransack the Spanish colonies, then 'singe the beard of the King of Spain' in 1587 by sailing into Cádiz and Corunna and destroying Spanish ships. He was vice admiral by the time the Spanish gathered their fleets to invade England, and he duly defeated them in a fury of fire and gunpowder. His seafaring continued into his mid-fifties, though his luck was running out. He died after an unsuccessful attack on fortified San Juan in Puerto Rico. Although he avoided the cannonball that tore through the cabin of his flagship, he succumbed to dysentery. Dressed in full armour, he was buried at sea in a lead-lined coffin, somewhere in shallow waters off Panama. Even today, divers continue to search for him.

Drake undertook his 'West Indian Voyage' in 1585, sailing from Plymouth with 21 ships and nearly 2,000 soldiers. He plundered Santiago in the Cape Verde islands (with flying fish) and captured Cartagena in Colombia (with lizard). The chart, hand-coloured by Italian draftsman Baptista Boazio, was created to celebrate the successful campaign.

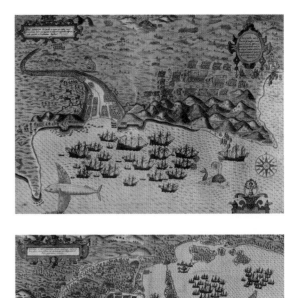

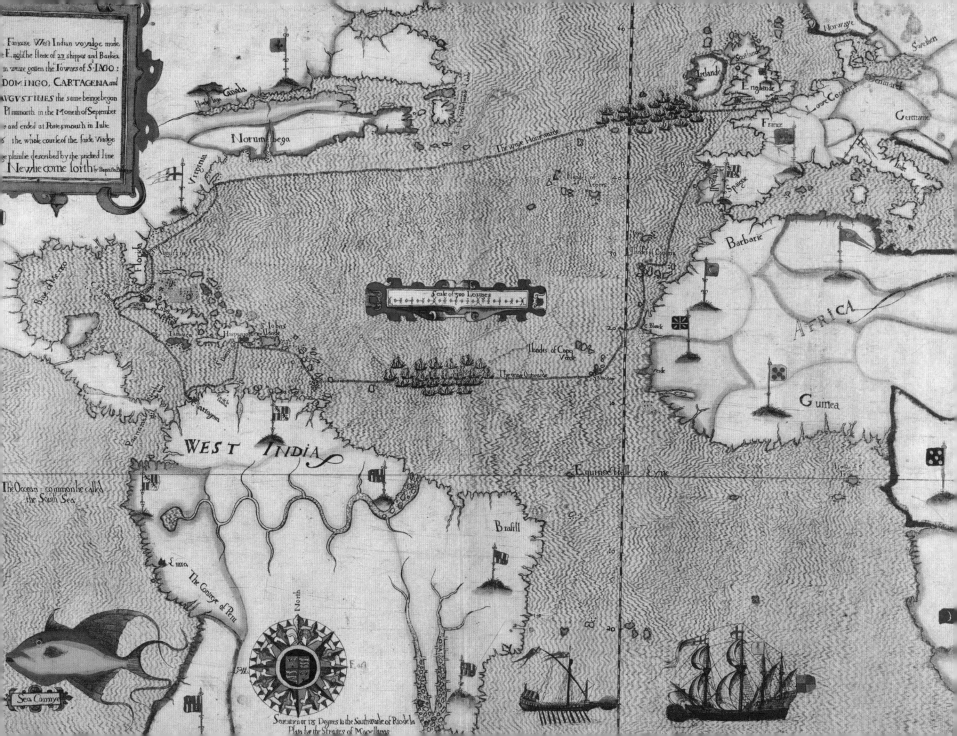

Canada

Norumbega

Virginia

Florida

Bay of Mexico

C. S. Anton

Iucatan

Iamaca

Hispaniola

S. Iohns Illande

S. Iuan

Cartagen

Panama

Panama

The Occean commonlie called
the Sowth Sea

Nueua

The Conttrye of Peru

Sea Cunnye

WEST INDIA

Brasill

The waye Homewarde

Illandes of Azores

Illandes of Canaria

Illandes of Cape Verde

The waye Outwarde

Equinoctiall Lyne

Irelande

Scotlande

Englande

France

Barbarie

AFRICA

Gumea

Norwaye

Sweden

Denmark

Germanie

Spaigne

North

East

South

West

Scale of 500 Leagues

Seuentien or 18 Degrees to the Southwarde of Rio de la
Plata for the Straites of Magellanus

OPIDVM S Augustini hures in hoc conspectum,
amœnissimas habuit hortos et sua fortuna simp
arabus vero cum suis succersteris unitis maris portum
currere reductum. Præsidium hic restit in defensum
stunts, item eodem numero ad quadrum Capitanorum
rursus fratres in loco S Helena latis dat super seq
felix quemadmodum tamen in profuganis ris existdis dignita
erund usi ad probibendas hostiles et Gallis as intervium
rationum quæ profuti mollicret, sequeretur.

S AVGVSTINI
gers et terra Florum
sub latitudine 30 gradu
ora vero meridiani
humilior est, litus
cartus et insu
lofam.

Opposite: 'Drake's Raid'. This hand-coloured view of St Augustine is the earliest known depiction of a European settlement in the United States. The English fleet lies at anchor, while infantry are attacking ashore. Boazio wrote of the dorado, or dolphinfish, on the edge of his image: 'he is very pleasant to beholde in the sea by day light, and in the night he seemeth to be of the coullour of gold'.

This page: Drake's last campaign to harass the Spaniards in Central America was in 1595. In this precious manuscript journal of the voyage, the pilot records indications useful to navigation for a later expedition and reports Drake's death off Panama.

JOHN EVERETT 1876-1949

The artist and the sailor have many things in
common. They are both vagabonds and wanderers.

John Everett was a tremendously private man and only
truly at home when at sea. He made more than sixteen
major voyages, but he never published his memoirs and
rarely exhibited or sold his paintings. As the only son of an
aristocrat and her country clergyman husband, Everett had
a modest private income and no interest in self-promotion:
he just wanted to paint.

Born Herbert Barnard John Everett, he chose to be called
John from about 1901. He studied at the Slade School of Fine
Art in London and the Académie Julian in Paris, but took an
unconventional path, signing on in the London docks as a
crew member of the sailing ship *Iquique* in 1898 and working
his way to Sydney and back. In London the following year he
returned to the Slade, made sketching excursions to Cornwall
and France, and then settled on making marine painting his
speciality. When he married, for the couple's honeymoon he
arranged passage to Tasmania on a 700-ton barque. Each
August he sailed to Cowes to paint the racing yachts, and
also worked on harbour scenes in France. His small cutter
Walrus took him away much of the time he was supposed to
be at home. Unsurprisingly, his family life suffered and the
marriage didn't last.

With the onset of the First World War Everett was unable
to sketch outdoors because of wartime security regulations,
but eventually the Ministry of Information asked him to
depict London river scenes. He received a permit to draw,
and spent every day one summer at the docks. In 1918 he
joined the merchant navy and in 1920 sailed from Bristol for
Texas, returning home on an Atlantic steamer. More ocean

voyages followed and his work reflects the knowledge he
gained from living on board a ship for long periods; there is
maritime nostalgia and yet a modernism too. He was a fine
draughtsman, seeing rhythmic beauty in the patterns of sail,
rope and rigging, and he experimented with photography, as
well as continually sketching in oils.

The Second World War marked an end to his ocean forays,
but he continued to draw on his memories and sketchbooks
to embark on many more imaginative voyages, including
pictures of *Cutty Sark*, which he had admired, but never sailed.
For a man like Everett, the sea meant freedom, and the empty
horizon was his true solace. Encouraged by his friends, on his
death he bequeathed to the nation practically his entire life's
output, some 1,058 oil paintings and hundreds of sketches.

Everett made his first sea journey in the sailing
ship *Iquique* in 1898 aged twenty-one. His generation
lived through a time of considerable change - seeing
the first flights across the Channel, the end of
sailing ships used for carrying cargo, new industries
and global conflict. He was commissioned by the
Ministry of Information in the First World War to
make drawings and paintings of the London docks
and the Thames; opposite is the *Greystone Castle*.

Opposite: Everett's sketchbooks are filled with quick drawings in pencil, ink, watercolour and wash. He voyaged widely as a deep-water sailor, but also sketched along the English coasts and for many years studied shipping in the Thames.

Right: From the 1920s Everett was experimenting with unusual compositions, rhythmic shapes and contrasting colours in an Art Deco style. He sailed on the barque *Birkdale* from Bristol to Sabine Pass, Texas, in 1920. This sunlit view is from the upper top on the foremast, looking back and down on the billowing sails. Shadows of the upper foresails fall upon the mainsail.

Dazzle was a type of camouflage developed by the artist Norman Wilkinson in 1917, in response to the heavy losses sustained by British merchant ships to German submarines. It involved painting ships in contrasting colours and shapes in angular patterns to create a distorted effect and deceive enemies about size, course and speed.

Opposite: Everett painted numerous sea studies to capture the effect of light on water. Here is a page of coastal views and seascapes, some with ships on the horizon, including a distant view of Jamaica and also Guadeloupe.

EDWARD FANSHAWE 1814-1906

The climate throughout is perfect, and being tropical is well suited to me. I hope to make some sketches.

An exceptional Royal Navy officer, Sir Edward Gennys Fanshawe was also in a sense fairly typical of many seafaring gentlemen in the nineteenth century. He went to sea aged fourteen and steadily rose up the ranks of the navy through talent and family connections. Six decades later, he was still active in naval affairs at Queen Victoria's Golden Jubilee in 1887. A knight of the realm, an Admiralty Lord and President of the new Royal Naval College in Greenwich, Fanshawe was also a talented amateur artist.

Generations of young officers were encouraged to draw in lessons at the Naval College in Portsmouth during their training in coastal survey and log keeping – mastering the arts of observation, care and precision. They illustrated their journals with views and coastal profiles as they passed from midshipman to lieutenant, but most did not continue to paint unless their interests lay in this direction. Throughout his service at sea, Fanshawe's paints were never far from hand, and he recorded his experiences on numerous voyages.

In 1840 he first sailed on the corvette *Daphne* in operations off the coast of Syria, taking part in the bombardment of Acre and venturing up the Nile; in 1844 he was in the East Indies and won his captaincy fighting pirates off Borneo. He took *Daphne* back to the Pacific on an extended voyage from 1848, with a book of Captain Cook's expeditions as his daily reading. He visited Pitcairn and heard tales of the *Bounty* mutineers, and also dined with Fijian royalty and Tahitian warriors. On his way home, at the request of the Bank of England, he earned a large reward by freighting Mexican silver back to London.

Fanshawe's career at sea witnessed many of the era's major changes in naval technology: from sail-power to steam and eventually the beginnings of submarine warfare. From 1861 on he was superintendent of Chatham Dockyard, during which time the first ironclad, the armour-plated *Achilles*, was built there. Towards the end of active service, Fanshawe was commander-in-chief of the North American and West Indies squadrons, and in 1878 commander-in-chief at Portsmouth, where he was much involved in the latest fleet invention: torpedoes. He died in London on Trafalgar Day, 21 October 1906, still following naval developments with a keen interest, though the years of wooden warships had long passed. His personal motto was *dux vitae ratio*, 'reason is the guide of life'.

Left: Seru Epenisa Cakobau, or 'Thakambau', was the eldest son of Tanoa, the chief of Bau. Fanshawe met him in October 1849. A man of considerable integrity and strength, he later became the first recognized ruler of a newly united Fijian kingdom.

Opposite: *Daphne* off Cape Horn in 1852, carrying a freight of Mexican silver. The ship was sailing on a reduced rig after her masts had been knocked flat in a hurricane at Mazatlán.

ROSE DE FREYCINET 1794–1832

Life is too short! I wanted to brighten it up as much as possible, and I shall never regret my decision.

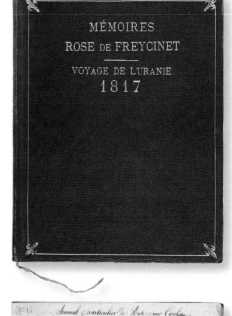

In the dead of night on 16 September 1817, a young woman crept through the streets of Toulon, France, towards the harbour. Disguised as a man, she intended to stow away on her husband's ship, the *Uranie*. This was embarking the next morning on a three-year scientific expedition to the Pacific and Australia, and would ultimately circumnavigate the globe. The woman mumbled the password at the entrance to the dock and climbed aboard, only to find herself faced with a crowd of officers. Asked to identify herself, she was saved from detection by a friend and co-conspirator, who declared that she was his son.

Rose de Freycinet's husband, Captain Louis de Freycinet, had colluded with her scheme, but when reports of the stowaway caused indignation in official circles in Paris the affair became front-page news. Journalists exaggerated the impudence of the young woman who had flouted convention, risking not only danger to herself, but also her husband's career. It was only when *Uranie* left Gibraltar that Rose believed her passage was safe, and she emerged as the commander's wife.

The long voyage was not without its challenges. Jacques Arago, the expedition's artist, wrote of her courage in the face of treacherous seas, months of monotony and the 125 men aboard. She survived close encounters with deadly snakes, danger of attack from pirates and life-threatening bouts of food poisoning and malaria. After making scientific observations and collecting specimens on several Pacific islands, the *Uranie* arrived in Sydney, where the de Freycinets were welcomed and enjoyed the entertainments offered by the best company.

Then on the way home disaster struck: *Uranie* hit a rock near the Falkland Islands. With seawater rushing in, the officers and crew grabbed supplies and scientific records, and abandoned ship. Arago recorded that Rose 'watched fearlessly as barrels of gunpowder floated by near her next to burning lanterns, and she forgot her own sad plight for the sake of the general misfortune.' By the time they were rescued ten weeks later, the privations showed: 'My thinness scares me', she wrote. 'I am pale, yellowish, and have sunken eyes; in short I look like a ghost.'

On their safe return, scandal forgotten, their story of love and adventure so captured the imagination of contemporary French society that the de Freycinets were fêted in the salons of Paris. Even King Louis XVIII showed compassion, remarking that Rose's act of conjugal devotion ought to be excused, as few would want to follow her. Despite being written out of the official accounts, a lasting, indirect reference to the presence of Rose de Freycinet appears in the naming of a new variety of dove, discovered on islands off New Guinea, and two species of ferns. Louis also named an island in the Pacific for her: 'It is done,' she wrote home in delight, 'my name has been linked with a small corner of the world.'

Rose kept a journal in the form of letters to her friend, Caroline de Nanteuil, providing an insight into life at sea at a time when women were strictly prohibited from French naval vessels. Opposite is a drawing of Shark Bay, as observed from the *Uranie*, by Alphonse Pellion, with Rose visible at the opening of the tent at the right.

Mr Pellion

Baie des Chiens-Marins,
Observatoire   l'Uranie

VASCO DA GAMA 1460–1524

I am not afraid of the darkness. Real death
is preferable to a life without living.

Sea voyages once had the potential to create a new world order. In 1498, as Vasco da Gama was sailing east into the Indian Ocean, an Italian maverick named Christopher Columbus sailed west for the third time and finally reached the mainland of the Americas, claiming a 'new world' for Spain. Both men were searching for the same prize: a sea route to Asia. This was not a quixotic quest to push the boundaries of human knowledge, but rather a very daring, and pragmatic, effort to reverse the global balance of trade with the East, then dominated by Islam.

Portugal had become a great maritime power, and da Gama enters this story as a gentleman of the king's household, aged about thirty-five, having trained as a navigator in the Portuguese navy. After some voyages proving his toughness, he became a kind of roving economic ambassador in the royal fleets for Portuguese interests overseas. More than making new discoveries, his paramount task was to establish good relations with local potentates, build trading networks and further the cause of Christianity. At his disposal when he set out in 1497 were four vessels: the *São Gabriel*, his flagship, and *São Raphael*, commanded by his brother Paulo, both square-rigged carracks, or nãos; a storeship; and the lateen-rigged caravel *Berrio*, commanded by Nicolau Coelho.

Tracking south from Lisbon, da Gama sailed down the west coast of Africa, rounded the Cape of Good Hope and entered uncharted waters. By January, as he neared the Muslim city-state of Mozambique, the expedition was forced to rest, repair and replenish. In April, between the monsoons, the ships left Malindi, in present-day Kenya, and sailed for Calicut, assisted by a Gujarati pilot named Ibn Majid. On 29 April they saw the North Star for the first time since leaving the Atlantic and finally, on 18 May 1498, 'after seeing no land for twenty-three days, we sighted lofty mountains at a distance of 8 leagues'. They had finally raised the Western Ghats.

After a voyage of ten months, the bold journey to India was complete. Arguably the greatest piece of sailing in the history of European seafaring up to that time, this was also the beginning of a new epoch, which saw the diffusion of ideas and a dramatic reshaping of relations between East and West. Da Gama then had to fight his way across the Indian Ocean in the teeth of contrary monsoon winds, with his crew riddled with scurvy, the first widely noted outbreak of the disease. In an effort to save supplies he even ordered one of his ships to be burned. His brother Paulo died on the return voyage, and when da Gama finally reached Portugal on 9 September he mourned for nine days before entering the capital to a triumphant welcome.

Right: A portrait of da Gama from the manuscript *Lives of Portuguese Viceroys in India*, of 1558, now housed in the Pierpont Morgan Library in New York.

Opposite: The Indian Ocean as imagined in the sublime Miller Atlas of 1519. A masterpiece, showing the state of Portuguese knowledge of the world, it was based on da Gama's sea journals and other pilot charts - a treasury of top-secret maritime knowledge.

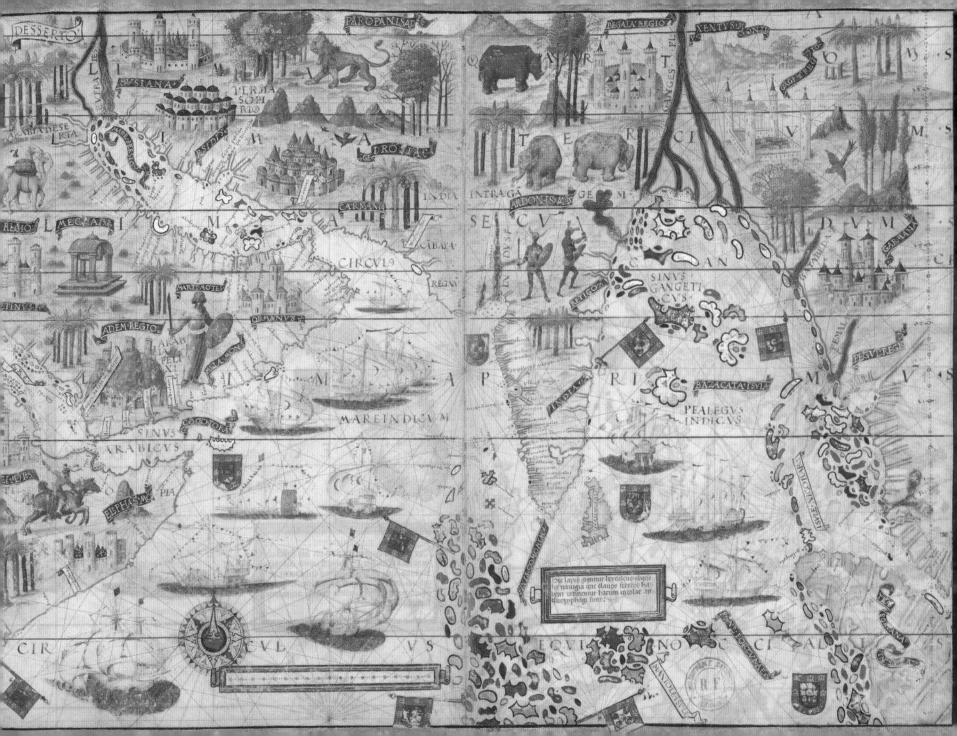

They are merchants, and have transactions with white Moors, four of whose vessels were at the time in port, laden with gold, silver, cloves, pepper, ginger and silver rings, and also quantities of pearls, jewels, and rubies ... we were told that further on, where we were going precious stones, pearls and spices were so plentiful that they could be collected in baskets.

The fleet of Pedro Mascarenhas and shipwreck of one of the vessels in 1554 from *Lives of Portuguese Viceroys in India* (right) and the caravels of da Gama's expedition round the Cape of Good Hope in 1497 (opposite right), as detailed in the *Memoria das Armadas* in the Academia das Ciencias in Lisbon.

Opposite left: This manuscript is the only surviving copy of a journal written during da Gama's first voyage to India in 1497. The lost original has been attributed to Álvaro Velho, though he did not immediately return to Portugal with the expedition, remaining for eight years in Gambia and Guinea.

OMPEDROMASQVARE

Partio Vasq da gama pera a jndia a oyto de Julho por capitão mor cō quatro vellas 3 pera requerir ho descobrimento da jndia e hūa carregada de mantimentos pera se cō elles e cō agente della Reformare, das quaes ∞ ões erão os capitaes /

S. Raphael.

C Paullo da gama D

Jrmão de Vasco da gama á tornada pera portugal, Varou e os Bayxos Antre quiloa e mōbaça, aos quaes chamão de S. Rafael por tes se da Nao ... e ssi se chamava, e agente della se Reparto pellas duas da compā fia. —

·S. gabriel·

C Vasquo da gama D

berrio

C Nicolao coelho D

C gonçallo nuñez D

Em Nome de ds Amen.

mandou ElRey dom manuell o pimo portugalle ...
navios os quaes ... á busca da Specearia, dos quatro navios hia por capitam mor Vº Dagama e dos outros hū delles paullo Dagama seu jrmão e ...

Partimos de Restello hūa ... de julho da era de 1497 nosso ...
nosso sōr leixe acabar a seu serviço amen.

primeiramente chegamos ao ... á vista das canarias ...
e na noute passamos á suea bento de ... e a noute seguinte ao amanhecer ...
... ds ora ... esta noute ...
... de perto paullo Dacunha e toda a frota por qual ...
pello outro capitam mor. E pois que amanheceo vou, ou
vemos vista delle nem dos outros navios, e nos fizemos ora ...
... desque ... esta porta No dia ... primeiro da
... ouvemos vista da ssa de ... e ...
ora ouvemos vista de tres navios, os quaes ... e moo da ...
... a nave dos martios e Nicolao velez e berrio ...
... e nossa companhia até ... os quaes
... tinham p dos o capitam mor. E pois ...
... nosso rota e fazemos o bem ...

UNLIKELY VOYAGES

Spider Anderson

Towards Darwin — grey green emerald sea with big black pilot whales

Only the voyager perceives the poignant loveliness of life, for he alone has tasted of its contrasts. He has explored the two infinities – the external universe and himself.

ROCKWELL KENT, 1924

As a marine artist I spend much of my life trying to paint what is often undepictable – to capture in a moment that which is ever-moving, restless and unending. This is what makes the sea such a deep source of inspiration for people all round the world. I think the uncertainties of this environment make it even more attractive. No matter how much you plan, your voyage will always sail into the realm of the unlikely. The winds and the waters are your master, the weather rules and the sea brings surprises that will defeat your pen and brush. I have felt whales beneath my hull and collected flying fish on my deck in the morning. At sea I have been near death, scared beyond measure and yet have never felt so alive. I have seen things that I still can't quite explain, let alone understand.

In my art I try to make some of the unlikely things at sea real to others. I render these sights in oil paint, water and lead and feel my way through a painting in miniature, every mark helping to make the whole. Having worked on or around the sea for over five decades, when I look at a sketch, or close my eyes and think back on a voyage, memories flood in like a tide. I know memories will also ebb as the years pass, and so my sketches become even more essential.

My first sea outing was at Christmas in 1964, launching in a gale. My father was a sailor and he built my brother and me a varnished jewel of a dinghy, a 'Sabot' pram, which we christened *Stormy*. We swamped, we bailed, we cried with excitement – with our father's hand on the tiller and his quiet words of instruction in our ears – as we reached back and forward, our mother watching from the shore. I was frightened on that first voyage, and overwhelmed by just how thrilling it all was. It has been much the same for my sailing life since. Exhilaration, fear and freedom combine. In that first year, many 'stormy' voyages followed, most just for an hour, some for a day.

Then a first trip out of sight of home, then another out all night. With a friend from school I paddled down the Brisbane River and camped on the riverbank under our canoe. A bed-sheet was our sail. I was ten and I was hooked. In my twenties I traded art school for life on a square-rigger, and fell in love with the tough life before the mast. I worked hard and stayed on *Eye of the Wind* as second mate during a scientific circumnavigation, and it introduced me to a fraternity of international sailors and expeditioners. As an artist, I joined a voyage to Papua New Guinea, building and then sailing an indigenous canoe along its traditional trading routes. For those two years I recorded everything in my sketchbooks.

Just before I turned thirty, I joined another, very different, expedition, this time as co-pilot in *Endeavour*, manning the world's first super-pressure helium balloon. It was totally untried, a new design. We had a few near-death moments, but got through because of the preparations we'd made. We were happy to calculate the risks and head beyond our comfort zone. And although I was up in the air, we were sailing, and some very lightweight journals came with me.

To be a good mariner you must have respect for the sea. It's a curious thing. It knocks off the pretensions of shore-life. The sea is uncompromising. It takes you away towards self-sufficiency and makes you believe more fully in yourself. I'm naturally a very shy person, but the sea has given me a confidence that I never knew I possessed. And it also gave me the courage to know I wanted more. I was exploring myself. The sea encourages the curious, and many of my sea heroes in this book – Chichester, Bligh, Knox-Johnston, Rodney Russ and my fellow Australian, Frank Hurley – possess curiosity as if it were their lifeblood. They have ventured into the unknown with conviction.

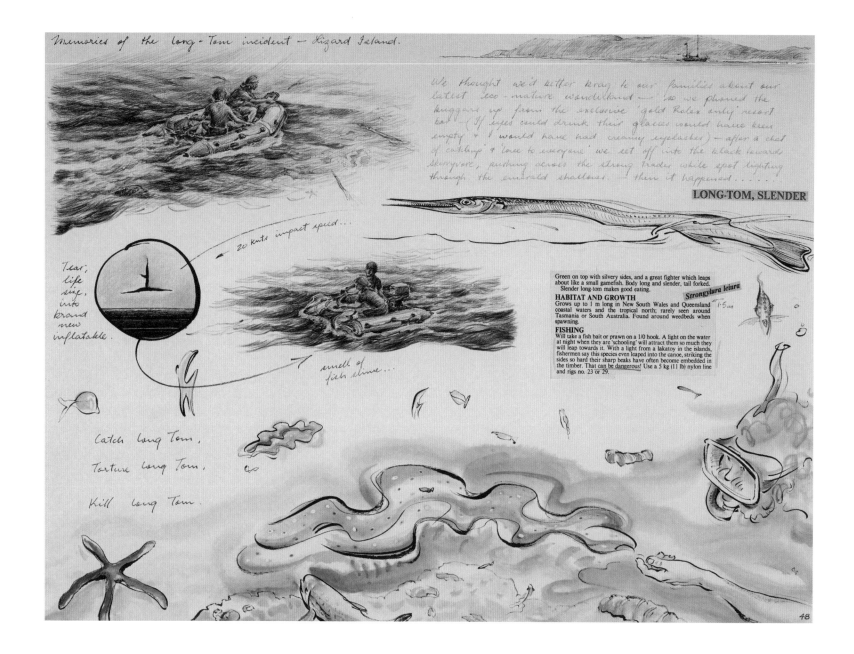

Memories of the Long-Tom incident — Lizard Island.

We thought we'd better brag to our families about our latest 'eco-nature wonderland' — so we phoned the buggars up from the exclusive 'gold Rolex only' resort bar. (If eyes could drink their glasses would have been empty & I would have had creamy eyelashes) — after a chat of cobblings & 'love to everyone' we set off into the black toward Skinnyvore, pushing across the strong trader while spot lighting through the emerald shallows — then it happened......

LONG-TOM, SLENDER

20 knts impact speed...

Tear; life size, into brand new inflatable.

smell of fish slime...

Green on top with silvery sides, and a great fighter which leaps about like a small gamefish. Body long and slender, tail forked. Slender long-tom makes good eating.

HABITAT AND GROWTH
Grows up to 1 m long in New South Wales and Queensland coastal waters and the tropical north; rarely seen around Tasmania or South Australia. Found around weedbeds when spawning.

FISHING
Will take a fish bait or prawn on a 1/0 hook. A light on the water at night when they are 'schooling' will attract them so much they will leap towards it. With a light from a lakatoy in the islands, fishermen say this species even leaped into the canoe, striking the sides so hard their sharp beaks have often become embedded in the timber. That can be dangerous! Use a 5 kg (11 lb) nylon line and rigs no. 23 or 29.

Strongylura leiura

1·5 m

Catch long Tom,

Torture long Tom,

Kill long Tom.

48

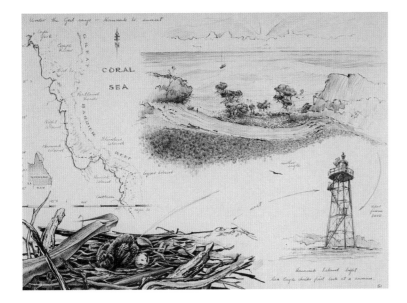

But you don't need to suffer life-threatening escapades for your journey to be meaningful, or for it to change your life. Of course not. I think immediately of Sandy Mackinnon and his *Unlikely Voyage of Jack de Crow* – which was as marvellous as it was unlikely. He was a restless art teacher and borrowed a small mirror dinghy in the holidays to make a journey from Wales through the canals to London. But he didn't stop there – he crossed the Channel, sailed and paddled his way up rivers and through locks all the way to the Black Sea, six months and some 6,500 km (4,000 miles) later.

A voyage like this is, to me at least, the perfect kind: small but adventurous, a little eccentric, but great fun. Things go wrong, they always do, so you must always be open to possibilities. That's why I respect Mackinnon as a sailor, as much as I love him as an artist. His boat was not big, but his horizons were huge. He voyaged with eyes wide open.

Being an artist at sea, an artist anywhere, is about being alert to possibility. Curiosity is the heartbeat of it. Always looking and making marks, suggestive little sketches, not necessarily masterpieces, but things to help you remember. A sketch is a visual quotation. It doesn't really matter what it looks like, just get something down with a pencil. Sometime later, perhaps even years afterwards, that sketch will help you recall the moment, the day, the environment, the way a sail fills in the breeze or the movement of a wave. Or, at the very least, it will inspire a memory and send you off on a new journey. This is why sketchbooks are so precious. They can carry us back and forward in time, taking us to all kinds of shores. If my boat was sinking, or my house was on fire, my sketchbooks would be the things I'd grab first. Everything else can be replaced.

Anderson sailed round the world on his honeymoon with artist wife Kim in the ketch *Skerryvore*. His sketches afloat and ashore detail a lifetime of wandering. 'I woke to the sea as a child', he relates, 'I dreamed of it through books. I wander on it, use the wind, collect the rain for drinking, and eat its fish … I try to leave no trace, and do what I can to look after it.' His advice is: 'You weigh anchor and go. Be prepared. You may be gone for some time.'

JOSEPH GILBERT 1732–1821

The country is very mountainous and entirely
covered with snow ... the land produces
nothing, only the haunts of amphibious birds
and sea monsters.

Though an expedition leader or ship's captain rightly wins the laurels for a famous undertaking, below decks, at the oars or up aloft, the common sailor was a vital part of the working of every ship. Generations of talented sailing masters guided their craft to all corners of the globe, but their names now are mostly forgotten. One such is Joseph Gilbert, master of *Resolution* on James Cook's second celebrated voyage of discovery.

The son of a farmer, Gilbert most likely went to sea as a boy, though almost no details survive of his early life. He joined the Royal Navy and steadily rose up the ranks, for by 1764 he was master of the 32-gun *Guernsey* and employed for many years on the survey of the coasts of Labrador and Newfoundland, like Cook. Gilbert returned home and made a new survey of Plymouth Sound in 1769, the accuracy of which again brought him to the attention of Cook. At forty years old, Gilbert was just a few years younger than his new captain, but his equal when it came to navigational skills. His 'judgment and assiduity' in surveying, wrote Cook to the Admiralty, 'as well as every other branch of his profession, is exceeded by none'.

The main task of *Resolution*, which sailed from Plymouth in the summer of 1772, was for 'further discoveries towards the South Pole' and to continue explorations of the Tropics. The expedition visited New Zealand three times, and after a series of probes into high latitudes was able at last to banish speculation of a vast continent connected to Australia, or stretching south somewhere from the Strait of Magellan. Further south still, through ice and fog, Antarctica lay undiscovered.

For much of the voyage it was Gilbert who was tasked with leading the boats in their inshore survey work. In Queen Charlotte Sound, New Zealand, as Cook was rowed in the pinnace on a shooting party, Gilbert went out to sea in the cutter to make soundings of rocks they had discovered on coming in. In Tahiti, he saved the ship from wrecking on a reef and then used the launch to recover their anchors. In Vanuatu in 1774, at Malekula, he was sent ahead in an armed boat to find a suitable anchorage as *Resolution* lay offshore, and when a fight broke out with the locals at Erromango, Gilbert managed to get his men safely back to the ship in a hail of poisoned darts and arrows.

Cook named Gilbert Isle for him, a small island off Tierra del Fuego, described as 'the most desolate coast I ever saw', though it was surely intended as a compliment. On their safe return, Gilbert produced many finely drawn charts of the voyage and Cook presented him with his watch. Gilbert then stayed ashore, though his eldest son George sailed with Cook on his fateful, final Pacific voyage. Gilbert's retirement was still very active, with appointments first at the naval dockyard at Sheerness and then at prestigious Portsmouth, and the busy yards of Woolwich and Deptford, both on the Thames.

Gilbert's log from *Resolution* details his voyage with James Cook from 3 January 1772 to 22 March 1775. Here is a page from their forays on Easter Island. The large-scale manuscript chart of the route of the *Resolution* voyage (opposite), with illustrations, was also drawn and signed by Gilbert.

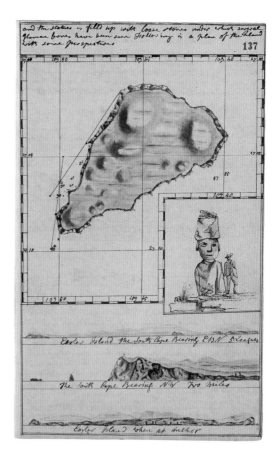

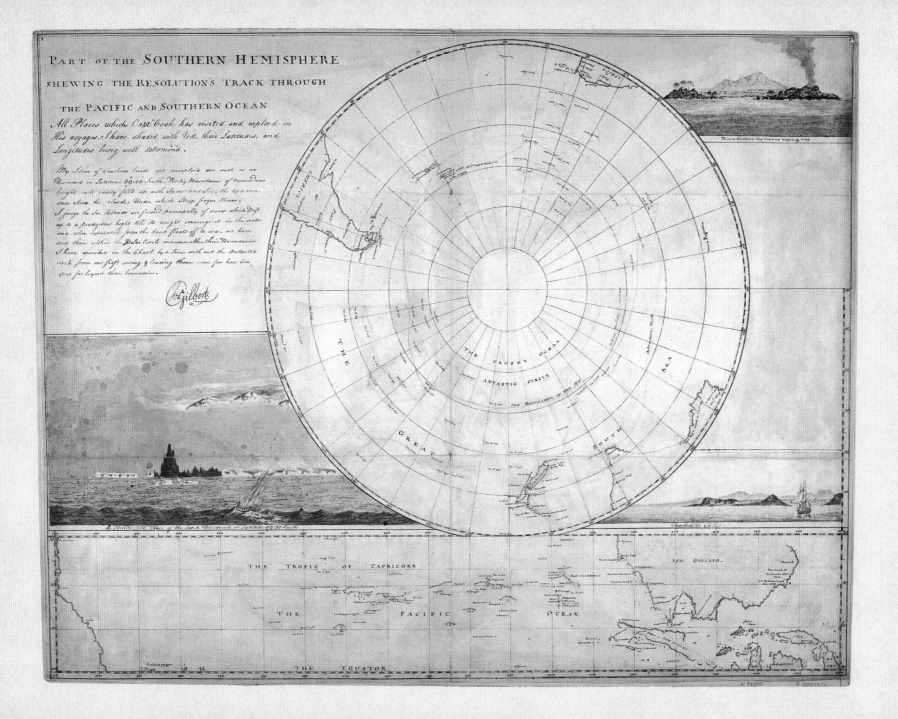

PART OF THE SOUTHERN HEMISPHERE

SHEWING THE RESOLUTION'S TRACK THROUGH

THE PACIFIC AND SOUTHERN OCEAN

All Places which Capt. Cook has visited and explor'd in
His voyages, I have shaded with Red: their Latitudes, and
Longitudes being well determin'd.

My Idea of Southern lands yet unexplor'd are such as we
Discover'd in Latitude 56:00 South, Rocky Mountains of tremendous
height such vastly filld up with Snow and Ice, the tops were
seen above the clouds; Under which Steep frozen shores.
I judge the Ice Islands are formed principally of snow which Drift
up to a prodigious hight till its weight immerge it in the water
and when separated from the Land floats off to sea, we have
seen them within the Polar Circle innumerable, their Boundaries
I have described in the Chart by a line with out the Antartic
circle from our first seeing & leaving them, some few have been
seen far beyond those bounaries.

THE TROPIC OF CAPRICORN

NEW HOLLAND

THE PACIFIC OCEAN

THE EQUATOR

THE GREAT SOUTH SEA

THE FROZEN OCEAN

ANTARTIC CIRCLE

THE BOUNDARIES OF THE ICE

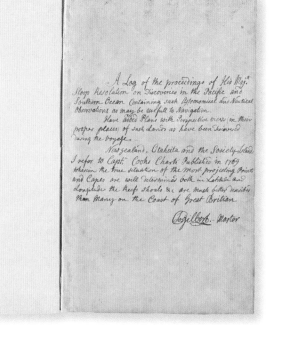

Chart labels: Saunders Island · C. Montague · C. Bristol · Freezland peak · Southern Thule · Candlemas Isles

Jan. 31st 1775 at 6 in the morning discovered the high rock off Cape Bristol. hauld our wind to the North. at 8 fact ship not being able to weather them sounded 175 fa. sand 2 miles from the said rocks saw high land bearing S½W an high mountain above the cloud ENE thick hazy went to just noon saw the land from SE to SSW many Ice Islands before the shore and the bays intirely fild up with snow at one SW ship and stood to the North and the wind freshening us we got off shore, in the morning saw Cape Bristol and Cape Montague on the 2 Feb. discovered Saunders Island and Candlemas Islands having the wind Northerly and an exceeding thick fogg we took to windward in the evening it cleared up the wind shifting to the SW we steered to the North and and got clear of the land

I believe the land to the East end of Saunders Island to have communicate with the land to the Southend of it, the weather being hazy and sometimes a thick foggy we could not distinguish the land in the bays. The Southern Thule takes a direction to the westward of south and I believe near to the coast we steered from the South ward, for in Lat. 60° we had much Ice saw many whales, penguins and abundance of other Birds sometimes the sea seemd coloured as it is in soundings the weat. was always thick and hazy, therefore we never could see beyond two leagues and sometimes not a mile I think we must have past near some parts of the coast before we saw it. This country has the most dreary starved appearance that can be imagined the spiral rocks and scraggy precipices forms the shore in land are snowy mountains of tremendous height high raise above the clouds. Following is a perspective view ———

A Log of the proceedings of His Majs.
Sloop Resolution on Discoveries in the Pacific and
Southern Ocean. Containing such Astronomical and Nautical
Observations as may be usefull to Navigation.
Have added Plans with Perspective views in their
proper places, of such Lands as have been discovered
during the voyage.
New zealand, Otaheita and the Society Islands
I refer to Capt. Cooks Charts Published in 1769
wherein the true situation of the most projecting Points
and Capes are well determined both in Latitude and
Longitude the Reefs shoals &c are much better described
then many on the Coast of Great Britian

Geo. Gilbert. Master

The neatly written title-page (above) of Gilbert's remarkable sea journal: 'A Log of the proceeding's of His Majesty's Sloop *Resolution* on Discoveries in the Pacific and Southern Ocean….' On the left is the first view of the rugged coasts of the South Sandwich Islands, while opposite are the volcano at Tanna in Vanuatu, and the desolate coasts west and east of Cape Horn and the Strait of Magellan, where Cook named a small island for Gilbert.

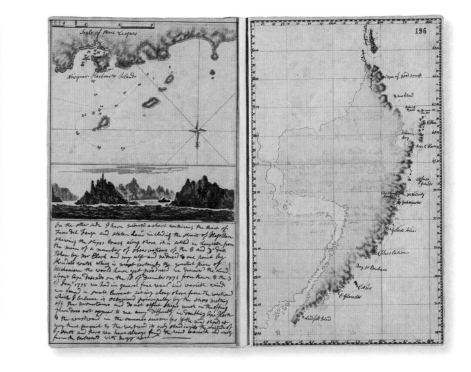

17 Jan 1773 ... 37 islands of ice in sight ahead of us. Sailed through a quantity of loose ice up to a large field ... continuing to the southward beyond our sight ... great number of whales seen to blow among the ice ... served a glass of brandy to the seamen as usual.

KONRAD GRÜNENBERG 1420–1494

The ship swayed so violently that many pilgrims got sick, and that night we went very carefully because there were many reefs.

'There are three things that can neither be recommended nor discouraged – marriage, war and a voyage to the Holy Sepulchre', wrote the Count of Württemberg on his return from Jerusalem in 1480. 'Each may begin well yet end very badly.' Invariably bloody and hazardous, the crusading movement was arguably the largest maritime endeavour of the Middle Ages: between the years 1000 and 1300 hundreds of thousands of men were transported from the ports of western Europe. This brought fortunes to ship owners and stimulated innovations in ship design across the Mediterranean. In the centuries that followed, new waves of pilgrims were keen to repeat the journey, risking dangers for the chance to witness the holy sites. A tourist industry was born, with souvenirs and guidebooks soon on sale. By the end of the fifteenth century a pilgrimage could be booked as a package trip from Venice.

Konrad Grünenberg, a German knight and social climber whose hobby was to paint coats of arms and describe jousting tournaments, possessed sufficient devotion and curiosity to join the medieval equivalent of an Adriatic cruise. Born to a merchant family, the patrician Grünenberg was a member of a local elite, though neither a baron nor a master builder as some accounts have it. His father was the mayor of Konstanz, a prosperous town on Lake Constance in southern Germany, on the trading route from Italy along the Rhine to northern Europe. Grünenberg himself was later elected as a *baumeister*, an elderman, sitting on a council to supervise municipal buildings. In his spare time he devoted himself to heraldry, and his sketches are some of the finest that survive.

On 22 April 1486 he embarked on a journey to the Middle East. He followed the standard route via Venice, from where, having stocked up on wine and live chickens, he shipped south on the *Jaffa*. He writes that the crew were mostly incompetent, his fellow passengers sleepless or seasick, while also adding some travel advice: 'Fill your bags well with Biscotti and two or three baked loaves that do not spoil.' The voyage itself was broken up with visits ashore – he admired fortresses on the Dalmatian coast, in Rhodes, and at Candia, now Heraklion, in Crete.

He spent twenty days or so in the Holy Land, travelling about on a donkey, avoiding robbers and 'wild beasts', and surviving the poor food and dirty hostels. After an absence of thirty-three weeks, he returned home triumphantly to write an account of his experiences. According to his diary, he was knighted in the Church of the Holy Sepulchre in Jerusalem one moonlit night, and he was certainly one of the lucky ones. Of the thirty fellow voyagers whose names he noted, at least nine are marked in red pencil with 'death' in the margin.

In his remarkable travelogue, completed in 1487, Grünenberg sketched many of the towns on the Dalmatian coast as he made his way from Venice to the Holy Land in the *Jaffa*. It was a large Venetian trireme galley which had been converted to a passenger ship, with three masts and generally three rowers on each of 58 rowing benches - some 174 rowers in total. It is estimated that around 120 pilgrims could be carried, as well as trade goods, luggage, supplies and a cargo of sheep.

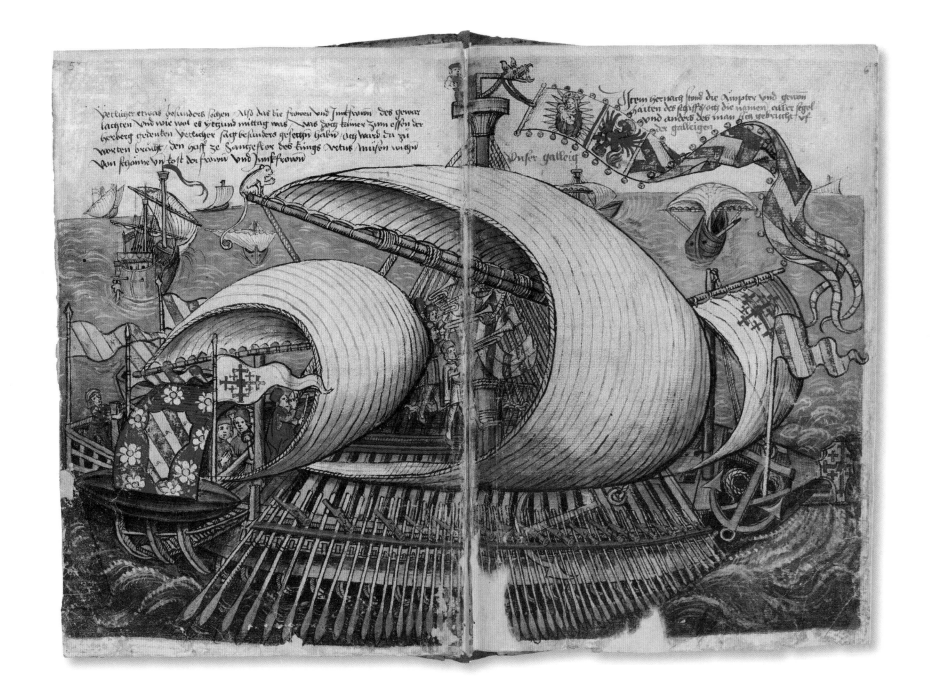

Vetlüger etwas besunders sehen Als das die frowen und Juncfrown des gewar
lachten und wie wol es yetzund mittag was was doch kainer zum essen der
herberg gedenken Vetlicher sagt besunders gesetzen habt Oth ward du zu
worten bracht den haff ze Sanchester des kings Artus müsen wichen
Von schöne und tost der frown und Juncfrown

Unser galleig

Item hernach stond die Ainster und gewon
hatten des schiffs och die namen aller segel
und anders des man sich gebruchet uf
der galleigen

ZHENG HE 1371–1435

We have traversed immense water spaces
and have beheld in the ocean huge waves
like mountains rising sky high.

A court eunuch of China's Ming Dynasty, Zheng He rose to the top of the imperial hierarchy as a kind of admiral-diplomat in command of a fleet of the largest wooden ships the world had ever seen. Nine-masted giant junks, which the Chinese called *bao chuan*, they were treasure ships, laden with porcelains, silks and fine art objects to be traded for all those things the Middle Kingdom desired: elephant ivory, rhinoceros horn, tortoiseshell and precious stones, rare woods and incense, medicines and pearls.

In a brief period from 1405, under He's command, the fleet made seven epic voyages throughout the China Sea and Indian Ocean, from Taiwan to the Persian Gulf and the eastern shores of Africa. The Chinese knew of Europe too from Arab traders, but had no desire to go there, as the lands in the 'far west' offered only wool and wine, which had little appeal. Admiral He must have kept some kind of journal and made charts, but these original manuscripts are lost. For centuries, few outside China knew of his travels, and in his own country much was suppressed. A new emperor did not want to finance more ships, forbade overseas travel and focused his funds on building a Great Wall, denying He's place in history. Later emperors feared others would be inspired by He's voyages to want to lead their own.

Chinese medieval records describe He's fleet, and if the chronicles are to be believed, the 1405 expedition comprised more than 27,000 men and a fleet of sixty-two colossal treasure ships, supported by two hundred smaller craft. This is barely imaginable, yet traveller Marco Polo and Moroccan scholar Ibn Battuta both clearly described multi-masted

ships of mammoth size, perhaps more than 120 m (390 ft) in length, carrying navigators, sailors, doctors, soldiers, scribes and artists. He's personal secretary, Gong Zhen, kept a diary, which later formed the basis of his book *Xiyang fanguo zhi*, 'The Annals of Foreign Nations in the Western Ocean', published in 1434. A few of He's officers also kept records, but they exist now only as part of more general narratives reproduced later in woodcut.

During He's lifetime, palaces and monuments were erected in his honour and stone tablets placed in locations recording his visits. One tablet was rediscovered in 1911 in Sri Lanka, commemorating He's second voyage to the island in 1409. Inscribed in Nanjing before the fleet set out, its text – in Chinese, Tamil and Persian – invokes the blessings of Hindu deities for a peaceful world built on trade, praises Buddha and records the lavish offerings the explorers made when they had safely stepped ashore. Today, a tomb in Nanjing honours He on the site of his original grave, but it only ever contained his headgear and clothes. It is thought his body was buried at sea off the Malabar Coast in western India, during a seventh, last voyage. Like so many other mariners, Zheng He did not make it home.

Zheng He brought back to China many trophies, including a giraffe from the Somali Ajuran empire as a gift to the Yongle Emperor in 1414. The stellar diagram (opposite left) gives instructions for navigation from Hormuz to Calicut. *Yi yu tu zhi*, the 'Pictures and Descriptions of Strange Regions', is said to be drawn from traveller's tales and eyewitness accounts from He's voyages (opposite right).

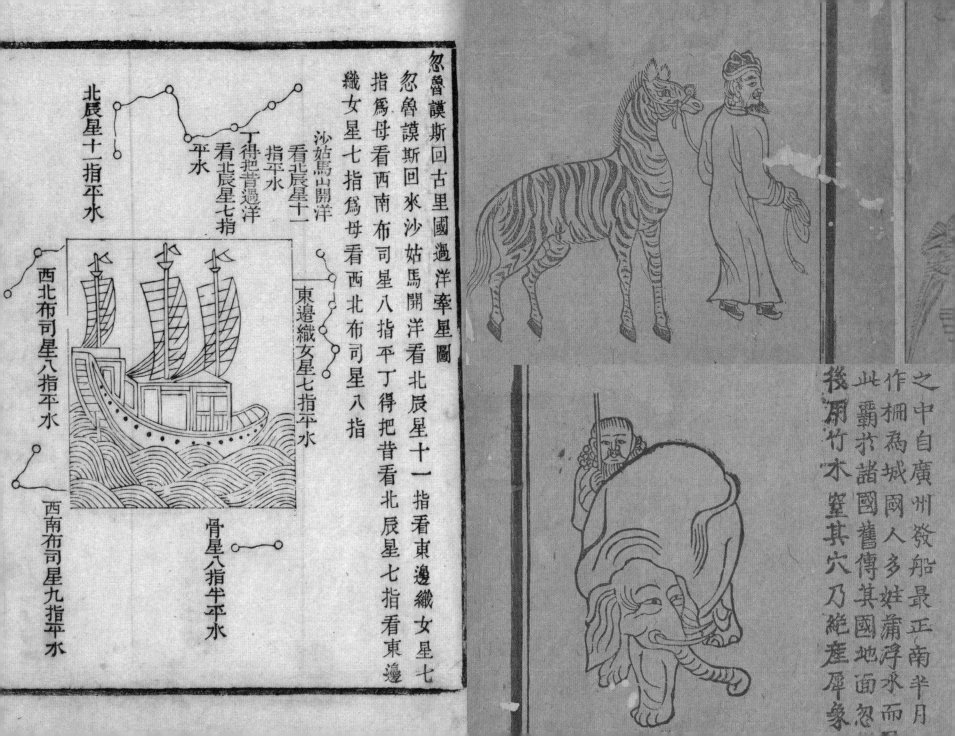

忽魯謨斯回古里國過洋牽星圖

忽魯謨斯回沙姑馬開洋看北辰星十一指看東邊織女星七

指為母看西南布司星八指平丁得把昔看北辰星七指看東邊

織女星七指為母看西北布司星八指

沙姑馬山開洋

看北辰星十一

指平水

丁得把昔過洋

看北辰星七指

指平水

平水

東邊織女星七指平水

北辰星十一指平水

西北布司星八指平水

西南布司星九指平水

骨星八指半平水

之中自廣州發船最正南半月

作柵為城國人多姓蒲浮水而

此霸於諸國舊傳其國地面忽

後用竹木窒其穴乃絕產犀象

ERIK HESSELBERG 1914–1972

Both air and water were so pleasant and warm that we went quite naked. Only whenever we took photographs we had to put on drawers.

There are many famous Norwegian mariners, including Roald Amundsen, hero of the South Pole, who was also the first through the Northwest Passage in 1906, or Fridtjof Nansen, humanitarian and oceanographer, who pushed for the North Pole from the *Fram*. One who sailed warmer waters was a seafaring artist who was brave enough to embark on a voyage that most thought doomed. The charismatic leader whose vision lay behind the challenge was fellow Norwegian Thor Heyerdahl. But Erik Hesselberg was the navigator, and his skills kept his companions alive. He also stayed positive, singing and sketching, even in the most challenging circumstances.

Born in Brevik, in Telemark, Hesselberg had known Heyerdahl since childhood. He trained at a sailor's school and worked as a professional seafarer for five years, making several trips around the world, and also studied art in Germany. Stuck there during the Second World War, he survived by working as a decorator, married a local woman and returned to Norway when peace came. In 1947, when he was working as painter, he was asked by Heyerdahl to join the balsa-wood raft *Kon-Tiki* as its navigator. He packed his sextant, sketchbooks and guitar, and never looked back.

For over a hundred days the six crew drifted with the currents and the southeast trade wind, sailing almost 4,500 nautical miles from Peru to Polynesia, to test the theory that prehistoric peoples from South America could have made the same journey. On 7 August 1947, *Kon-Tiki* was shattered on a reef at Raroia, an atoll in the Tuamotus. The six men swam and scrambled to safety, then waded ashore, bearded and bedraggled. In time, villagers arrived from another island in the group and they feasted and danced into the night. The voyage thought impossible had been achieved.

The islanders gave Hesselberg the name 'Tane-Matarau', after a navigator famed in their own stories. After the expedition, he built and lived on his own ship, *Tiki*, taking her to the Mediterranean while working as a painter and sculptor, and composing music. In the Riviera, he befriended Pablo Picasso, met Jean Cocteau and Georges Simenon, and collaborated with another gifted Norwegian artist, Carl Nesjar, before returning home to Norway to live out his final years.

After the *Kon-Tiki* expedition Hesselberg published a book of his sketches in 1949, based on his sea diaries, called *Kon-Tiki og Jeg* in Norwegian. It was translated into several languages, including English.

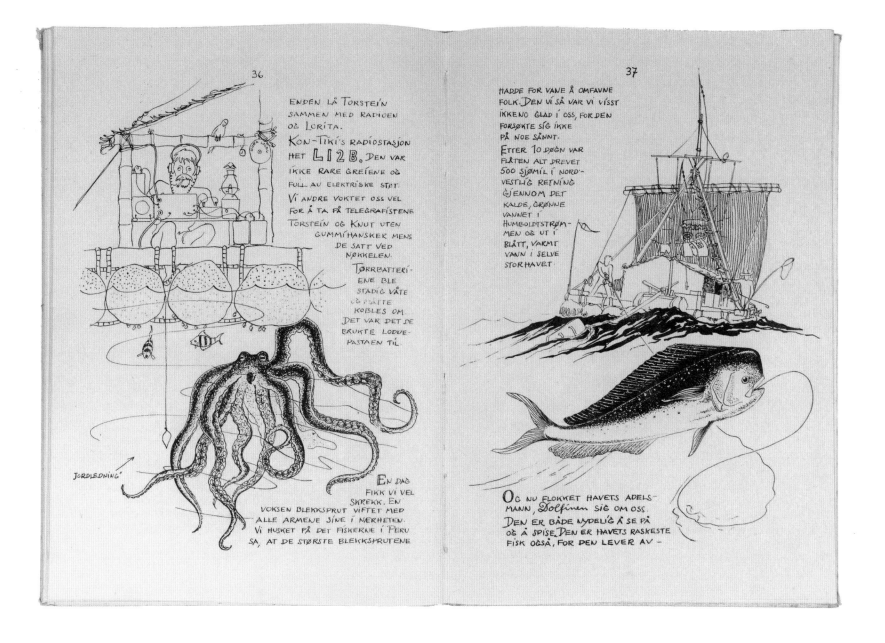

36

ENDEN LÅ TORSTEIN SAMMEN MED RADIOEN OG LORITA.

KON-TIKI'S RADIOSTASJON HET LI2B. DEN VAR IKKE RARE GREIENE OG FULL AV ELEKTRISKE STØT. VI ANDRE VOKTET OSS VEL FOR Å TA PÅ TELEGRAFISTENE TORSTEIN OG KNUT UTEN GUMMIHANSKER MENS DE SATT VED NØKKELEN.

TØRRBATTERIENE BLE STADIG VÅTE OG MÅTTE KOBLES OM. DET VAR DET DE BRUKTE LODDE-PASTAEN TIL.

JORDLEDNING

EN DAG FIKK VI VEL SKREKK. EN VOKSEN BLEKKSPRUT VIFTET MED ALLE ARMENE SINE I NÆRHETEN. VI HUSKET PÅ DET FISKERNE I PERU SA, AT DE STØRSTE BLEKKSPRUTENE

37

HADDE FOR VANE Å OMFAVNE FOLK. DEN VI SÅ VAR VI VISST IKKE NO GLAD I OSS, FOR DEN FORSØKTE SIG IKKE PÅ NOE SÅNNT.

ETTER 10 DØGN VAR FLÅTEN ALT DREVET 500 SJØMIL I NORD-VESTLIG RETNING GJENNOM DET KALDE, GRØNNE VANNET I HUMBOLDTSTRØM-MEN OG UT I BLÅTT, VARMT VANN I SELVE STORHAVET.

OG NU FLOKKET HAVETS ADELS-MANN, DOLFINEN SIG OM OSS. DEN ER BÅDE NYDELIG Å SE PÅ OG Å SPISE. DEN ER HAVETS RASKESTE FISK OGSÅ, FOR DEN LEVER AV –

Thor Heyerdahl married his bride Liv on Christmas Eve in 1936; he was twenty-two years old and she was twenty. They sailed in a Tahitian schooner to the Marquesas for a year-long honeymoon, wanting to get back to nature. These are pages from his original journal.

GLORIA HOLLISTER 1900-1988

It matters not whether fishes are rare or common ...
each one is studied at Nonsuch.

Hollister emerges from the waves with a sea fan as
her heavy diving helmet with oxygen supply tube is
lifted above her head. She also made record-breaking
descents in the bathysphere.

All hands watched as the winch strained and bubbles roiled over the surface. The metal sphere emerged, streaming with water, and was hoisted over the rails and on to the deck. The hatch was unscrewed and a woman crawled out, her face beaming. It was 11 June 1930, Gloria Hollister's thirtieth birthday, and she had just descended deeper in the ocean than any other woman.

As chief technical assistant to the famed naturalist William Beebe, Hollister was among the team of scientists stationed at Nonsuch Island on his Bermuda Oceanographic Expedition. Their objective was to discover and categorize all forms of aquatic life in the area. In subsequent dives, Hollister would descend an astonishing 368 m (1,208 ft) – a women's record that would remain unbroken in her lifetime. Sealed in the cramped quarters of the bathysphere, she had gazed through the tiny fused-quartz windows to observe an alien world, marvelling at eel larvae and leptocephalus, noting how much more graceful they were in their own world than in the aquarium in her lab.

After graduating from Connecticut College for Women in 1924, Hollister gained a masters degree in zoology at Columbia, then worked as a cancer research assistant at the Rockefeller Institute. In 1928, however, she applied for a position with Beebe in his Department of Tropical Research at the New York Zoological Society. Beebe was looking for a professional naturalist, skilled at dissecting, to join his team on an expedition to Bermuda. Hollister soon became invaluable to Beebe, not only as the person he entrusted to be on the other end of the communication line as he descended in the bathysphere, but also as an experienced ichthyologist. Hollister invented her own system of preparing fish specimens so they were rendered transparent and could be studied more closely – a method the Bermudians called 'fish magic'.

Hollister accompanied Beebe and his research team on two further projects before leading three expeditions for the Department herself. In 1936 she embarked on her Guiana Expedition to the Kaieteur Falls, leading a team through dense tropical jungle to discover 43 waterfalls previously known only to the indigenous people, as well as many species of jungle fauna, including a tiny golden frog and the Canje pheasant, or hoatzin – part bird, part reptile.

Like her mentor, Beebe, Hollister understood the fragility of the world's ecosystems and was determined to do what she could to protect them. In the early 1950s, with her husband Anthony Anable, she created the Mianus River Gorge Conservation Committee – a project that saved the habitat from development. It saddened her that humankind was such a destructive force, yet turned to nature when life became too stressful. 'Man', Hollister wrote, 'has an urge to run away from what he had made for himself in order to renew his contact with the world as it was before he put his mechanical mark on it.'

The cover of a logbook and pages of notes dictated by William Beebe to Gloria Hollister via telephone from his bathysphere. When Beebe invited Hollister among other female scientists and artists on to his research staff in 1928, his decision was questioned. He responded that it was irrelevant whether members of his team were men or women: 'What matters most in a researcher', he stated, is 'what is between the ears.'

THE LOG
of the
BATHYSPHERE
1934
HOLLISTER

THE BERMUDA BOOKSTORES

FRANK HURLEY 1885–1962

Seals and penguins are exceptionally
accommodating creatures to the polar castaway.

Had his mother got her way, Frank Hurley would never have become an explorer. Mrs Hurley was so adamant he shouldn't leave on a voyage that she sent a secret letter trying to persuade the leader not to take him. 'He has never roughed it', she wrote, 'and has lung trouble so bad that I do not think he would come back if he started.'

James Francis Hurley was born in the suburbs of Sydney. He ran away from school, found a job in an ironworks and saved enough money for his first camera, a Kodak box brownie. Within a year he had turned professional, soon bought a plate camera and at twenty was part of a thriving postcard business. In 1910, aged twenty-five, he applied, despite his mother's protests, to join an expedition to Antarctica under the leadership of Douglas Mawson. His successes there led to an invitation to join Ernest Shackleton as official photographer and filmmaker on *Endurance*, a voyage that turned into an epic of survival.

Shackleton's ill-fated *Endurance* expedition, 1914–17, is one of the most famous in history, and Hurley recorded every step of the perilous Antarctic voyage in his journals. It is remarkable that the men ever made it home, let alone Hurley's precious leather-bound diaries and glass photographs too. The expedition's aim was to cross the Antarctic continent via the South Pole for the first time. Despite warnings of heavy pack ice ahead, the team on *Endurance* left the remote whaling station of Grytviken in South Georgia in December 1914 for the Weddell Sea. During January and February 1915, the ship became inexorably trapped in the ice and, having drifted helplessly, on 27 October 1915, was crushed.

For most of the retreat across the floating pack ice, Hurley shared a tent with Shackleton. They camped on ice floes for months before making a desperate bid for land and temporary safety. In three of *Endurance*'s lifeboats the party braved treacherous seas to reach Elephant Island on 15 April 1916. One of the boats, the *James Caird*, was strengthened and Shackleton, together with five companions, sailed 1,300 km (800 miles) across stormy seas to South Georgia to bring about the rescue of the men left stranded on the remote island.

It was a harrowing voyage, but what is less well known is the hard reality of survival for Hurley and the remainder of the party. They lived on Elephant Island in a structure of two upturned boats fastened together with canvas. These makeshift quarters, termed 'the snuggery', housed twenty-two men in cramped and freezing conditions for four months. As Hurley wrote: 'We had at last arrived at a condition of filthiness in which it was impossible to become any dirtier.' They survived on a diet of penguin and seal until they were finally rescued by the Chilean trawler *Yelcho* on 30 August 1916 and reunited with Shackleton, the man they called 'The Boss'. Hurley wrote and sketched in his journals almost every day, and his cheerfulness, as much his courage, was of great help to his crew-mates.

Undeterred, Hurley went on to serve Australia as an official photographer in both world wars and he returned to the Antarctic with Mawson in 1929. By the time of his death in 1962 he had justly earned a reputation as one of the great photographers of the twentieth century.

Hurley's journal details the daily struggle for survival on Elephant Island in 1916, where the men made their home underneath two lifeboats edged around with rocks. An evocative first-hand account, it is stained in places with the blubber from their stoves and the action of sun, storm and snow.

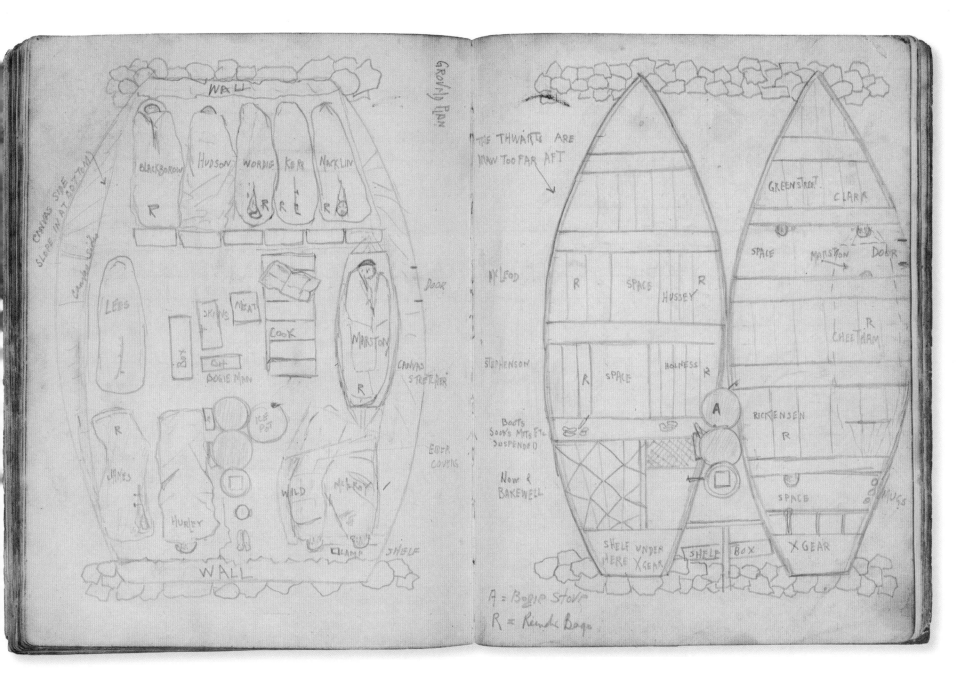

GROUND PLAN

WALL

CANVAS SIDE (SLOPE IN AT BOTTOM)

BLACKBOROW R
HUDSON
WORDIE R R E
KERR R E
MACKLIN R

CANVAS SIDE

LEES

SKINS
MEAT
BOX
COT
BOGIE MAN

COOK

MARSTON R

LEGS

R
JAMES

HURLEY

ICE POT

WILD

McILROY

DOOR

CANVAS STRETCHER

EIDER COVERS

LAMP SHELF

WALL

THE THWARTS ARE NOW TOO FAR AFT

McLEOD

STEPHENSON

BOOTS SOCKS MITS ETC SUSPENDED

NOW & BAKEWELL

GREENSTREET
CLARK

SPACE
MARSTON
DOOR

R
SPACE
HUSSEY R

R
CHEETHAM

R
SPACE
HOLNESS R

A

RICKENSEN
R

SPACE
BOD MUGS

SHELF UNDER HERE X GEAR
SHELF
BOX
X GEAR

A = BOGIE STOVE
R = Reindeer Bags

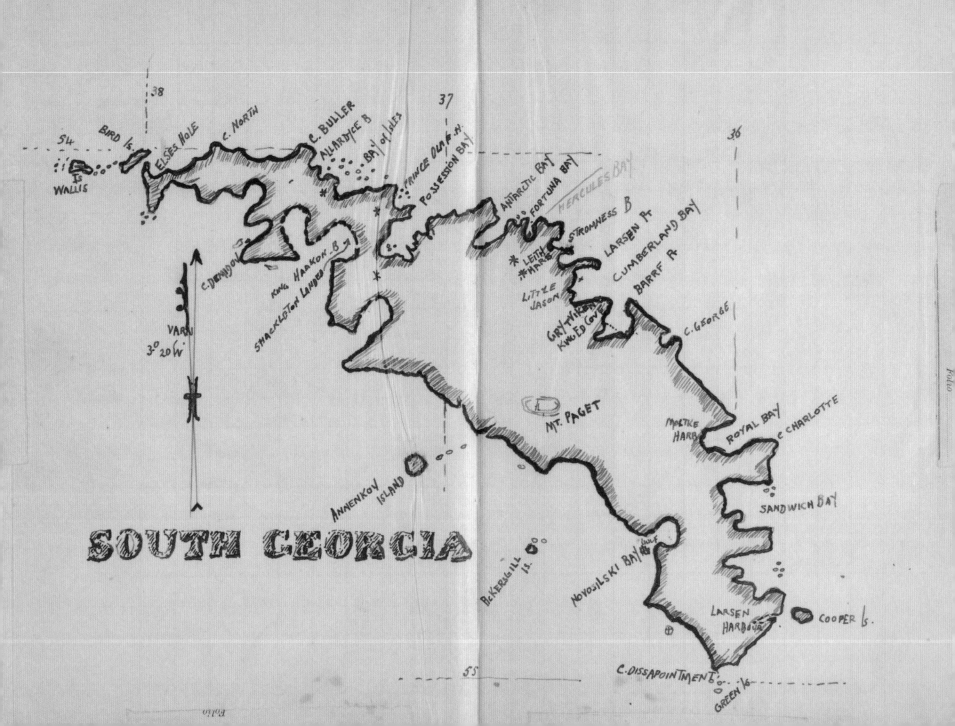

SOUTH GEORGIA

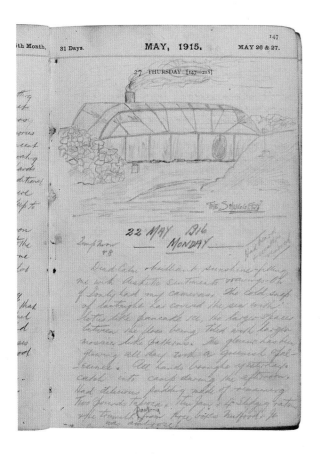

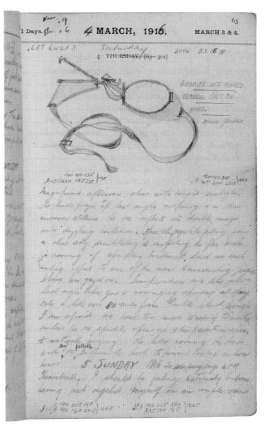

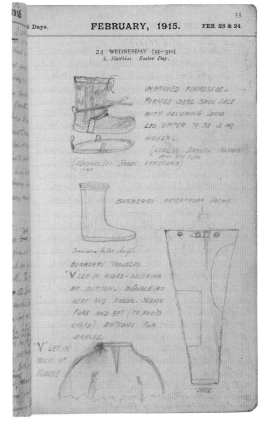

A later sketch of South Georgia (opposite) shows the bay on the west coast where Shackleton managed to make landfall, before his arduous trek over the interior to the whaling station at Stromness. Hurley was an innovator, constantly working on improvements to his gear and clothing (above). He returned to South Georgia himself in 1917 to shoot more footage for an Antarctic film.

Monday 1 May 1916 … take up residence in the boat shelter … The roof is formed by two overturned boats resting on two low walls fore and aft … The walls are covered in with canvas taken from the tents. The small blubber bogie is installed, which radiates a pleasant warmth.

Many years later, Hurley returned again to the
polar regions, this time on the *Discovery*, with
Douglas Mawson in command. Hurley's journal is
filled with photographic prints, which he developed
himself then cut and pasted inside. The portraits
of each of his companions decorate the edges of
their Christmas Day menu.

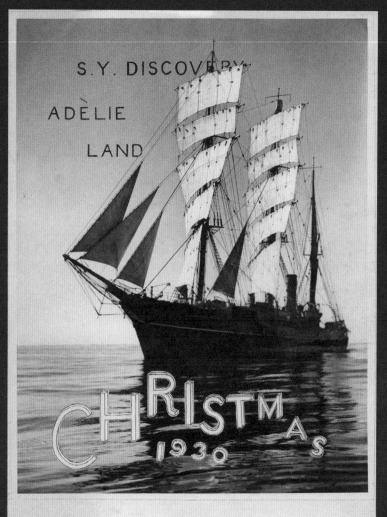

S.Y. DISCOVERY
ADÈLIE
LAND
CHRISTMAS
1930

The second voyage of the
Discovery to Antarctica
1930-1931   by Frank Hurley

25 Dec〉 Christmas Day. Dearie me what divine reveries come crowding in on me as I write in the cosy warmth of the darkroom, listening to the sweet strains of the gramophone coming in through the lower laboratory, from the wardroom. Christmases spent in many strange parts. Christmases to

MENU

Olives   Salées
Sprat   Guerri
Potage   Glaçon

Blanchaille

Anse de l'antarctique. Jambon
Petit Pois   Chou-fleur
Pommes de terre
Asperges au beurre fondu
Pouding Noël . Sauce Cognac

Champignons "DISCOVERY"

Champagne - Great Western
Port - Yalumba Punch - Suedoise

café
Cigars - Embassy Cigarettes · Variés
Selections H.M.V.

group is a symbol. a punctuation at the termination of civilization which stays emotions with an abrupt stop & makes one ponder — not over past chapters, but the blank pages of the future.

A gentle swell from the waiting sea sways the ship ere those last cheers die. They echo strangely, like a far off call from all the world — not merely cheers, but whisperings from everywhere. This is the significance: The well wishes of the world go with you, but civilization sits in judgement of your actions & achievements. Go forth

"To seek, to find and not to yield".

SOUTHWARD TO THE CROZETS

HEAD OF BULL SEA ELEPHANT

1858 MILES

After disembarking the pilot, we round the breakwater and emerge into a flat calm blue and silver sea.

Scarcely have I enjoyed a prospect more tranquil and attuned to my nature. Our ship, drowsing leisurely along, creates the only disturbance on the sun burnished blue. Gently she parts the waters, hustling them in sparkling foam, which lapping against our sides make pleasant whisperings.

The 'hospitable city' has passed behind the land, and only its outlying borders, straggling over the foot slopes of Table Mountain are visible. The mountain is a vision of loveliness. Through an almost imperceptible haze, which diffuses details, it rears like a superb

KUMATARO ITO 1860-1930

Count that day lost whose low descending sun,
finds no new nudibranch described, drawn,
and done.

Embarking on one of the most thorough marine surveys the United States had ever mounted, the steamer *Albatross* set out in 1907 on a voyage to explore the aquatic resources of the Philippines, its neighbouring islands and seas. The leader of this enterprise was Hugh McCormick Smith, a renowned ichthyologist and head of the US Bureau of Fisheries, and later curator of zoology at the Smithsonian. With him was Kumataro Ito, a Japanese artist with a passion for the intricate beauties of the underwater world.

Ito had studied under the artist Gyozan Nakajima and had established himself as a natural history painter at the Department of Zoology of Tokyo University. He met Smith through their shared interest in goldfish. The *Albatross*, despite its age, was still the best research vessel in the American fleet – perhaps in the entire world – for undertaking such a voyage, but the magnitude of the operation dwarfed anything the ship had attempted before. The Philippine archipelago comprises some 7,100 separate islands, ranging from mountainous mini-continents like Luzon and Mindanao to scraps of rock barely awash at high tide.

The ecological diversity is equally great: rocky shores, coral reefs, mangroves, estuaries, deep ocean basins, and freshwater lakes and rivers. The small scientific team used all manner of methods to sample the aquatic life, including bottom trawls, dredges, plankton nets, beach seines, hand-lines and night-lights. Reef fish were usually collected with explosives, a practice frowned on today. Many valuable specimens were also obtained by buying them, often from local fishermen in their boats or in markets ashore.

Little is known of the details of Ito's life, but his sketches and notes speak volumes for his skills as an artist and for his patience. After each fish or marine creature was brought on board it was preserved in alcohol and all the relevant data were recorded in an endless array of journals and notebooks: where, when and how collected, what kind of gear, ecological habitat, water temperature, and so on. Reliable colour photography was still several decades away, so accurate sketching was vital. All specimens lose their vivid colours over time, particularly those stored in ethanol. Ito made quick drawings on rice paper and worked up studies with careful annotations.

By the time the *Albatross* returned to San Francisco in May 1910, the team had made 487 bottom trawls, 272 dynamite stations, 117 pelagic tows, 102 seine hauls, 75 night-light stations, 17 gill net collections, 6 poison stations – copper sulphate, used in tide pools – in addition to daily fishing with regular traps and handlines. The voyage was one of most productive oceanographic expeditions ever conducted: it is estimated a staggering 490,000 specimens were collected.

Nudibranchs are often casually called sea slugs, but they are in fact marine gastropod molluscs that shed their shells. They come in an extraordinary range of colours and forms and have been given nicknames to match, such as 'Clown', 'Splendid', 'Dancer' and 'Dragon'. At the invitation of Hugh McCormick Smith, Ito also travelled to Washington to work on the collections, sketching and painting every day for a whole year.

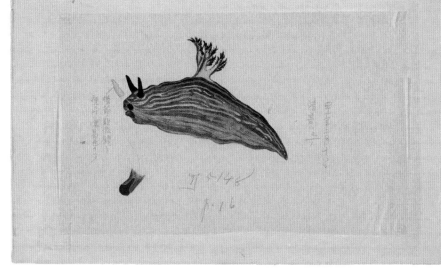

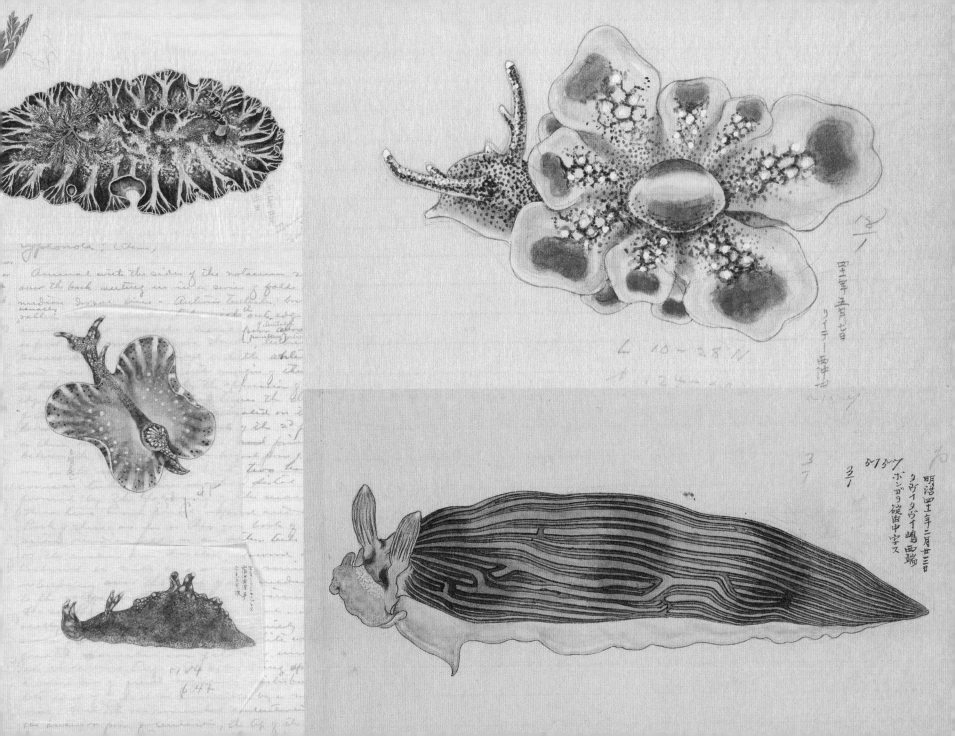

ROCKWELL KENT 1882-1971

On deck, a hurricane. I'd never felt such wind before. The sea was beaten flat, with every wave crest shorn and whipped to smoke.

Few can match the endeavours and complexities of Rockwell Kent, as an illustrator, writer, designer, seafarer and adventurer, though today his name is little remembered beyond the world of book collectors. Called a 'wandering mystic' and a maverick of early modernism, Kent was a rugged individualist who defies easy labels. At the height of his career his artwork was virtually everywhere.

He was born on the banks of the Hudson, north of Manhattan, and was a student of many influential painters, in particular William Merritt Chase at the New York School of Art. He also later studied architecture at Columbia. In 1905 he first ventured to Monhegan Island off Maine, where the elemental beauty of its coasts became a sustaining theme, and he exhibited his paintings soon after. Kent was drawn to remote places, including Newfoundland, navigated the difficult waters around Tierra del Fuego and lived in the hunting community of Illorsuit, on a tiny island off the western coast of Greenland.

He found freedom beyond his studio walls and liked to feel the burden of a heavy pack or the lash of salt water whipped by a fierce wind. In the late summer of 1918 he took his nine-year-old son Rocky to the American frontier of Alaska. His book *Wilderness*, the first of many memoirs, earned him plaudits as a new Walt Whitman. In 1926 he suggested to his publishers that he illustrate *Moby-Dick*. His three-volume edition, filled with haunting brush and ink drawings, sold out immediately. A trade edition quickly followed, which did much to resurrect Melville's reputation and to establish Kent's fame.

As war loomed, he turned his attentions to progressive politics. While his patriotism never wavered, his vocal support for socialism caused controversy. Post-war, he advocated nuclear disarmament and continued friendship with America's wartime ally, and now rival, the Soviet Union. His views placed him on the wrong side of the Cold War consensus and though never a Communist his passport was suspended in 1950. Following a decade of lawsuits, his right to travel was reinstated and after a well-received exhibition at the Pushkin Museum in Moscow he donated eighty paintings and hundreds of prints to the Soviet people. This was fortunate, for some years later his farmstead was struck by lightning and burned down. In 1967 he was awarded the International Lenin Peace Prize.

His reputation in America never recovered. He set about rebuilding his house, but his strength was gone. When he died of a heart attack in 1971, *The New York Times* described him as 'a thoughtful, troublesome, profoundly independent, odd and kind man', who had made an 'imperishable contribution to the art of bookmaking'; a fairly sedate summary for someone so adventurous. As he once told a reporter 'Do you want my life in a nutshell? It's this: that I have only one life, and I'm going to live it as nearly as possible as I want.'

Above: With 'Willie' Ytterock, a Norwegian sailor, Kent tried to sail round the Horn in a converted lifeboat bought for $25. Fog and gales forced them back. Kent created this self-portrait commemorating his hike across Tierra del Fuego.

Opposite: Kent visited Greenland several times, in 1934-35 living in the village of Illorsuit in a hut he built himself; this drawing shows the area where he over-wintered.

DISCOVERIES

[see Chapter XXXVIII] of the Kent Greenland Sub Polar Expedition, 1931-2. Lest the backers of the expedition be disappointed with its results it must be explained that someone, unfortunately, had already given names — and whose names! — to the larger bodies of land and water. We have, however, done our best with what remained. But, the expedition — continuing its work through 1934-5-6 — is faced with a deficit in cash and supplies. Should there be generous souls or corporate bodies desirous of furthering the aims of the expedition we should feel that it would be advancing the glory of America to write their names upon the map — even if we have to scratch out the old ones. Think of a Liggett & Meyers tobacco co. "peninsular"! Or ———'s Applejack sea!

Inland Ice

Disko Id.

Nugsuak

Umanak

Satut

Appat

Uvkusigsat

Ikekrtat (of Emanuel's story)

Umanak Fiord

Nugssuak

Kangerdluarsuk

Kangerdlugssuak

Mt. Hoyt

Upernivik

Sarkak (of Emanuel's story. There are no houses there now)

Mt. Jas. N. Rosenberg

Pan American Airways Corp. Ice Cap

General Electric Co. Ice Cap

Mt. Regals

Mt. Walsh

Mt. Zigrosser

Point Steff.

H. J. Crooks-Ripley

Igdlorssuit

Igdlorssuit Sound

Ubekjendt Eiland (Unknown Island) now Kjendt Eiland

Inqid

Peter Freuchen Point

Umiako

Karrat Id.

Karrats Fiord

Mt. Bill Kittredge (H. R. Donnelley and Sons Co. The Lakeside Press, Chicago)

Nugatsiak

Motor boat of the expedition

"City of Ausable Forks" (Essex County, N.Y.)

To Arthur — Christmas 1967

Rockwell Kent

BACK FOR MORE

Arved Fuchs

When preparing for a voyage, I'm always asked the same questions: 'Why are you going out again on the rough ocean?' or 'Don't you want to go somewhere warm this time?' And I often struggle for words to explain why I go, why I find the Southern Ocean calling me. The vague answers that I usually give – 'because it's wonderful', 'because the coastlines we're navigating are interesting' – rarely satisfy me, let alone those asking. It's hard to explain something that casts such a spell. The sea is beautiful and terrifying. It brings joy and despair.

I grew up in Germany, close to the North Sea. My grandparents lived on the island of Sylt and that's where my memories start: at the water's edge, looking out across the waves. What is beyond the horizon? From that moment on the sea has always represented adventure, fun and freedom – even in later life on voyages when the situation was difficult and dangerous. Surrounded by the stormiest ocean in the world, the approach to Antarctica on any ship is an adventure. But anyone sailing a yacht to Antarctica alone, or with a small crew, has to do so with deep conviction. When I first came here in 1989, I flew in on an ancient DC-6 chartered from Chile. It felt like landing from a spacecraft on another planet; my senses were overwhelmed. But it was all too instant. Arriving by ship is different, it's slower and expectation builds.

In 1989, Reinhold Messner and I, hauling heavy sleds behind us, walked 2,500 km (8,200 miles) across Antarctica, the first time this had been done on foot without dogs or machines. We had created a part of polar history, but I still felt that we had got there the easy way. Ernest Shackleton, who also wanted to cross Antarctica, never even reached solid land, and he and his men were forced to survive on the ice after their ship *Endurance* had been crushed. Their legendary journey in small boats to reach Elephant Island, and then out again in *James Caird* to seek a rescue at the whaling station in South Georgia, is incredible. I have sailed the route in a replica boat and my admiration for Shackleton and his navigator Frank Worsley is boundless. I made my voyage willingly and well prepared – these men had no choice. And the seafarers who ventured into unknown waters before Shackleton came south in wooden ships, with sextants and their charts mostly blank. What extraordinary bravery and skill.

When sailing in these seas I also think of German mariner Eduard Dallmann, who was fifteen went he went to sea on whalers and freighters. By 1859, and a captain, he voyaged to the Pacific and up into the difficult ice of the Bering and Chukchi seas. The only time I've ever felt afraid at sea was when I was beset near Wrangel Island. It was a very close call and we worked hard to find a way to save our boat, and ourselves. Dallmann also commanded the steamer *Grönland* in Antarctica, exploring parts of the Peninsula to try to discover new whaling grounds. Although I don't approve of the whaling industry, Dallmann has my respect as a seafarer for keeping his men and ship safe in an exacting environment.

James Cook on *Resolution* crossed the Antarctic Circle for the very first time in 1773, seeing numerous icebergs but never land. His ships were the best of their time, filled with the latest nautical technology and skilled sailors, but they had no radios or electronic navigation equipment. Cook took with him artists including William Hodges and Henry Roberts, whose sketches help us to imagine what such a voyage must have been like. It was not until January 1820 that ships' crews finally caught a glimpse of Antarctic coasts through the mists – sailors from Britain with William Smith and Edward Bransfield, and Russians under Fabian Gottlieb von Bellingshausen, and then later in November an American sealing

The Resolution & Adventure 4 Jan.^ 1773. Taking in Ice for water. Lat 61. S.

W. Hodges

Above: James Cook's *Resolution* and *Adventure*, as sketched by William Hodges on 4 January 1773 'taking in Ice for Water, Lat 61°S.' Cook recorded how once this 'yielded fifteen tons of good fresh water'.

Opposite: William Hodges produced many dramatic images of the wild Antarctic seas and icebergs, or ice islands as Cook called them. The ships sailed through ice-fields, fog and freezing cold, and once narrowly escaped being wrecked on an iceberg, but never sighted Antarctica itself.

Ice Island

W. Hodges

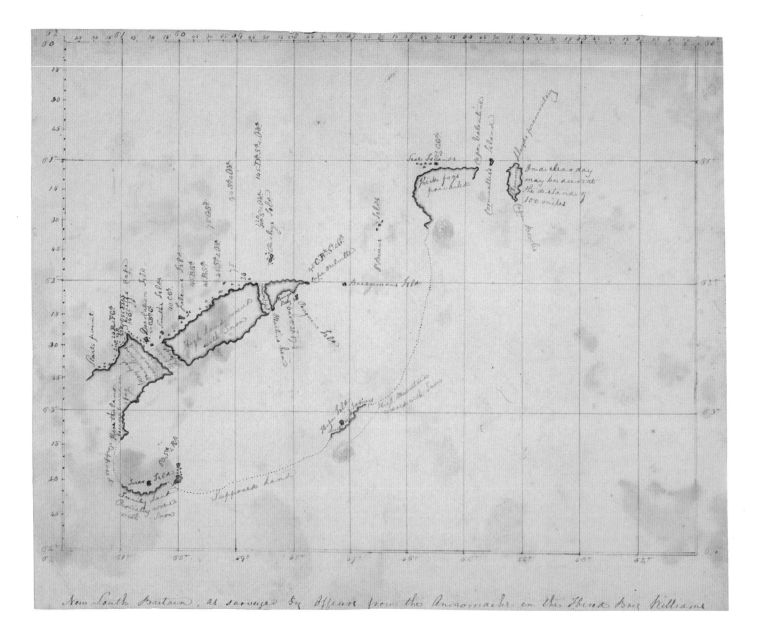

Opposite: Charles Poynter was midshipman on a truly pioneering voyage exploring the South Shetlands on the brig *Williams*. In January 1820 the crew were the first people to sight Antarctica, and this is Poynter's chart, the earliest to show the coast of the continent.

Below: The title page of the journal kept by George F. Emmons during the Wilkes Expedition of 1838-42 on board *Peacock*, which discovered and explored the Antarctic continent. In it Emmons, who later had a distinguished naval career, describes and illustrates Pacific harbours, an overland journey from Vancouver to San Francisco, the Antarctic and the South Seas.

Drawings Made While Attached To The South Seas Surveying & Exploring Expedition on board

THE U. S. SLOOP OF WAR "PEACOCK"

BY

GEORGE F EMMONS

Overleaf: The pages of the journal of Jan Brandes are filled with curiosity and wonder. Embarking in 1778 in the employ of the Dutch East India Company, he portrays shipboard activity, curious sea creatures, coastal profiles and a supply of bananas for snacking on while reading in the cabin.

expedition with Nathaniel Palmer in the ship *Hero*. A young man named Charles Poynter, sailing with Smith in the brig *Williams*, was the first to sketch out the faint coastline of Antarctica in pencil.

Antarctica is a beautiful and serious environment, encircled by a harsh ocean. The interior is desolate and empty, but the coasts are filled with variety. In the penguin colonies, the birds crowd in hundreds of thousands. Elephant seals nap sluggishly and fat in the sun, fur seals defend their territory and chase anyone who dares to come too close. The animals are not afraid; a carelessness that was once fatal to them. Between 1904 and 1964, around 50,000 seals were killed annually to boil their fat to oil. During the same period, over a million large whales were slaughtered and utilized at the stations. Even the penguins suffered – incredibly they were sometimes used as fuel for the cauldrons. The scars of this bloody story can still be seen on the coast: dilapidated whaling stations, rusty machinery, half-sunken fishing vessels and sun-bleached bones.

A cruise to Antarctica from South America today begins where others ended fatefully: near the stormy Cape Horn. It is about 1,000 km (3,300 miles) from the Cape to the Antarctic Peninsula, and even though modern ships have stabilizers and high-tech navigation systems, the journey over the Drake Passage is still a challenge. Passengers huddle in sheltered corners on deck and look in wonder at the flight of the albatrosses skimming the crests of the waves, their huge wings gliding over the troubled sea without touching it.

As the first icebergs appear drifting in the stormy sea, all seasickness is forgiven. I have photographed thousands of icebergs, but a picture is nothing in comparison to reality. Nowhere else in the world have I felt such humility before creation than here. The huge expanses of empty sea, ice and open sky are everything to me and always changing. In a few minutes you can learn more about yourself and the world than any university can teach.

There will always be people who say: 'What can a cold ocean, an iceberg, or a whale teach you? Why bother? And why on earth would you want to go back for more?' Those who ask why will never know the seafarer's secret: the sea is where we want to be.

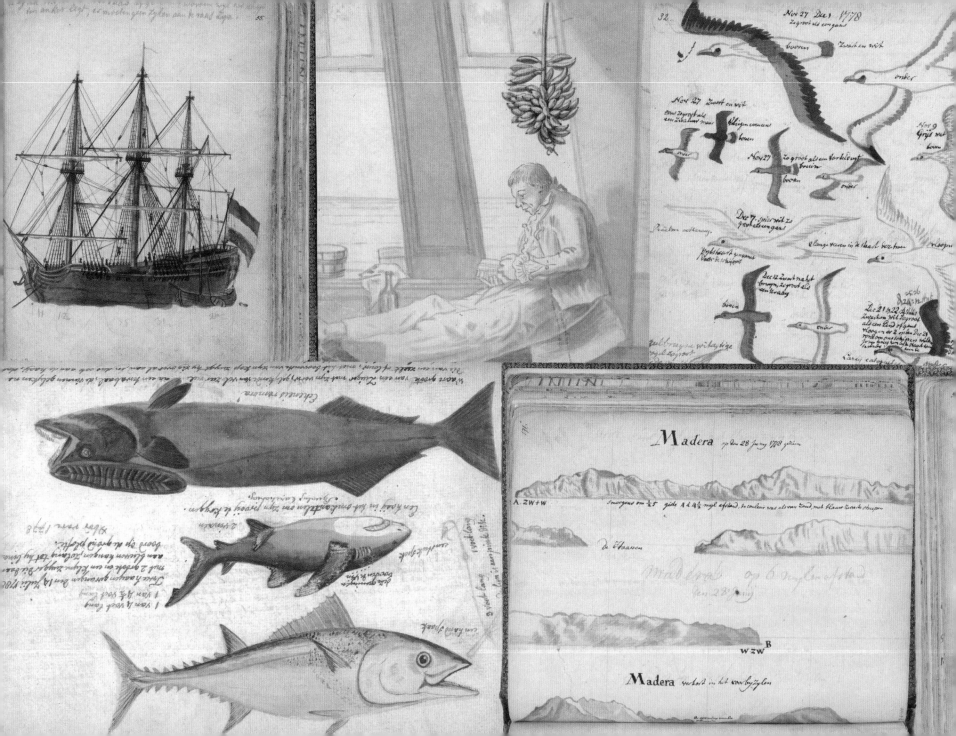

De Blauwe Berg over de Stad Batavia te zien van de Rheede
geprojecteerd naar een teekening van een Stuurman die niet al te schoon was.
N: 1788 Jan: 18.

Het IJland Java uit de Bogt van Anger

Een Loetsmannetje (visch) zwemmende altyd nagt en dag naast ons Schip (Holland genaamd door
gekeetend te als hy nog in de Zee Stroom, om dat wy er geen gevangen hebben, Zie de bugten het welk by zwem...

Gasterosteus ductor

De Bogt van Anger ...

Dajong of roeijaen ...

BENJAMIN LEIGH SMITH 1828-1913

All well. No one has any doubt
that we shall get home all right.

Danger came in on the tide. Frozen floes pinned the wooden ship against the ice ashore. A hull plank ruptured and the water rushed in. All hands had just two hours to haul supplies on to the ice before the vessel sank like a stone. For many months afterwards the tops of the masts could be seen breaking the surface, but it was scant consolation. The Arctic winter would soon be upon them and they urgently needed shelter to survive the long night. It would be the first time men had overwintered on Franz Josef Land, in a hut of turf and stone they built by hand, with cut sails stretched over to form the roof. With quiet confidence their leader Benjamin Leigh Smith calmly declared: 'I will do my best for you all.'

The son of a radical politician, Leigh Smith was able to follow his interests as a man of means. He studied in Cambridge and was called to the bar at Inner Temple in 1856, but instead dedicated his life to science and travel. An able sailor with his own master's ticket, in 1871 he took the yacht *Sampson* to Spitsbergen and the Seven Islands, and voyaged there many times not merely to hunt but also undertaking valuable oceanographic work on the Gulf Stream. In 1880 he built the *Eira* and headed north through heavy ice conditions to the archipelago of Franz Josef Land, recently discovered but only partly mapped. It was on his second voyage there in 1881 that the *Eira* was caught in the ice at Cape Flora off Northbrook Island.

The crew endured the winter in their makeshift hut, hunting polar bears and waiting for the return of the sun to make their escape. Leigh Smith faithfully kept a log

throughout, creating a factual, understated record. Every Saturday after supper, and with a double ration of grog, the men played music and sang shanties. On Sundays divine service was usually followed by a large breakfast of polar bear curry. Then on 21 June 1882 the party set out on the perilous voyage south in four boats, using tablecloths and spare shirts for sails. After forty-two days, they sighted the coast of Novaya Zemlya. Near the entrance of Matochkin Strait they met the Scottish whaler *Hope*, commanded by Sir Allen Young, who had sailed from England in search of them.

Leigh Smith was a polar explorer of the first rank, but unlike many other adventurers of the age, he was a man of genuine modesty. He refused accolades, sent others in his place to public gatherings and published no account of his expeditions. It is said by his family that he always kept the key to the house in his waistcoat pocket. Arriving home in the early morning, after being presumed lost for many months, he quietly let himself in so as not to disturb anyone. He had few regrets, though the loss of a waterproof box containing his measurements of deep-sea currents frustrated him. It was knocked overboard as the boats struggled to reach safety. Yet, most important, every man had survived.

Leigh Smith's ship *Eira* - Welsh for snow - was a three-masted barquentine with a 50hp steam engine and a crew of twenty-five. Its second voyage to Franz Josef Land in 1881 was a disaster. On 21 August the pack ice came in with the tide and the ship was crushed, filled with water and quickly sank. The watercolour above is by an unknown artist, but Leigh Smith's own sketch (opposite left) provided a clear eyewitness account for an engraving later published in the *Graphic* newspaper.

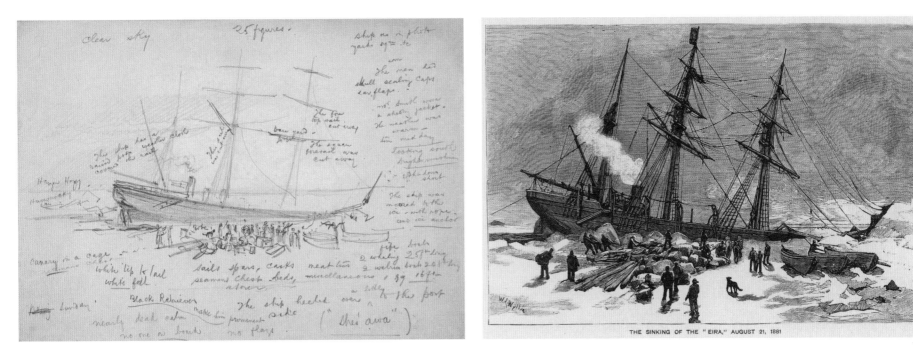

THE SINKING OF THE "EIRA," AUGUST 21, 1881

HENRY MAHON 1809-1878

Discharged Cured. Lime juice was continued
to the end of the month.

Scurvy is now known to be caused by a deficiency of Vitamin C. In 1740, the high numbers of men who died on Anson's circumnavigation (p. 20), most from scurvy, attracted much attention in Europe. According to Scottish physician James Lind, scurvy caused more deaths in the British fleets than French and Spanish arms combined. Lind conducted the first ever clinical trial on the condition in 1747, as ship's surgeon on *Salisbury*, experimenting while on patrol in the Bay of Biscay.

Many other ships' surgeons helped to develop and test the theory that citrus fruits cured the malady. Some more enlightened seafarers, Captain Cook most notably, also argued for the health benefits of better ventilation aboard ships, eating greens such as cress and pickled cabbage, improving the cleanliness of sailors' bodies, clothing and bedding, and below-deck fumigation with sulphur and arsenic. Some experimented with distilling seawater for a supply of fresh water and brewing beer for its antiscorbutic properties, as much as for morale. Exploring the coasts of Dusky Sound in New Zealand, Cook's men made beer from rimu bark and spruce needles, with a touch of tea plant. Increasingly lemon juice was also added to the sailor's daily ration of grog, the origin of the American nickname for British sailors as 'lime-juicers', later shortened to 'limeys'.

Irish ship's doctor Henry Walsh Mahon was another advocate for best practice. He studied at the Royal College of Surgeons in Dublin and the École de Médecine in Paris. In 1835 he became a surgeon in the Royal Navy, and in 1846 gained the annual prize for the best journal kept afloat.

In 1840 he served on the convict ship *Isabella*, and in 1842 was with *Barossa*, arriving in Van Diemen's Land (Tasmania) with 348 male convicts. He later joined *Samarang* on a four-year survey voyage to Borneo and the South China Sea, turning his talents to zoology, describing and sketching new species in his journal with medical precision. Latterly he was Staff Surgeon to European military pensioners in New Zealand. Having saved countless lives during his career, he died in Dublin, causes unknown, though probably simply old age. He is buried in Mount Jerome Cemetery where his headstone bears the words: 'Rest for the Weary'.

Mahon's journal from the frigate *Samarang* for
1 January 1846 to 18 January 1847, when surveying
the coast of Borneo. Dabbling in zoology in his
spare time, he was kept busy as medical officer
caring for the crew of two hundred.

Opposite: A page from Mahon's journal showing the
effects of scurvy, from his time as surgeon on the
convict ship *Barossa*, 1841-42. Sailors suffering with
scurvy found their limbs growing stiff and their
skin bruised and ulcerous, and long-healed broken
bones unknit themselves. It has been estimated that
scurvy killed over two million people serving on
ships between 1500 and 1800.

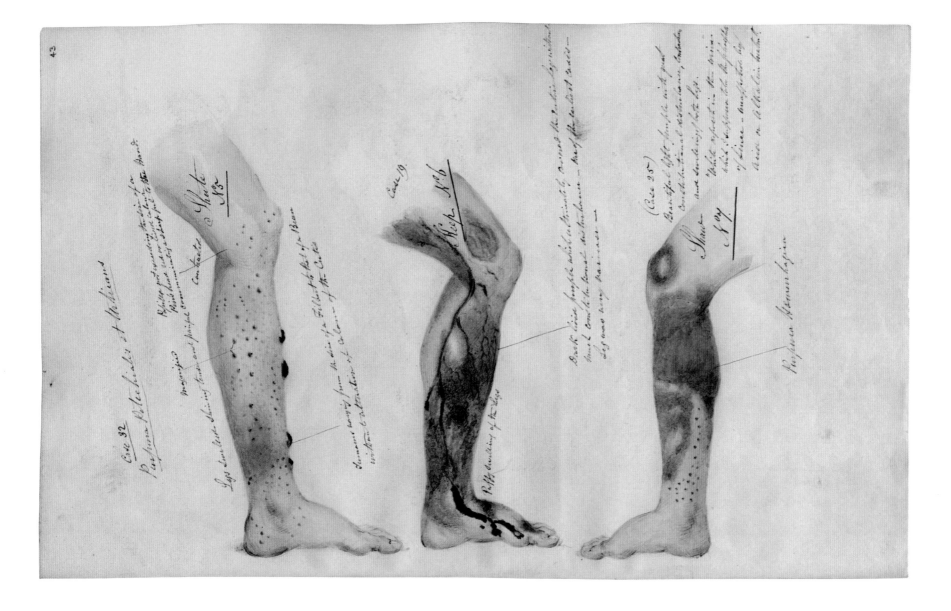

The Cassia Alata or
Acapulco of Manila

Leguminosæ   Tribe Mimosæ

Arthur Adams delt.

Opposite: The leaves of the medicinal plant *Cassia alata*, or Senna, known as *akapulko* in the Philippines, were used for their 'laxative, purgative and anti-fungal properties'. Assistant surgeon and naturalist Arthur Adams made this sketch in Mahon's sea journal, having collected a supply for the ship.

Left: Sketch in Mahon's journal of three sea snakes. The banded *Hydrophis belcheri*, though timid, is extremely poisonous - its venom is 100 times more deadly than the most poisonous land snake. Mahon noted, 'one of these snakes bit an officer of the *Woolf* who died within a few hours'.

NEVIL MASKELYNE 1732-1811

*A bad observation, or an observation which
is given without the means of verification,
is worse than no observation at all.*

On a voyage to Barbados in 1763 a young vicar with a passion for maths held the fortunes of men, and nations, in his hands. He had been sent to test new technologies in a navigational race, the outcome of which would transform the world. He later produced a celebrated *Nautical Almanac* to tabulate the heavens, helped by a network of human 'computers'. Yet at this stage, his days are spent alone with his journals, minutely inking in calculations while his ship lurches across the Atlantic.

As the global ambitions of the European nations grew, through exploration, expansion and trade, accurately determining longitude became an area of focused effort, with mathematicians, navigators, astronomers and instrument-makers all applying their energies to the problem. Dead reckoning – estimating the ship's position relative to its last known location by tracking speed and heading, and a host of other factors such as currents and wind – had been a useful past technique, with observations of the altitude of the Sun or pole star used to determine latitude. Observing the Sun or stars could establish local time whether on land or sea, but the secrets of longitude remained elusive.

New instruments and new methods were needed. Spain offered royal rewards from 1567, and the Dutch not long after. The British government passed the Longitude Act in 1714, which promised rewards of up to £20,000 if longitude could be determined to within half a degree. John Harrison eventually produced marine timekeepers to the required level of accuracy, but they remained rare and expensive and it took decades for seafarers to trust them.

Nevil Maskelyne first entered this story as an energetic Cambridge graduate, sent in 1761 on a voyage to St Helena to observe the transit of Venus across the face of the Sun. Though cloud thwarted his efforts, Maskelyne refined a technique of observing the angles between the Moon and stars with a sextant and reckoning longitude. He would help pioneer the creation of simpler, pre-computed tables of the Moon's future positions, and devised a series of nautical almanacs vital to navigation and cartography for several years ahead. The lunar-distance method required complex mathematics and careful application, but it was reliable and was ready to use.

Maskelyne was a champion for getting marine timekeepers and scientific observers on naval expeditions. When Cook sailed on his first voyage in *Endeavour* in 1768 he used the lunar technique, yet later relied on improved chronometers too. After his voyage to Barbados, on which he tested various methods, Maskelyne became Astronomer Royal in 1765 and remained so for almost fifty years. He was a quiet man, dedicated to his craft for the betterment of others. Night after night at his hilltop observatory in Greenwich Park he studied the skies. And with each careful record, and each mammoth calculation, the hard life of ordinary navigators around the world was made a little easier. Though his name may not be attached to a grand discovery or breakthrough invention, as an organizer of people and prodigious amounts of useful data, his maritime legacy is considerable.

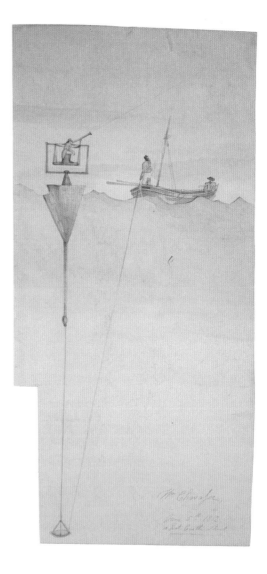

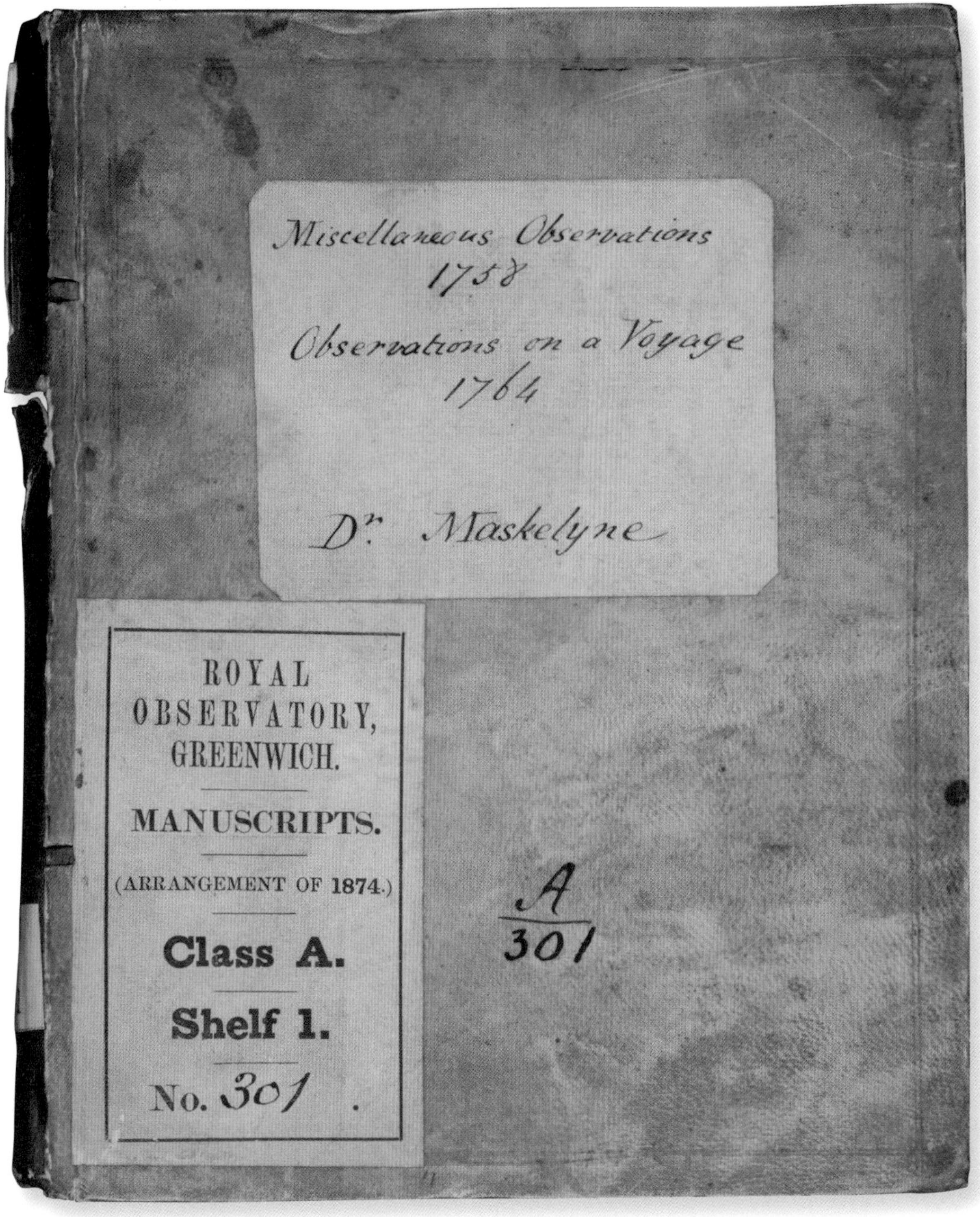

Miscellaneous Observations
1758

Observations on a Voyage
1764

Dr. Maskelyne

ROYAL
OBSERVATORY,
GREENWICH.

———

MANUSCRIPTS.

———

(ARRANGEMENT OF 1874.)

———

Class A.

Shelf 1.

No. 301 .

A
301

Opposite: The Board of
Longitude considered many
alternative methods for
finding longitude at sea,
and Maskelyne often offered
his expert opinion. Here is
Lieutenant William Chevasse's
design for a marine chair to
observe Jupiter's satellites.

A notebook of Maskelyne's
observations made in 1758,
when he held a curacy, and
those made in 1764 on the
return voyage from Barbados.

4

1770	Watch H		Watch K		Thermom.	
	Time by Watch H M	Time too fast of Clock H M S	Time by Watch H M	Time too fast of Clock H M S		
☽ march 19	2. 10	1 57 49	2. 8	1. 55. 49	37	10:h:34
♂ 20	0 15	0. 6. 0	0 14	0 5 20	35	
☿ 21	0 26	0 20 30	0 28	0 23 12	33	
♃ 22	0 10	0 7 56	0 14	0 12 59	34½	10B
♀ 23	0 20	0 21 25	0 17	0 19 49	34½	10B
♄ 24	0 26	0 30 53	0 31	0 37 41	30½	WB
☉ 25	0 16	0 24 19	0 14	0 24 30	39	
☽ 26	0 21	0 32 47	0 15	0 29 23	40	10B
♂ 27	0 16	0 31 12	0 10	0 36 17	30½	10B
☿ 28	0 20	0 38 39	0 16	0 38 9	38	
♃ 29	0 26	0 40 5	0 23	0 49 2	38½	WB
♀ 30	0 13	0 30 29	0 12	0 41 54	42	WB
♄ 31	0 18	0 41 57	0 10	0 43 49	46	WB
☉ Apr. 1	0 29	1 1 28	0 28	1 5 48	47	
☽ 2	0 24	0 59 55	0 15	0 56 42	47	WB
♂ 3	0 42	1 21 26	0. 30	1 15 41	43	
☿ 4	0 33	1 15 53	0. 25	1 14 36	44	
♃ 5	0 45	1 31 22	0 41	1 34 34	43	
♀ 6	0 30	1 19 40	0 23	1 20 26	43	W B.
♄ 7	0 25	1 18 17	0 23	1 24 21	43	W B.
☉ 8	0 32	1 20 40	0 19	1 24 15	42	W B.
☽ 9	0 17	1 17 16	0 13	1 22 9	44	W B.
♂ 10	0 33	1 36 49	0 21	1 34 5	41	
☿ 11	0 31	1 30 19	0 10	1 34 59	43	W B.
♃ 12	0 41	1 51 51	0 27	1 47 55	41½	W B.
♀ 13	0 26	1 40 19	0 15	1 39 47	42	W B.
♄ 14	0 22	1 39 49	0 8	1 36 40	42	
☉ 15	0 16	1 37 19	0. 6	1 38 34	44½	
☽ 16	0 18	1 42 51	0 7	1 43 30	49	
♂ 17	0. 19	1 47 22	0 5	1 45 26	50	
☿ 18	0 19	1 50 52	0 5	1 49 22	50	
♃ 19	0 17	1 52 22	0 6	1 54 19	49	
♀ 20	This day the watches went down, having been forgot to be wound up; H stopped at 5.31.19 & K at 5 13 42					
☉ 22	Mr Glendal came down & wound up both watches and set them going nearly with mean time.					
	2. 0 4 0 44		2. 4 4 4 45		46	

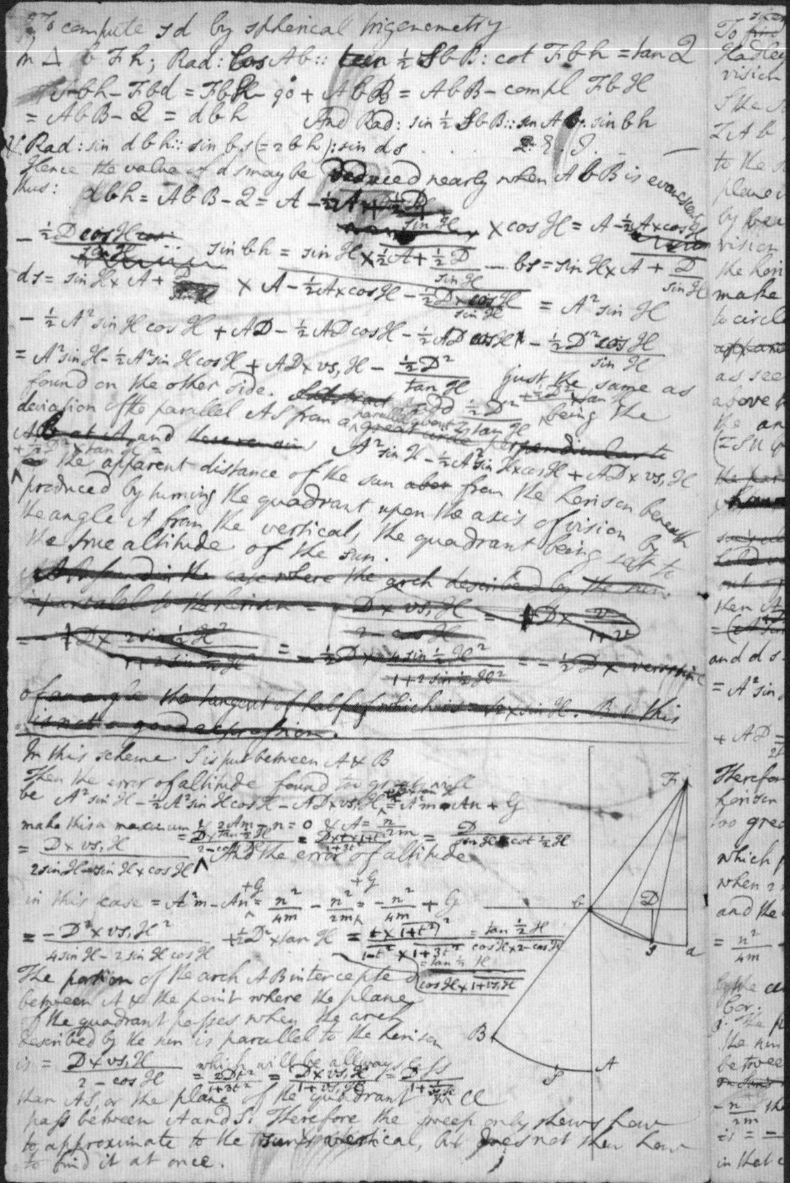

To compute ꝺd by spherical trigonometry

In △ dbℌh; Rad : Cos Ab :: tan ꝺ Sbℌ : cot Ⴔbℌh = tan ꝺ

Ⴔbℌh − Ⴔbd = Ⴔbℌh 90° + AbꝺB = AbꝺB − compl Ⴔbℌ
= AbꝺB − ꝺ = dbℌh

And Rad : sin ꝺ Sbℌ :: sin bℌ (= ꝺbℌh) : sin dꝺ . . . . . Q.E.I.

Hence the value of dꝺ may be reduced nearly when AbꝺB is evanescent
thus: dbℌh = AbꝺB − ꝺ = A − ½A ...

[remaining derivation illegible]

In this scheme S is put between A & B
Then the error of altitude found in the vertical
be A²·m sin ℌ − ½ A²·m sin ℌ cos ℌ − AꝺB × vs. ℌ, A·m × tan + G
make this a maximum ...
And the error of altitude ...

in this case = A²·m − A·m + ...

The portion of the arch AB intercepted
between A & the point where the plane
of the quadrant passes when the arch
described by the sun is parallel to the horizon
vs = D + vs. ℌ which is the plane ...
then AS, or the plane of the quadrant, will
pass between A and S. Therefore the sweep only shews how
to approximate to the truly vertical, but does not then shew
to find it at once.

Opposite left: Maskelyne and his assistants conducted many trials of marine chronometers at the Royal Observatory, Greenwich, on behalf of the Board of Longitude. In 1770 they tested the now celebrated timepieces of John Harrison and Larcum Kendall. Maskelyne's journals are filled with workings, constantly trying to simplify and improve the calculations necessary to turn observations at sea into longitude and latitude.

In 1763 the Board of Longitude sent Maskelyne to Barbados to oversee the official trial of three contenders for the prize: John Harrison's marine timepiece (now known as H4), a system of lunar calculations and a marine chair for observing Jupiter's satellites (such as that shown on p. 174). With Harrison's watch, Maskelyne measured Bridgetown's longitude to within 10 miles. This was a considerable advance that rightly earned Harrison a reward.

WILLIAM MEYERS 1815-n.d.

Feel very bad this morning, so much so that
I drink wine and lemonade together with about
½ gallon of salts.

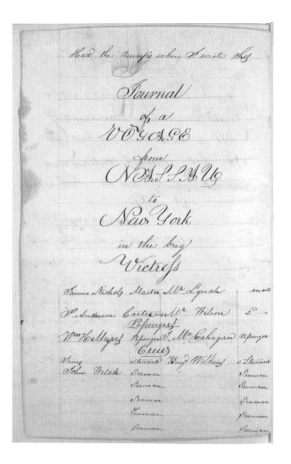

Seasickness, tropical fever, war and storm – artist William Meyers experienced it all. He was born in Philadelphia and first went to sea on trading vessels to the West Indies in 1838, and also worked as a civilian at the Washington Navy Yard. In 1841 he joined the US Navy as a gunner, and was assigned to the sloop *Cyane* for a three-year Pacific cruise. He served under Commodore Thomas Jones' Pacific Squadron, taking part in the presumptuous American seizure of Monterey in 1842, and during the Mexican-American War was a gunner on the *Dale*. Despite all this action, Meyers was able to keep a journal and sketched scenes of life on board and ashore. He resigned from the Navy in 1848 having developed a trapped nerve in his face, which he said was due to his time working at the naval lab in Washington making rockets and firework flares. A note in his journal reveals he'd also contracted venereal disease after a dalliance in Hawaii.

After returning ashore, Meyers tried unsuccessfully to rejoin the navy. Instead, in New York, he came up with the idea of creating a moving-picture panorama of a sea voyage to California, based on his original sketches. East Coast performances like this stirred the wanderlust of would-be gold seekers. With the help of a theatrical scene painter, his show opened in 1849 at the Stoppani Hall on Broadway, with 'splendid views of the principal ports on the Atlantic and Pacific Oceans'. It was said to be particularly popular with women 'whose husbands, brothers, lovers, etc. have gone'. The following year it was on display again at the Bleecker buildings on Morton Street, a stone's throw from the wharves on the Hudson. For many people prior to the invention of film, watching a painted panorama like Meyers' was their first taste of a long sea voyage, before they embarked on their own journeys by following the 'forty-niners' out west.

President Roosevelt later bought one of Meyers' original sketchbooks. 'In many years of collecting sketches, paintings and engravings relating to the Navy of the United States, I had found virtually none which had connection with naval operations in the Pacific', he noted, 'thus the very dearth of adequate contemporary literature adds much to the historical value of Gunner Meyers' brush.'

This is the first of Meyer's sea journals, from 1838, recording his voyages from Baltimore to Cuba on the schooner *Ajax*, and to Nassau in the Bahamas, as master of the brig *Lucy*. He returned to New York as a passenger on the brig *Victress*.

19

taking an observation of the Sun

at 9 oclock at night we are boat Nicaragua

Monday commences fine weather nothing particular
Jan 7th 1839

Course	Dist.	Dep. Lat.				Departure
N W	48	34			34	
NWW	21	12			18	
S W	17			12	12	
N W½	8	7			5	

53-12-41 69

at 1 oclock at the main top gall...

Lucy meeting ... Nicaragua by moonlight

Meyers drew his self-portrait before and after he suffered from fever on a voyage: 'heavy chill and hot fever this morning'. Later, as it was Christmas Day 1838, the crew had 'an antiquated fowl for dinner'. Opposite is a selection of glimpses from his sea journal, including mending breeches, smoking, taking observations with a telescope, *Lucy* off Cuba (bottom left) and 'Natural Cascades SE from Cape Henry … Seasick Gentry' (top left).

GEORG MÜLLER 1646–1723

This water is so utterly poor, yet it tastes
as good to me as the best wine.

As a child, Georg Müller was fuelled by curiosity and a longing to explore distant lands. After his apprenticeship as a gunsmith in Alsace, aged fourteen he left his parents' home in Rufach, Germany, and began a travelling life. He wandered from Breisgau to Mainz, from Trier to Cologne, then further afield, working his way through Austria, Hungary and Italy. On learning that the Dutch East India Company was looking for recruits, he emigrated to the Netherlands and, in 1669, boarded the *Gouda* as a midshipman and mercenary and set sail for Batavia on Java, the administrative centre of the Dutch trading empire, now modern-day Jakarta.

Sailing west of Gibraltar, *Gouda* was attacked by two Turkish ships, resulting in 28 dead and 46 injured. Numbers on the *Gouda* dwindled further as passengers and crew were either swept overboard in violent storms or succumbed to scurvy and dehydration. With water running out, rain was collected in the sails and any spare cloth; every drop was precious. As they crossed the Indian Ocean the wind dropped. Drifting slowly in stifling heat, Müller wrote of the exposure and sunburn they had to contend with.

In August 1670, over three hundred days after they had set sail, *Gouda* finally reached the island of Java – 'paradise', according to Müller. During his twelve years of service he travelled throughout Java and various other islands of Indonesia. He learnt the Malay language and spent all his free time drawing and exploring. He had an eye for the unusual, creating a vivid record of the native flora and fauna and the people whom he met, along with some fanciful creatures copied from the books he read, accompanied by strange descriptions told in verse.

Now housed in the Abbey Library of St Gallen in Switzerland, Müller's extraordinary journals provide a colourful and vivid glimpse of a young man's experience of seventeenth-century colonial life and the creatures of the oceans at that time.

Little is known about the life of Georg Müller, though it is clear that he was an enthusiastic and curious individual. He filled his journal with colourful, playful observations of everything he found of interest, from a pineapple to a huge variety of marine specimens, including a flying fish, a puffer fish and yet other more fanciful creatures.

Ein frembdes Meer Monstrum

34.

Meer Minsch

Eine Seekuhe

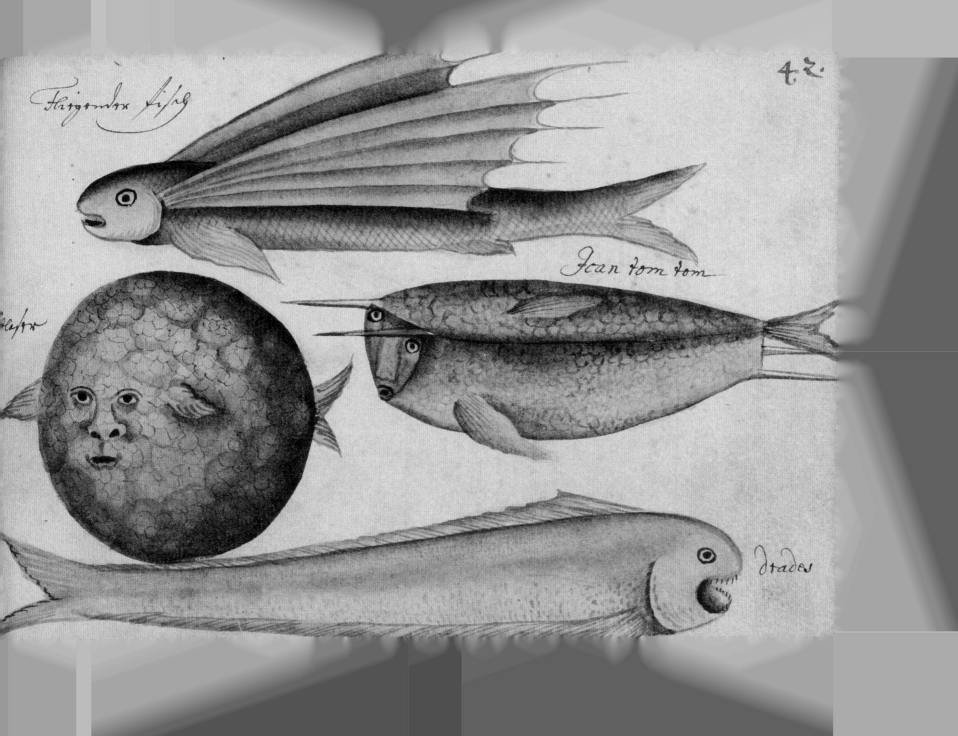

Fliegender fisch

42

Jcan tom tom

Trades

Das wüste wild gesalzen Meer
Die Wellen sach wie berg stehen
Septentrion auch occident
Sind mir gar wol bekant.

Grausam sab sehen wüten
rechenklich auff nider gehen
Meridien und Orient

Auff grossen schiffen gefahren Ich,
Auß Europa, America
Dem wind und wasser gott betraut,

Manch tausend meil glaubts sicherlich
von Africa in Asia
Auff Pelus und Neptun gebaut

Shortly before his death, Müller presented his two illustrated travel journals to the Abbey Library of St Gallen, Switzerland, along with a collection of everyday objects from seventeenth-century Batavia, such as a Chinese teapot and silk purses, reflecting the multicultural nature of the Dutch trading centre.

Müller spent several months in South Africa and records that many animals, such as lions and leopards, were caged and transported back to the Netherlands. His sketch right shows his first sight of some birds, including parrots and cockatoos, and his idea of a penguin.

HORATIO NELSON 1758-1805

Duty is the great business of a sea-officer;
all private considerations must give way to it,
however painful it is.

Sailors in the eighteenth-century faced mortal danger with regularity. The very act of going to sea exposed them to fatal diseases and myriad ways to die. To which was added the prospect, as Horatio Nelson's seafaring uncle once put it, that in battle 'a cannon ball may knock off your head'. In Nelson's private letters we can read how he was reconciled to his own death. Wounds were just a hazard of his profession.

Even during his lifetime, Nelson's skill and daring were extolled in story and song. He is the man who struck fear into his enemies, and who disobeyed orders, the man who fell in love with a married woman, and collapsed on the deck of his ship, his spine shot through, as his men fought for their lives in the waters off Cape Trafalgar. His ships, though burnt and splintered, emerged from the storm triumphant, but their gallant commander was dead. He was the naval hero who gave his life doing his duty; his signal on the eve of battle, 'England Expects', became a mantra for a maritime century. The ascendancy secured by Nelson's sailors at Trafalgar enabled Britain to rule the waves as never before.

It's a remarkable life story for a parson's son born in Norfolk. His first sea voyage was to the Caribbean, as a boy of twelve on the 64-gun *Raisonable*, and with it a first encounter with seasickness, from which he suffered for the rest of his life. In 1773 he joined a voyage in search of the North Pole, where it is said he absconded from his ship and hunted a polar bear on the ice. He caught malaria in the Indian Ocean and it recurred in the jungles of Nicaragua, almost killing him; he was stricken with yellow fever, food poisoning and

dysentery off San Juan; he came down with scurvy crossing the Atlantic in 1782. At the siege of Calvi during the capture of Corsica in 1794 he was blinded in his right eye.

To Nelson a combat mission could simply end one of two ways: glorious victory or death. Yet in his dashing commando raid on the defences of the town of Santa Cruz in the Canary Islands in July 1797, neither happened. His attack was repulsed with significant casualties among his force, and Nelson was hit by grapeshot in the right elbow, which led to his arm being amputated.

At the Battle of St Vincent earlier that year, Nelson had proved his tactical acumen and moral courage by leaving the line of battle prescribed by his admiral and sailing alone into the enemy's fire. Eighteen months later, the Battle of the Nile raised his renown yet higher and he became Lord Nelson of the Nile. At Copenhagen, with the battle hanging in the balance and fire from the Danish batteries fierce, he calmly sent a note to the Danish Commander proposing a truce, beginning with the words 'Lord Nelson has directions to spare Denmark'. The bold move succeeded and firing ceased.

Despite romantic scandal ashore, on ship at least Nelson was a man of true integrity. In an age of 'cruelty and barbarity' at sea, he stood out as a highly civilized commander and one who was genuinely willing to put his body on the line for the cause. No surprise then, that he was beloved by his officers and men.

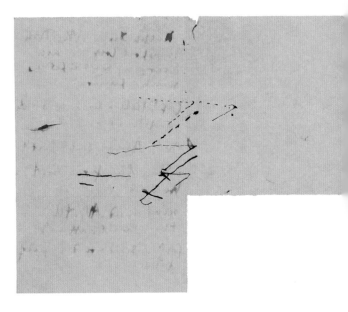

Above: This sketch, hastily made on the back of
a scrap of paper, appears to outline Nelson's plan
for the Battle of Trafalgar, showing the enemy line
cut in two places.

Opposite: The cover of Nelson's own signal book and
a page from his will written before Trafalgar in 1805.

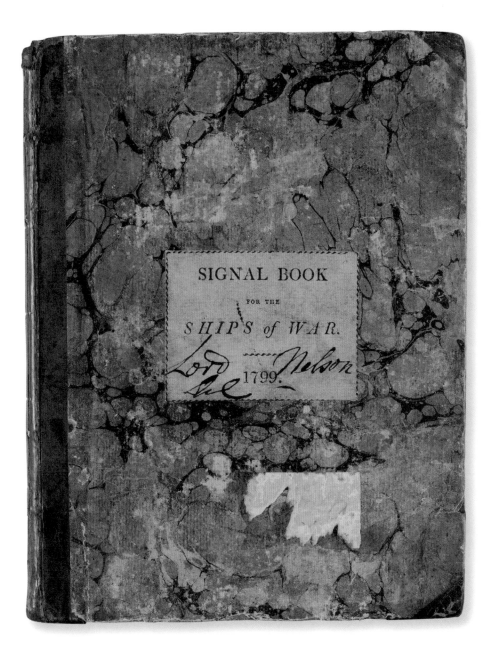

Friday Night at half
past Ten I rose from
dear dear Merton
where I left all which
I hold dear in this World
to go to serve my King
& Country may the
great God whom I adore
enable me to fulfill
the expectations of my
Country and if it is his
good pleasure that I
should return my thanks
will never cease being

Above: Nelson's private weather log kept during the early stages of the Mediterranean campaign in 1803, said to have been pinned up in his cabin during the voyage. As is usual, the log records the date, several barometer readings per day, with times for each, and brief notes on the weather.

Opposite left: A page from an album of an unknown admirer, showing the plan of the Battle of Trafalgar, with Nelson's portrait on the right, and on the left, Cuthbert Collingwood, second-in-command on *Royal Sovereign*.

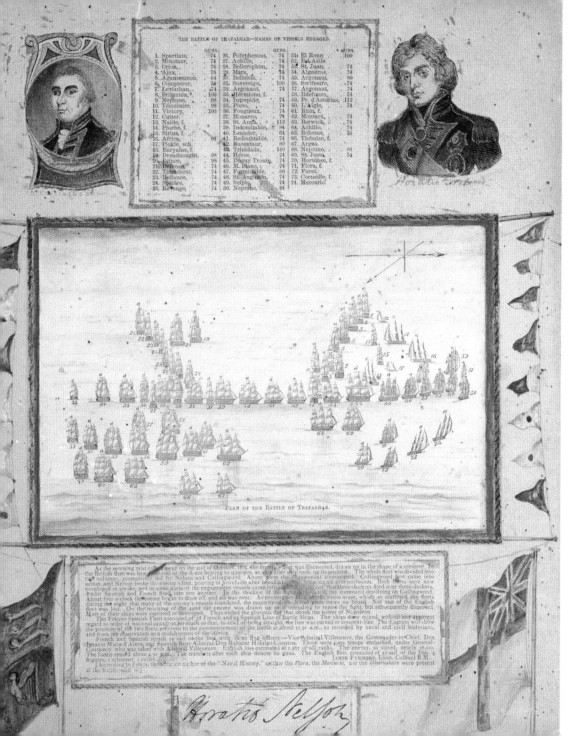

Above: This remarkable sketch of Trafalgar is by
Paul Nicolas, a marine lieutenant on HMS *Belleisle*.
During the battle *Belleisle* was badly damaged
in action with the *Fougueux*, but despite being
completely dismasted, she refused to surrender.

PAUL-ÉMILE PAJOT 1873-1929

Whenever it's bad weather, I draw at home
and lend a hand to raise my little boys.
They will never know what we are doing
to give them everything they need.

Among countless sketches in Pajot's journals is
this one showing the lifeboat of Les Sables-d'Olonne,
which capsized three times during the rescue of
Reine des Cieux. Opposite is a later drawing
of the four-masted barque *Fleur de Strasbourg*
coming from Chile loaded with nitrates.

Fisherman artist Paul-Émile Pajot was a man whose life was defined by the cruel sea. In later years, as he came to be more widely known, he was styled as the 'marin-pêcheur et peintre de bateaux' ('fisherman and painter of boats'), but he was never interested in being famous. 'He does not paint boats for people who love painting, but he is a painter for people who love boats', as author and artist Jean Cocteau said of Pajot in 1925, at the first exhibition of his work in Paris.

Pajot was born in La Chaume on the Vendée Atlantic coast of France, the eldest son of a fisherman and a seamstress. The family led a modest existence, living six in one room, and when the weather was too bad to fish Pajot's father earned a few cents by cutting the wooden needles used for mending nets. But their quiet existence was shattered on 27 January 1881. That night a terrible storm devastated the port of Les Sables-d'Olonne: eleven boats missing and fifty-one men drowned, leaving more than a hundred orphans. At first light in the morning, empty boats lay stranded and broken on the beach. Wives and children came down to the shore to search for the bodies of their loved ones. Pajot's father was one of the victims, lost at sea.

When he was eleven Pajot had to leave school and work to support his family, joining the sardine boat *Beauséjour*. After a first summer fishing, his old teacher offered him lessons in the evening. By the age of twenty and in military service he began to perfect his drawing. In 1896 he married Dalie Merlen, a childhood friend. A year later, their first son was born, and the happy couple had six more children.

At the dawn of a new century, in February 1900, Pajot began writing a journal entitled 'My Adventures'. Five large volumes survive, with five hundred pages each and endless illustrations of the boats he'd worked on, of schooners encountered in the Bay of Biscay, and portraits of family and friends. There are more than a thousand gouaches and ink drawings, with images cut from the popular press also serving as inspiration. It's a mixture of his own experiences and the maritime dramas of the day, just as Les Sables-d'Olonne was being transformed into a bustling seaside resort for the wealthy.

With many mouths to feed, Pajot worked as much as humanly possible, out for sardines, on trawlers and the dangerous deep-sea tuna runs. In 1906 he was finally able to buy a boat of his own, *Anna-Maria*, and though his eyesight was failing he also began to make larger works for sale. His paintings were discovered by the artist Albert Marquet when he was on holiday and were admired by Cocteau, who was a driving force behind the exhibition; orders came from buyers all over France.

Pajot was also writing poetry. Whenever there was need for a story at a town meeting or banquet, especially if there was a drink to be had, Pajot was on hand and came armed with his accordion. But in 1929, just as the art world was beginning to recognize his talents, he tragically died ashore. Having problems with his lungs, he went outside for the sea air, stumbled on some steps and broke his skull.

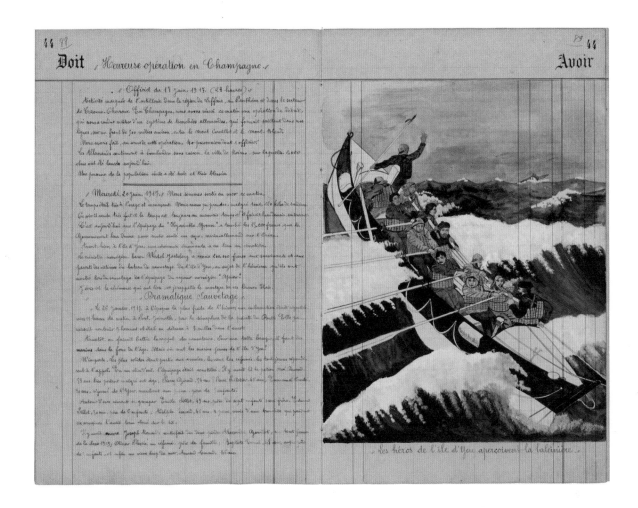

Les héros de l'île d'Yeu aperçoivent la baleinière.

Opposite: The Dundee ketch *Si J'étais Roi* returning with 350 fish caught off Santander; the *Honneur et Dévouement* commanded by Aimé Vigier, running near the wind with 280 fresh tuna taken on the line; the snail sloop *Ami du Drapeau* arriving; and the shipwreck of the *Petit Florent* with a fishing boat coming to the rescue in the winter of 1929.

Above: Pajot's diary records this dramatic lifeboat rescue on 26 January 1917 in deep winter, in both words and a vivid image.

Overleaf: Pages from Pajot's journals showing his range and mastery - from scenes of peril at sea to marine life and portraits of sailors and fishermen.

The wind was blowing from the sea, sometimes furious, And I complained about the poor sailors Who face the sea to make a living And who, too often, find their tomb ...

...au que le patron me félicita, car il avait la même idée que moi.

Le Poulpe géant.—

La Baie des Trépassés. (côte du Finistère).

Aussi, comme nous avons passé de bons moments ensemble chez ...ire Kersire, avec ses enfants et chez Marie-Yol.

Nous fûmes trois jours en calme, après avoir comme sous dix ... mal le temps, une journée, l'on vit un poisson monstrueux, se promener ..mir de bord. Le poisson mesurait au moins cinq mètres de longueur.

Il était, qui, comme une barrique.

Il avait au moins huit ou dix rangées de dents énormes, ... nous des crochets. Le patron installa quatre hameçons de thon ...é ... un morceau de lard pour servir d'appât.

Un Squale monstrueux...

Aussitôt, les pilotes du monstre (ils étaient deux), se dirigent sur l'appât, et le poisson monstrueux les suit.

D'un seul coup de ses mâchoires, il brisa l'appareil.

Fin du 7ème Chapitre.

L'IPNOPS, le seul poisson des profondeurs, qui est-peut être privé d'yeux.

Le TRACHYPTERUS, arborant ses plumets et ses houpettes.

3. Le Cératias, caché dans les profondeurs, agite son hameçon et pré-cipite ses victimes dans sa gueule en chausse-trappe.

4. Le Melano-cétus, pêche à la ligne et met ses proies en réserve dans son volumineux estomac.

5. L'APHYONUS, vit à 3.000 mètres de fond.

6. L'ACANTHONUS, tout en tête, rejette ses excréments..... sous sa gorge .....

POISSONS DES GRANDES PROFONDEURS.

Hommage à nos Héros.

Chapitre 2.

Sommaire: Officiels. — Le beau temps revient. — Le départ Paul-André pour Toulon. — Venï à la Rochelle. — Communiqués.

Officiel du 16 Juin, 1918. (14 heures).

Des actions locales au nord-est du bois de Genlis, au sud de Dammars dans la région de Vinly, nous ont permis de faire 70 prisonniers et de capturer des mitrailleuses. Une tentative ennemie pour franchir le Matz en ... de l'Oise a échoué sous nos feux.

Nuit calme sur le reste du front.

Officiel du 16 Juin, 1918. (23 heures).

En Woëvre, l'ennemi qui avait réussi ce matin, à prendre pied dans le villag ...de Xivray au cours d'une vive attaque, en a été rejeté peu après par nos trou ...qui ont rétabli leur position. Nous avons fait des prisonniers dont un officie ...Rien à signaler sur le reste du front.

Nous continuons à rectifier nos lignes.

Officiel du 17 Juin, 1918. (14 heures).

Entre l'Oise et l'Aisne, nous avons réussi, ce matin, une opération de ... qui nous a permis d'élargir nos positions, au noir et au nord-ouest de Hé ... ...bleraye. Nous avons fait une centaine de prisonniers et capturé des mitra ... ...leuses. Au bois des Carrières et dans les Vosges, nous avons repoussé ...des coups de main ennemis. Rien à signaler sur le reste du front.

Officiel du 17 Juin, 1918. (23 heures).

Entre Oise et Aisne, nous avons repoussé des contre-attaques ennemies au nord de Hautebraye et consolidé nos gains de ce matin.

Le chiffre des prisonniers que nous avons faits dans cette région atteint 37 ...25 mitrailleuses et 8 mortiers de tranchées sont restés entre nos mains.

Officiel du 18 Juin, 1918. (14 heures).

Au sud de l'Aisne, nous avons réussi une opération locale.

Théodore perdit son grand canot.

Au sud d'Ambleny et à l'est de Montgobert, nous avons fait une centaine de prisonniers, dont deux officiers.

Entre l'Ourcq et la Marne, nos patrouilles ont fait des prisonniers.

Nuit calme sur le reste du front.

Où nous faillîmes y périr tous.

Officiel du 18 Juin, 1918. (23 heures).

L'activité de l'artillerie a été assez vive au nord-ouest de Montdidier, ainsi

WHERE THE ROAD ENDS

Philip Marsden

Sing to me of the man, Muse, the man of twists
and turns driven time and again off course.
THE ODYSSEY, HOMER, TRANS. ROBERT FITZGERALD, 1961

Two nautical maps, two ages. One is a chart of the British Isles and a portion of the Atlantic drawn in 1473 by Grazioso Benincasa, a prolific cartographer from the Italian port of Ancona. It is a portolan, a piece of parchment marked with ink and tempera and used to guide ships along the coast and out into vast areas of featureless ocean, to help open up the world to the restless spirits of post-Renaissance Europe.

The other is on my phone. It is the Navionics Boating app. It covers a similar sea, and is also, by chance, from Italy. I'm deeply attached to this app, purchased for not very much at all, capable of zooming in and out with the merest movement of finger and thumb. 'We start where the road ends', the tagline declares. I love its clean graphics, the little arrow that shows my boat's position. I love the crisp red line that runs out from it, projecting the heading and what will happen if I run my course. I love it for the reassurance it gives me as a single-handed sailor. I have paper charts and a Raymarine chart-plotter on board, but neither gives the instant picture of Navionics, the snapshot necessary for establishing position, depth, hazard, when several things are happening very quickly and all at once. The touch screen is no good if spray is sloshing into the cockpit and everything is wet, but on rock-scattered passages and the approaches to many tight harbours it has been a godsend.

Benincasa's portolan was, in 1473, also state-of-the-art. It pooled all available knowledge. It offered the same reassurance, the same essential information in passage-planning, with the marking of major and minor ports and anchorages. Navionics uses satellites and GPS to fix position – no need to worry about a poor phone signal – and the cursor can be placed over any destination to plot distance and bearing, and is time-synced to give tidal streams and state of tide. The portolan

uses compass roses and straight lines. It takes no account of the Earth's curvature but in its time was practical and accurate and beautiful by association, offering relief from the navigator's lot of ceaseless anxiety.

But there is something else about Benincasa's portolan. Little more than a day's sail off the west coast of Ireland is an island where no island should be. Adding fictitious islands is, in navigation terms, a lot less dangerous than marking nothing where there *are* islands; and it's easier to prove a mid-ocean feature than disprove it. So mythical islands littered charts for years – in 1875, the great hydrographer Sir Frederick Evans purged 123 of them from the Pacific (including three that did turn out to exist). As recently as 2012, Sandy Island in the Pacific was finally scrubbed from charts when a ship sailed through its position and found the water to be 1,300 m (4,265 ft) deep.

The island on Benincasa's chart was more than just a rumour or cartographic tic. Roughly twenty miles across, it's marked 'Brazil'. As Hy Brazil or Hy Brasil, it had been floating around the fringes of European cartography for some time, attracting to its mythical shores a flotsam of stories and notions. The Spanish ambassador in England reported on the zealous efforts that were then being made to try to find it: 'for the last seven years the people of Bristol have equipped two, three, four caravels to go in search of the island of Brazil and the Seven Cities'.

The island of the Seven Cities – or Antillia – was also a phantom. It cropped up on a great number of contemporary charts, including those of Benincasa, some way to the west of the Azores. Its shape was usually strikingly regular, resembling a giant postage stamp with seven perforations for its seven bays. Like Hy Brasil, its promise had helped to generate a great deal of wharfside activity along Europe's seaboard. These were not so much places as ideas – hopes, fantasies – demarcated by imaginary shorelines. Hy Brasil held the elixir of life; it was the Isles of the Blessed, the islands of St Brendan's quest, even the place of King Arthur's burial. Antillia and its seven cities likewise embodied the hopes and projections of the Christian world. During the Moorish invasions of the eighth century, seven bishops and their people had fled Spain and sailed west, to Antillia in the Atlantic. On the island each bishop had established a colony. Now, seven centuries later, those communities were waiting to be rediscovered.

The story of the portolan and the app is of the acquisition of knowledge, the ever-sharpening awareness of the physical world around us. Navionics is now automatically accumulating data, in real time: readings from subscribers' instruments are fed back into the charts to improve the hydrographic picture. In comes precision measurements, the Earth's surface minutely known – out goes open-ended possibility, utopias, the sustained existence of entirely made up islands.

And with them goes a certain magic. We now have no *terra incognita*, no watery edges to our charts to mark *hic sunt dracones,* 'here be dragons'. We know that there is nowhere on Earth where gryphons live or rivers flow on three days a week, no island of giant sheep, no island of laughter or sirens or flesh-eating demons, nowhere that fulfils the promise of Elysian joys or the guiltless pleasures of Eden, nowhere beyond the horizon where the souls of the dead reside in eternal peace.

Every era gets the maps and charts it deserves. Ours are astonishingly efficient, moving towards a state of omniscience and total safety; they are also literal-minded and utilitarian. Spend a few hours with fifteenth-century portolans, look closely at the details, the marginal drawings, and you enter a world where there is no line between the real and the fantastic. You find yourself pulled into a world of sea voyages on creaking caravels packed with men, an uncomfortable mixture of privation, risk and terror – but all floating on the gambler's hopes of bounty and fortune.

Last summer I sailed up the west coast of Ireland. Even with my Navionics, a nautical almanac, a depth sounder and log, it remained hazardous. Rocks were unbuoyed and unlit, the weather often vicious, the scale of the Atlantic swells alarming. A Donegal mariner told me that he still comes across rocks that do not appear even on electronic charts. The faint thrill of that was reactionary; there will come a time when it is no longer true, when every rock is known. But maps are never purely functional. They are an abstraction, an edited version of the real world. Like a story, they involve a certain imaginative reassembling to move from the page back to the scenes they represent – and in that reassembling lies their enduring pleasure.

It is winter now. I am writing up my journey. On my phone I flit up the coast, zooming in to check the layout of a certain island harbour. I am reliving the passage there, and the night on a mooring caught in a gale; I am remembering the story a man told me of St Columba's conversion of the island to Christianity and his banishing of its demons by turning them into pigs, which then ran over the cliffs to their death. The electronic map conjures it all up. Sitting here at my desk, those distant days and far-off shores glow with the pleasure of recollection. I yearn for them – as others before me gazed at the portolans of Benincasa and yearned for the harbours of Antillia, for the out-of-reach coastline of Hy Brasil.

Page 198: The Dutch private navigation manual of Matheus Rogiers, 1680-83, currently in Het Scheepvaartmuseum, Amsterdam.

Opposite: Grazioso Benincasa produced portolan charts in Venice in 1473, which were bound into a small atlas - this opening shows the navigable coasts of Europe, from Spain up to Scotland.

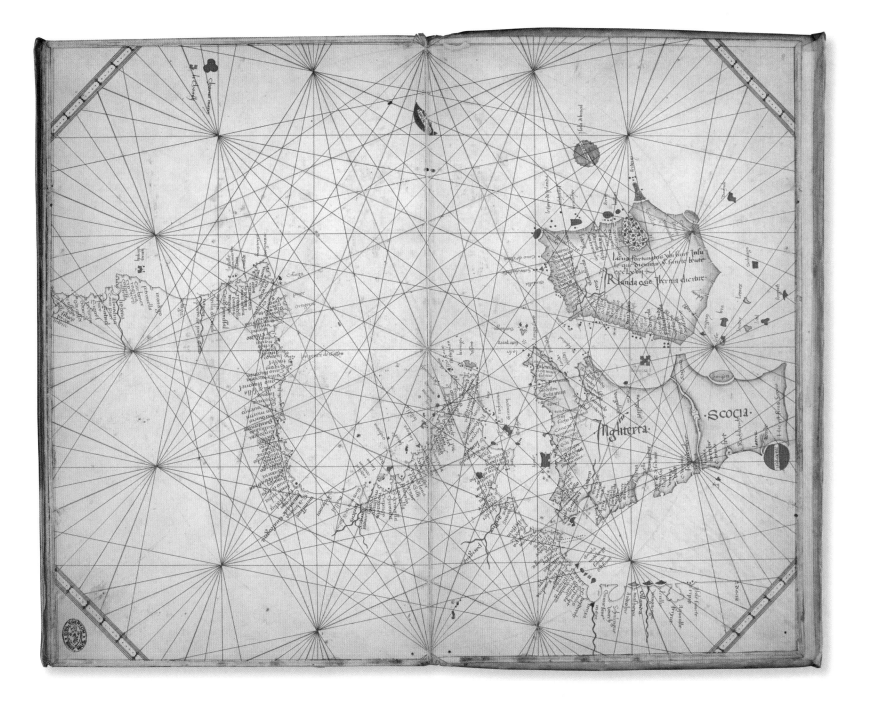

JULIUS PAYER 1841–1915

The eye-lids freeze, even in calm weather.
Great cold as well as great heat generates
the great evil – thirst.

Imagine the surprise and sheer relief to come upon land after drifting powerlessly for more than a year at the mercy of the elements on a ship trapped in the ice. On 30 August 1873 the men of the Austro-Hungarian North Pole Expedition saw in the distance, through a break in the low clouds, an unknown shore, a black fragment rearing from the chaos of ice stretching to the horizon. They named the new land Franz Josef in honour of their emperor, and toasted their fortune in grog hastily made on deck. This had never been the plan. Their goal had been to sail effortlessly on a warm current from northern Norway right over the Pole.

One of the members of the expedition, and its co-leader, was Julius Payer. Born in Teplice, a small town in Bohemia, now part of the Czech Republic, Payer was the son of a cavalry officer. He was a scholar at the Austrian Theresian Military Academy, and even before his eighteenth birthday had fought at the Battle of Solferino. He returned to his role as history professor at the academy, but a life of books was not enough. He was also a talented mountaineer, and in 1868 he was invited to join the German North Polar Expedition as surveyor and glaciologist. His climbing skills were useful in East Greenland in opening up new areas for charting. With his friend naval lieutenant Karl Weyprecht, he also sailed to Novaya Zemlya, as preparation for the later Austro-Hungarian voyage.

It was on that voyage that their ship, *Tegetthoff*, reached the ice in August 1872 and never left it, beset through dark months of winter and wet, foggy summer. After their surprise landfall, Payer led a sledging party through the new Franz Josef Land, reaching 82 degrees, essentially the most northerly point of Europe, and disproving the theory of a warm, ice-free, polar sea.

Still unable to break free, the ship was abandoned on 20 May 1874 and the men began an arduous retreat across the ice towards open sea, hauling equipment and provisions on sleds and boats. Journals and natural history items were welded into watertight metal cases. They left four bottles, each containing a letter, on four icebergs, in the hope that the world would learn of their discoveries if they failed to make it back. One of these messages was found almost fifty years later by a Norwegian expedition. Of the *Tegetthoff* there is no trace.

Despite returning to Europe with precious sketches and maps, critics still doubted if Franz Josef Land existed. Payer resigned from the army in frustration. When later voyages reached the islands he was vindicated, but he had already moved on, enrolling as an art student in Frankfurt. He was elevated to the Austrian nobility as Ritter von Payer, and for many years he worked as an artist in Paris. He returned to Austria in the 1890s, founding a painting school for ladies in Vienna. In 1912, at the age of seventy, he proposed another expedition to the North Pole, this time by submarine. His spirit of adventure had clearly not left him.

The first chart of the islands never before seen - newly discovered Franz Josef Land - explored by Payer by sledge across the frozen sea in May 1874. Opposite is his sketch of the Middendorf Glacier and the memorial cross raised at the grave of engineer Otto Krisch who had died of scurvy.

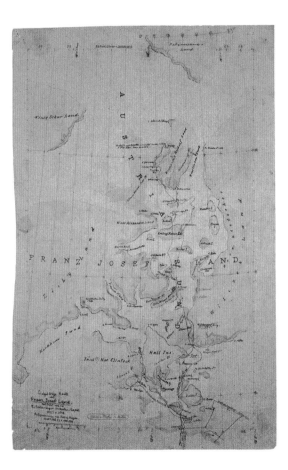

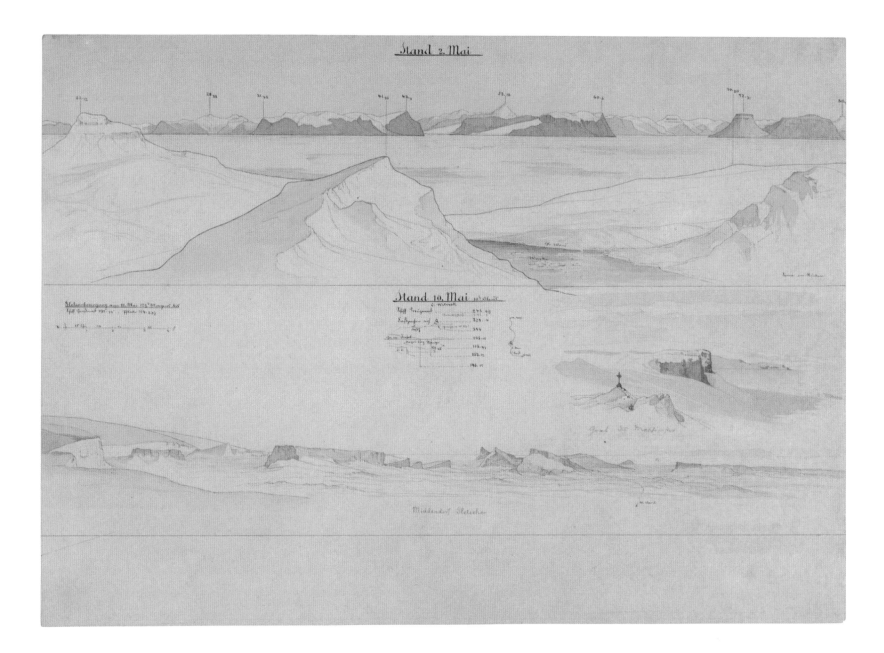

THE MOON WITH ITS HALO.

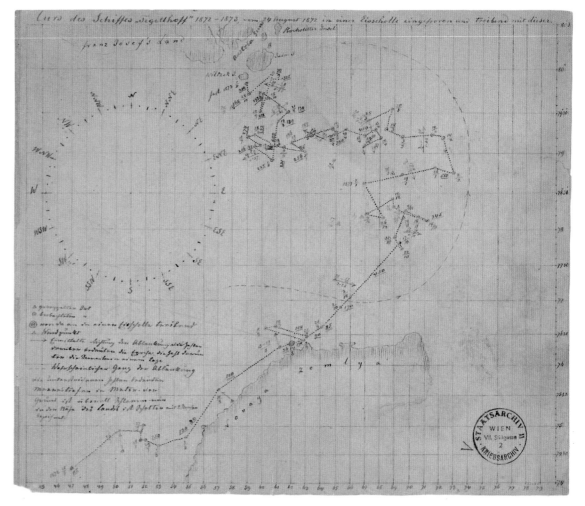

Moving with sledges over the sea ice and along frozen coasts, Payer and the expedition members advanced through Franz Josef Land as far north as 82°N on 12 April 1874. They then had 265 km (165 miles) to retreat through violent gales and over difficult ice to try to find their ship again.

The manuscript chart above shows the drift of the *Tegetthoff*, a wooden steamship sheathed in iron and powered with a 100hp engine. The expedition sailed from Bremerhaven in Germany on 13 June 1872, rounding Norway and entering the Barents Sea, before becoming ice-bound on 20 August off Novaya Zemlya. By the following August the ship had drifted northwest towards the unknown island group which they later named Franz Josef Land. Engravings based on Payer's sketches and memories of their experiences made for an exciting account when published after a safe return home (opposite).

TWILIGHT AT MIDDAY, FEBRUARY 1874.

Die Schlittenreisenden unter Julius Payers Führung
kommet auf der Rückreise zu einem Kreuz.

FRUITLESS ATTEMPT TO RESCUE MATOCHKIN.

AN OCTOBER NIGHT IN THE ICE.

ANTONIO PIGAFETTA 1491-1531

I will see with my own eyes the magnificent
and dread things of the ocean.

They said at first the men were ghosts. Barefoot and bedraggled, the few who could walk made their way slowly through the crowds up from the quayside to Seville cathedral. Skeletally thin, their ravaged bodies were covered with boils and open sores, their gums blue and bleeding, most teeth gone. They had seen horrors enough for many lifetimes and yet they were the lucky ones. Mutiny, cannibalism, torture, scurvy, starvation and drowning were some of the fates that had befallen their companions on this, arguably, the greatest maritime voyage in history: the first circumnavigation of the globe.

Of the five ships and some 260 men that had set out from Spain in September 1519, only a single vessel and eighteen crew returned. One of the survivors was a Venetian scholar named Antonio Pigafetta. The leader, Fernão de Magalhães – the Portuguese navigator now generally remembered as Ferdinand Magellan – had died half-way through the three-year voyage, hacked down while fighting knee-deep in water on the shores of an island in the Philippine archipelago. It had taken them 98 days to cross the vast Pacific, with supplies running so low they were forced to eat sawdust and hardtack maggots, and pieces of ox leather. Rats captured on board, roasted or raw, became a vital part of their diet.

The one ship, the *Victoria,* that eventually made it home brought back spices and land claims, and tales to astound the world. A passage from the Atlantic into a new ocean had been discovered, the fabled Spice Islands were reached, and curious new peoples – including 'Patagonian giants' – had been encountered. After Magellan's death a Basque mariner, and sometime mutineer, Sebastián Elcano was in command, and he won the laurels Magellan richly deserved: royal renown and a coat of arms featuring a globe with the inscription *primus circumdedisti me*, 'you were the first to encircle me'.

Not much is known of Pigafetta, but without his journal even less of the successes, or sufferings, of Magellan's voyage would be recorded. His account is based on the detailed diary he kept throughout the voyage, and on his return to Spain he presented himself to King Charles V, the Holy Roman Emperor, bringing not 'gold, silver, or any other precious thing worthy of so great a lord', but 'a book written first hand'. The Emperor was apparently not that impressed, and Pigafetta received no honours beyond his meagre wages. He took his story to the Portuguese and then French courts; in Italy the Pope was impressed enough to give him lodgings while he prepared his manuscript and worked on his illustrated maps. These are the first depictions of many unknown coasts.

Pigafetta never saw his book into print. He joined the famous Philippe Villiers de l'Isle-Adam, Grand Master of the Order of Rhodes, and became a knight-errant. It is thought he died fighting the Turks. As for Elcano, he was so overwhelmed with troubles on land that he also returned to sea. He died of scurvy in 1526, having piloted a ship through the Strait of Magellan a second time.

Pigafetta's original journal kept on ship is lost. However, he also wrote a full account of the voyage, which survives in four manuscript versions, of which this is the most complete.

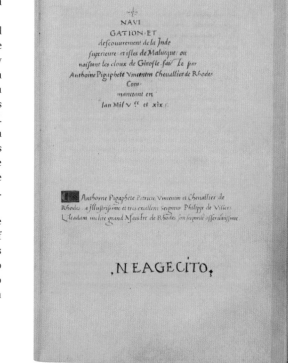

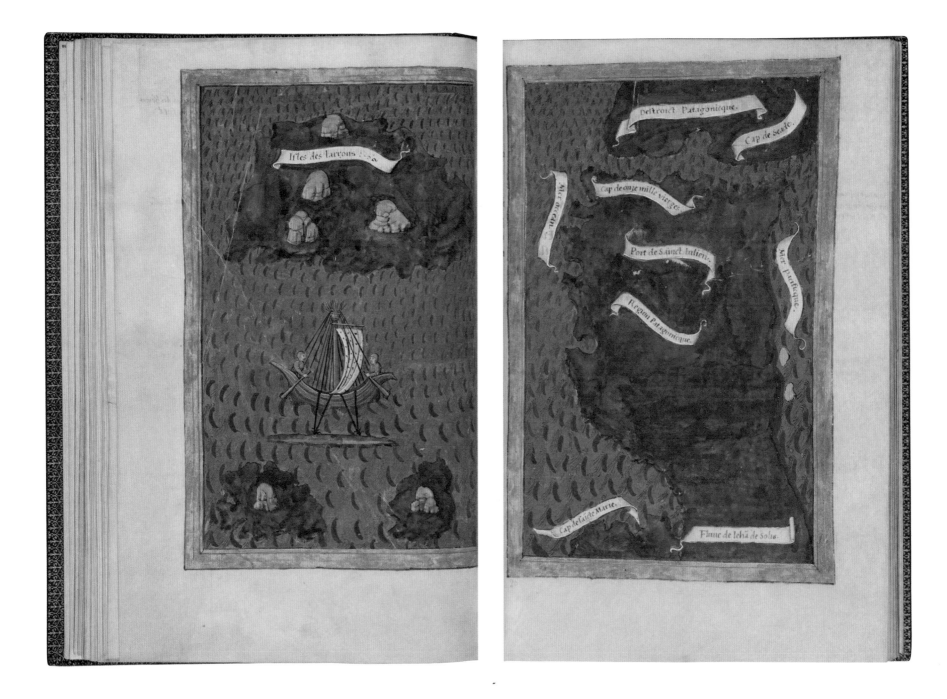

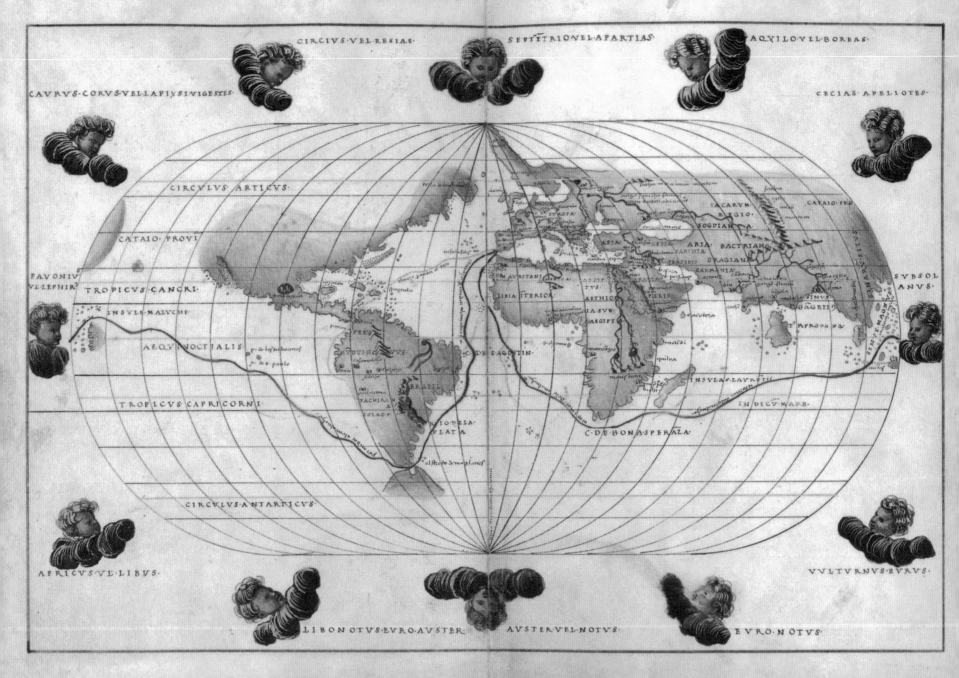

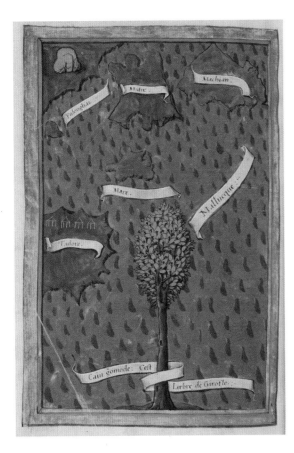 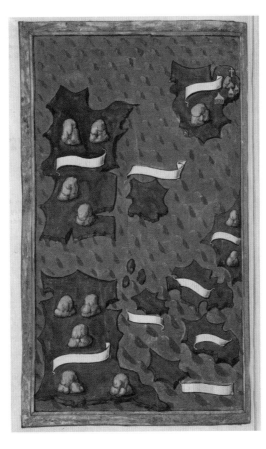

Opposite: A portolan atlas produced by Battista Agnese, one of the most important cartographers of the Italian Renaissance, drawn in 1543 in Venice. Agnese was careful to include the latest discoveries. The voyage of Magellan's expedition round the world is inscribed in pure silver, and in pure gold is the route of the famed treasure ships from Peru to Spain. The cherubs represent the classical twelve-point winds, from which modern compass directions evolved.

The maps in Pigafetta's manuscript are the first depictions of many unknown coasts. The one of Guam (page 207, left) also contains the first depiction of Pacific islanders, with the naked Chamorro shown as strangely hooded warriors, afloat in their *proa* with its lateen sail. The Strait of Magellan is also drawn for the first time (page 207, right): the upper part is south, bottom is north.

The *Victoria* reached the Moluccas on 8 November 1521. Pigafetta's depiction of the fabled Spice Islands, the ultimate goal of Magellan's voyage, shows a distinctive clove tree (above left). The few survivors of this extraordinary circumnavigation finally arrived back in Seville on 8 September 1522, after almost three years at sea.

NICHOLAS POCOCK 1740-1821

The Action continued very violent till near one o'clock and the ships dismasted seemed to emerge from the Smoke.

A self-portrait made sketching before a mirror, perhaps sometime around 1790, after Pocock had moved from Bristol to London.

Far out in the Atlantic a fierce battle was raging. For the British it became known as the 'Glorious First of June', but at that moment the reality was the deafening roar of cannon, splintered masts, human cries and shattered bodies, and dense, drifting smoke. Standing at the rail of the frigate *Pegasus*, a fifty-four year old mariner followed the action against the French closely. He lifted his telescope to read signals in the vanguard and reached for his sketchbook.

It is not known exactly how merchant captain turned professional painter Nicholas Pocock came to be there in 1794. No record has been found to tell us whether he was invited aboard as a war artist, an official observer or perhaps the guest of an officer friend. It is incredible that his journal, which contains his eyewitness account, survives. Never before had a British fleet action been captured in such intricate and original detail.

Pocock's career at sea started as a boy, apprenticed to his father. By his early twenties he had served on countless Bristol trading vessels and risen through the ranks. From 1766 he captained ships for the Champion family of merchant seafarers on a dozen voyages, mainly to the east coast of America and the West Indies. Like many ships' masters, he was a meticulous log keeper, yet Pocock's journals are different. Besides the usual columns detailing speed, bearing and wind direction, are wonderful vignettes. Pocock taught himself to draw and his sketching became both a hobby and a habit. He was also training, thinking ahead to a life ashore when he would try his hand as a professional artist. He submitted paintings for the Royal Academy exhibition in London in 1780, and though they arrived too late to be considered, he received an encouraging letter from its President, Sir Joshua Reynolds, advising him to paint from nature and carry 'palette and pencils to the waterside'.

In 1782 he showed his first paintings at the Academy and had an unbroken record of exhibition there until 1812. His first pictures were marine views and the quays of Bristol, where he lived for fifty years before moving to London. In the capital a considerable number of wealthy new patrons – and retired sea captains and Admiralty lords – provided Pocock with a ready clientele.

His knowledge as a seaman and his intricate brushwork found him favour with Admiral Lord Hood, a naval hero of the War of Independence, and after the death of Dominic Serres in 1793, Pocock became the leading English maritime painter through the long French wars, chronicling all the major sea engagements. Veterans came to tell their tales at his studio and his research was assiduous. Many of his works were engraved, and he created illustrations for celebrated biographies of Nelson, William Falconer's epic poem *The Shipwreck*, and the widely read *Naval Chronicle* journal. In 1817 he suffered a stroke, and seems to have stopped painting. His death occasioned just a few brief notices, but his contributions to marine painting deserve greater attention.

Saturday October 3d 1767

H	K	HK	Courses	Winds
2	4	..	EbN	North
4	4	..	ENE	NtW
6	3	1	East	NbE
8	3	1		NbE
10	2	..	EbE	NE
12	2			
2	2	..	SE	ENE
4	2			
6	2	1	NEbE	NEbN
8	3			
10	3	1		
12	2	1	NNW	NE

The Most part Light Airs and Variable with fair Weather a Ship and Brig Standing to the Northward

Course	Es Et S.
Distance	60
Xlatt..	23 South
Depart	56 East
DLong..	1n 0 E.
Long in	67 46 W
Me. D..	567 E
L. Me.	10 51 E.

Tack'd

Latt. Observd 34 .. 10 .. N.

Sunday October 4th 1767

H	K	HK	Courses	Winds
2	3	..	NbW	NE
4	3			
6	4			
8	3	1	North	ENE
10	2	1	NbW	NEbE
12	2	1		
2	2	..	NbE	EbN
4	2	..	NbW	NEbE
6	2	1		
8	3	..	North	EbN
10	3			
12	2	1		

The most of this 24 hours Light Breezes and Fair Weather with Smooth Water &c as Flag at 8 AM a schooner in Sight to Leward.

Course	NbW
Dis..	68
Xlatt..	63 North
Dep..	24 West
XLong..	30 t..
Long in	68 18 d..
Me. D..	531 East
L. Me.	10 .. 28 d..

68 Miles Flog

Latt. Observd 32 .. 22 .. North

Monday October 5th 1767

H	K	HK	Courses	Winds
2	2	1	North	EbN
4	2	1		
6	3	1		
8	3	1		
10	2	1	NbE	NbW
12	2	1		
2	2	1	NNE	East
4	1	1	NbE	EbN
6	1	1	NNW	NEbE
8	3	1	North	EbE
10	1			
12	1	..	NbE	EbN

Light Breezes and Variable with Pleasant Weather Smooth Water &c as Flog

Latt Observd 33 .. 28 No.

Course	North
Distance	66
Xlatt..	66 No..
Depth..	00
XLong..	00 ..
Long in	68 18 W.
Me. D..	531 E..
L. Me.	10 .. 28 E..

68 Miles Flog

Tuesday October 6th 1767.

H	K	HK	Courses	Winds
2	3	1	NbE..	EbN
4			NbE S.. E	
6	3	1	NbE	
8	3			
10	2	1		
12	2			
2	2	..	North	
4				
6	1	1	NbW	NEbE
8	2	1	North	EbNE
10	1			
12	1	..	NNE	

Light Airs with Pleasant Weather Smooth Water &c as Flog

Course	North
Dis..	65
Xlatt..	65 No..
Depart..	00
XLong..	00 .. 00 ..
Long in	68 .. 18 W.
Me. D..	5.31 E..
L. Me.	10 .. 28 E..

65 Miles Flog

Latt. Observd 34 .. 33 .. North.

Wednesday October 7th 1767

H	K	HK	Courses	Winds
2	2	1	NbW	NEbE
4	3			
6	2	1	North	EbE
8	2	1	NbE	East
10	2	1	NbE	EbN
12	2	1		
2	4	1	NEbN	EbS
4	4			
6	4	1	NE	NE
8	4	1		
10	4	1		
12	4	1		

Light Breezes and Variable from East to NE with very Smooth Water &c as Flog at 2 P.M. a schooner in Sight Standing to the Westward.

Course	NbE N
Dis..	72
Xlatt..	59 Miles
Depart..	40 East
XLong..	49 d..
Long in	67 .. 29 W..
Me. D..	57.1 East
L. Me.	11 .. 17 d..

53 Miles Flog

Latt. Observd 35 .. 32 .. North

Thursday October 8th 1767

H	K	HK	Courses	Winds
2	4	1	EbN	EbN
4	4	1		South
6	4	1		
8	4			SSW
10	5	1		SW
12	7			
2	6			
4	5	1		NtW
6	5	1		
8	6			
10	5	1		
12	6			

The first part of these 24 hours Light Breezes & Clear Weather Set our Steering Sail & Driver, the Middle and Latter part fresh Breezes and Hazey with a Following Sea.

½ point Variation Westerly

Course	ENE ¾ E
Dis..	129
Xlatt..	61 North
Dep..	114 East
XLong..	2 .. 21 ..
Long in	65 .. 8 W
Me. D..	68.5 E..
L. Me.	13 .. 38 E..

129 Flog

Latt. Observd 36 .. 33 .. North

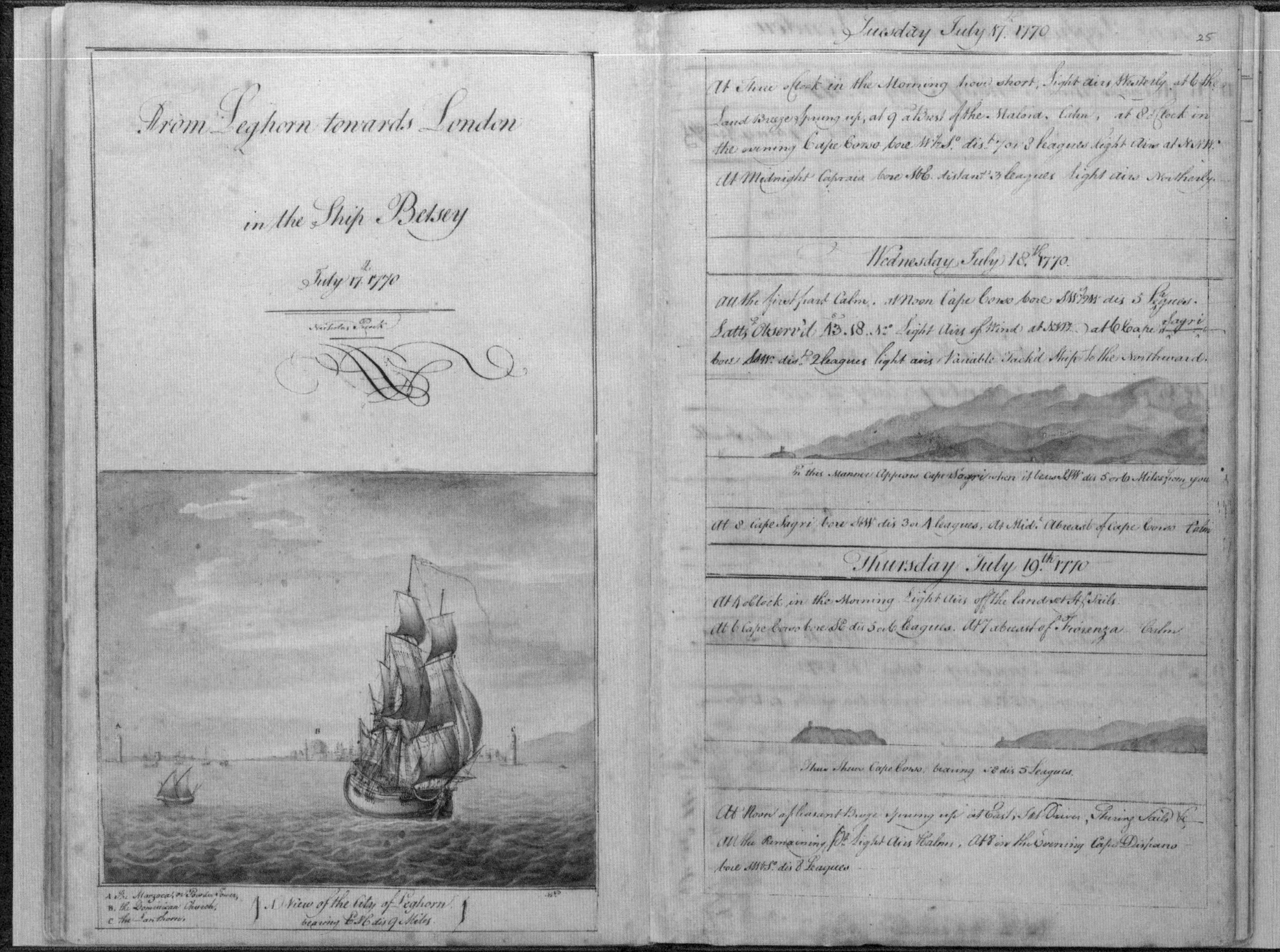

From Leghorn towards London

in the Ship Betsey

July 17 1770

Nicholas Pocock

A. B. Margaret or Pisaton Tower.
B. St Dominican Church.
C. the Lanthorn.

A View of the City of Leghorn
bearing E.S.E. dist 9 Miles

At Three oClock in the Morning hove short, Light airs Westerly, at 6 the Land Breeze sprung up, at 9 at West of the Maloni, Calm, at 8 oClock in the evening Cape Corso bore N.E.S° dist 7 or 8 leagues light Airs at N.N.W.

At Midnight Capraia bore S.E. distant 3 leagues Light airs Northerly.

Wednesday July 18th 1770

All the first part Calm. At Noon Cape Corso bore S.S.W ½ W. dist 5 leagues. Latte Observ'd 43.18. N° light Airs of Wind at S.S.W. at 6 Cape Sagri bore S.S.W. dist 8 leagues light airs Variable Tack'd Ship to the Northward.

In this Manner Appears Cape Sagri when it bears S.S.W. dist 5 or 6 Miles from you

At 8 Cape Sagri bore N.S.W. dist 3 or 4 leagues, At Midt Abreast of Cape Corso Point

Thursday July 19th 1770

At 4 oClock in the Morning Light Airs of the land set all Sails At 6 Cape Corso bore N.E. dist 3 or 6 leagues. At 7 abreast of Fivenza   Calm.

Thus Shews Cape Corso, bearing N.E. dist 5 leagues.

At Noon a pleasant Breeze sprung up at East, Set Steering Sails &c. AM the Remaining part light Airs Calms. AM or the Evening Cape Distano bore N.N.E. dist 8 leagues.

Monday the 11th of April

H	K	HK	Course	Winds
2	7		EbN	NW
4	6	1		
6	6	1		
8	6	1		
10	6	1	WNW	
12	6	1	SWbS	
2	3	1		
4	6			
6	6			
8	6			
10	5	1		
12	5			

The first and Middle part Strong Gales & Squally the latter Moderate with a large Swell from SE at 4 AM out 3d RF Set Mainsail Topsail at 8 out all RF Set Small Sail.

Course	EbN ½ N
Dist	148
D Latt	26 North
Depar	148 East
D Long	2°58 d°
Long in	53.16 West
M D	1268 East
L Mr	

L att Observd 35.49 — 25.30 d°

Tuesday April 12th 1768

H	K	HK	Course	Winds
2	4		EbN	NbE
4	3		ENE	North
6	2		EbN	
8	1			
10	Calm			
12				
2	1		NbE	SEbE
4	1	1		
6	3		North	EbN
8	4			
10	4	1		
12	4	1		

The first part of this 24 hours light airs & cloudy the Middle Calm the latter fresh Gales with Rain at 2 PM up Maintopsail Yard Set topgallant sail at 9 PM handed Maintopsail handed Jibb & topsails at 8 PM in 1st and 2d RF at 9 handed fore & Mizen topsail Strong Gales.

Course	NEbN ¼ N
Dist	16
D Latt	12 North
Depar	19 East
D Long	24 d°
Long in	52.52 West
M D	1287
L Mr	25.54 d°

Wednesday April 13th 1768

H	K	HK	Course	Winds
2	3		NW	NbE
4	2	1	North	ENE
6	4		South	NNW
8	d°			d°
10	d°			d°
12	d°			d°
2	d°			d°
4	d°			d°
6	2	d°	NNW	NbE
8	3	1	EbN	NbE
10	2		East	
12	2	1	EbN	

The first and Middle parts very Strong Gales with Rain at 2 PM Lowrd Fore & Mizen topsail & at 3 PM handed Mainsail at 6 AM more Moderate Sail Set Mainsail at 3 Set Main F at 6 Set topsail Ship at 8 Set Jibb & topsails at noon out all RF Sun Wt d°

Course	NNW
Dist	20
D Latt	28 North
Depar	11 West
D Long	14 d°
Long in	53.6 d°
M D	1276 East
L Mr	25.40 d°

L att Observd 36.59

Thursday 14th April 1768

H	K	HK	Course	Winds
2	2	1	EbS	NW
4	3			NW
6	4			
8	4			
10	4	1		
12	4		NNW	WNW
2	3	1		NW
4	3	1		
6	6			
8	6			
10	7		SWbW	
12	7	Mid Gg		

The first and Middle Parts light Breezes Midd Fair Weather the latter fresh Gales and Cloudy at 8 AM Set driver along Swell from ye Eastward 6 degrees Variation Westerly

Course	ENE ½ N
Distance	110
D Latt	30 North
Depart	97 East
D Long	2°0 d°
Long in	51.6 West
M R	1373 East
L Mr	27.40 d°

L att Observd 37.19 North

Friday 15th April 1768

H	K	HK	Course	Winds
2	7		ENE	WNW
4	7			
6	6	1		NNW
8	6	1		
10	6	1		
12	6	1		NW
2	6	1		
4	7		NNW	
6	7	1		WNW
8	6	1		
10	6	1		
12	6	Mid	North	NW

The Most of this 24 hours fresh Gales with a great Tumbling Sea, hard showers Rain & Lightning & at 2 AM double Reef'd Main F at 6 out 2d Reef at 8 in 2d RF & at 6 AM Set fore & Mizen Staysail Main Sail & Mizen Sail at 10 out 2d RF & Set Main topmast Staysail

Course	EbN ¼ N
Dist	162
D Latt	34 North
Depart	140 East
D Long	2.58 d°
Long in	48.8 d°
M D	1513 East
L Mr	30.28 d°

Saturday 16th April 1768

H	K	HK	Course	Winds
2	4		ENE	NW
4	4			
6	4	1		
8	2			
10	5			StbS
12	7			NE
2	7	1		NW
4	8			
6	8			
8	6			
10	6	1		
12				

The first part of this 24 hours light airs and cloudy with a large Swell from ye Northward at 6 AM set all Sail Jibb & topsails the Middle fresh Gales & Cloudy the latter Strong Gales with heavy Showers Rain at 4 double Reef'd handed Mizen topsail at 3 AM handed Jibb & Main topsail at 11 Set Mainsail.

Course	NEbE ¾ E
Dist	156
D Latt	70 d°
Depar	117 East
D Long	2.31 d°
Long in	45.37
Mr	1630 East

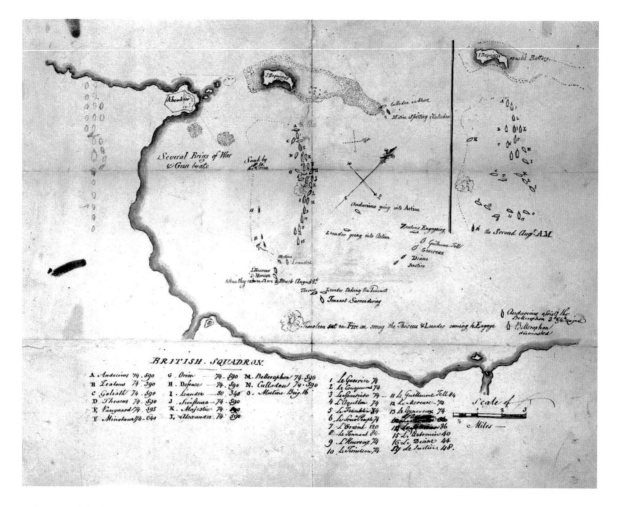

Above: Chart of the Battle of the Nile in August 1798. Pocock often prepared small watercolours and plans of action like this, showing the position of the ships, with wind and compass direction and the point of view from which his oil paintings might be created. His research was meticulous.

Previous pages: By 1766 Pocock commanded the merchant ship *Lloyd* and he made six voyages from Bristol to the colony of Charles Town, now Charleston, South Carolina. However, hostilities with the American colonists, culminating in the War of Independence of 1776, compelled British ship owners to trade elsewhere, and in 1770 Pocock sailed to the Mediterranean as captain of *Betsey*. On all his voyages, Pocock kept a detailed record, with illustrations, of his position and the weather conditions.

Opposite: Present at the Glorious First of June in 1794, Pocock is one of the first artists to draw in a 'war zone' - one sketch (above right) shows the *Royal Sovereign* and the *Terrible*. He also made an *aide-mémoire* table of the flags of the British fleet at the battle. A later work (below right) depicts the capture and destruction of Spanish frigates in 1804.

Van Division		Center Division		Rear Division	
Main		**Mizen**		**Fore**	
Caesar *pasley*		Invincible *Bowyer*		Ramillies	
Bellerophon		Barfleur		Bellona x	
Leviathan		Theseus x		Alfred *J. Alx. Hood*	
Russel		Gibralter		R. George	
Malborough		Qn. Charlotte *Lord Howe*		Montague	
R. Sovereign		Brunswick		Majestic	
Audacious		Valiant		Glory	
Defence		Orion		Hector *Montague* x	
Impregnable		Queen		Alexander x *Absent*	
Tremendous		Ganges x		Thunderer	
Culloden		Arrogant x			
Latona		Phaeton		Rebe x	
Niger		Southampton		Pallas x	
Venus		Pegasus		Comet	
		Aquilon		Charon	

Royal Sovereign almost before the Wind

PIRI REIS 1465-1554

This harbour is where we wintered our warships ...
a fine haven, safe against all winds.

The fate of nations has often rested on the outcome of fierce battles at sea. Little remembered now, but arguably one of the most influential engagements of all, the Battle of Lepanto in 1571 had repercussions for centuries. The Ottoman navy, previously unstoppable, was routed by a coalition sailing under the banner of the Holy Roman Empire near the Greek port city of Corinth. It would be the last major battle between oar-driven galleys, involving ferocious deck-to-deck fighting and ramming with prows. No fewer than 187 Ottoman ships were destroyed, and with them any remaining hope of Turkish westward expansion into Europe.

In the long maritime history of the Turks, one sailor in particular stands out: the commander cartographer Hadji Muhiddin Piri Ibn Hadji Mehmed, known usually as Piri Reis, literally 'Captain Piri'. Born in Gallipoli, he first sailed as a privateer with his uncle Kemal, and then fought in the naval wars against Spain and rival trading republics. He was at the Battle of Modon in 1500, when the Ottomans bombarded the fortress and later overwhelmed most of the Venetian possessions in Greece. He also sailed many times transporting Muslim and Jewish refugees to safety from the western Mediterranean. When his uncle died in a shipwreck, Piri withdrew to Gallipoli. It was there, in 1513, that he devised his first world map.

His greatest achievement, however, is his *Kitab-i Bahriye* – the 'book of maritime matters' – a compendium of charts drawn from his decades as seafarer. A new sultan was on the throne and Piri hoped to gain favour. He made two versions, the first in 1521 and a second a few years later, while other copies were created in the following decades. It was a pioneering resource of integrated knowledge, the expression of a dominant naval force, its pages filled with texts and images of strategic value to Ottoman commanders. Piri carefully described the ports and landmarks of major trading partners, the castles and fortifications of potential enemies, while also warning of dangerous shoals and reefs, the patterns of local winds, or where a sailor might find shelter and fresh water.

Back at sea, Piri was a commander in the campaign against Egypt and served as a captain under the notorious admiral Hayreddin Barbarossa. In 1522 he joined the siege of Rhodes, defeating the Knights of St John and securing the island's surrender. He rose up the ranks to lead the Ottoman fleet, fighting the Portuguese in the Red Sea and out into the Indian Ocean, with his headquarters at Suez. In 1548 he recaptured Aden and later occupied the Qatar peninsula to prevent others setting up bases on the Arabian coast. By the time he returned to Egypt he was almost ninety years old, battle-worn and weary. Court intrigue fuelled a rumour that he had secretly amassed a great treasure and, when he refused to put to sea to wage yet another campaign in the Persian Gulf, he was arrested. Despite all his years of loyal service, his charts were confiscated and he was swiftly beheaded.

God has not granted the possibility of mentioning all the aforementioned things – the cultivated and ruined places, harbours and waters around the shores and islands of the Mediterranean, and the reefs and shoals in the water – in a map since, when all is said and done, a map is a summary.

Opposite left: Piri Reis produced his first world map in 1513, of which only this fragment remains. It was rediscovered in the Topkapi Palace in Istanbul in 1929 and is one of the oldest surviving charts to show the Americas. It is said the western portions were drawn from charts made by Columbus, which Piri's uncle had seized in 1501 when capturing Spanish ships.

Opposite right: A fine copy of the *Kitab-i Bahriye* is held in the Walters Art Museum, Baltimore. Originally composed in 1521, it was dedicated to the new sultan, Suleiman the Magnificent, under whose rule the Ottoman fleet dominated the seas from the western Mediterranean to the Persian Gulf. This shows the western hemisphere within a windrose.

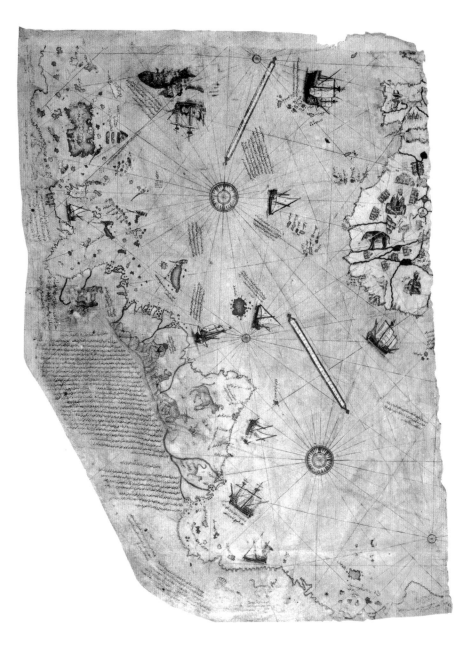

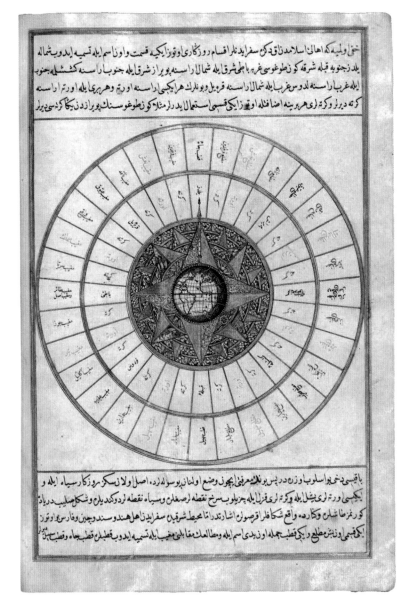

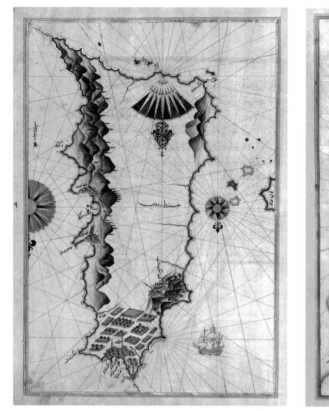

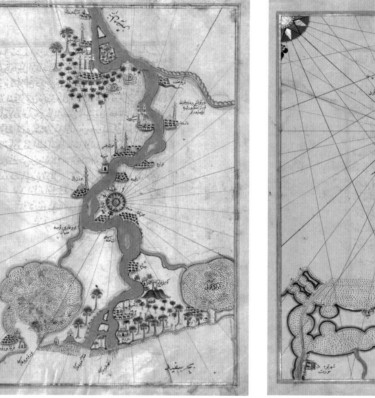

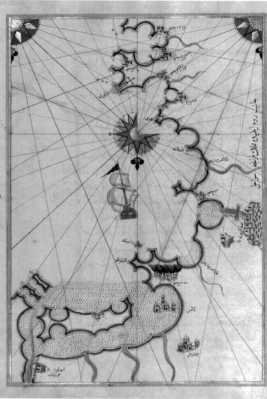

Left to right and opposite: The island of Rhodes, the River Nile from its estuary, the French coast around Narbonne and the Venetian lagoon. Reis sailed up the Nile to Cairo to present the Sultan with the new world map he had created. At its height the Ottoman empire was one of the most important cultural and economic powers in the world and for much of this time Venice was a major trading partner. The Ottomans sold wheat, spices, cotton, raw silk and ash (for the glass industry), in return for finished goods such as soap, paper and textiles.

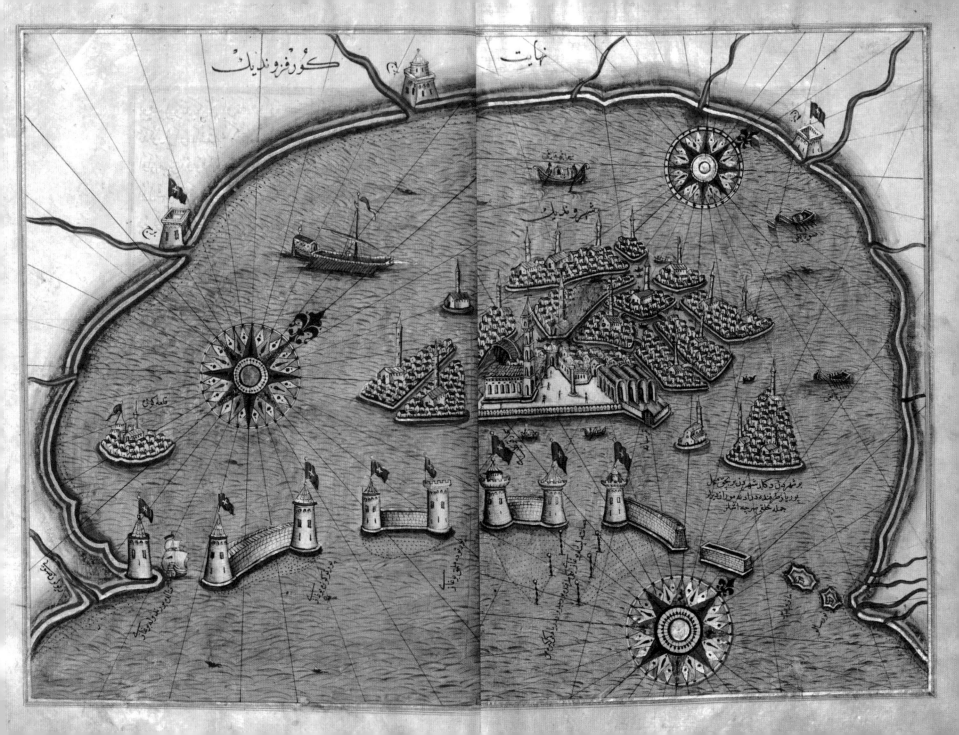

BARTHOLOMEW SHARP 1652–n.d.

In this prize I took a Spanish manuscript
of a prodigious value.

Many seafarers sought fortune and glory in the Spanish Main, or South Sea, of the Americas, with the hope of treasure in their minds. Whether legitimate privateers or lawless pirates, in England they won huge fame, if not wide admiration, for vying for a share of the spoils of this new world. For most of these mariners, voyages ended not with riches but in disappointment, with imprisonment for some and for many more a painful death. Bartholomew Sharp was a pirate and proud of it. 'Well versed in the underworld of maritime skulduggery', he was both a scoundrel and a skilful sailor. And strangely, a journal saved his life.

We know little of his early years. He claimed that he had served under the well-known pirate Henry Morgan in the sacking of Panama in 1671, and was in the gang that destroyed Porto Bello in 1679. On an expedition in 1680–82 he became the first to round Cape Horn in an easterly direction, sighting no land between his hideout at Juan Fernández and Barbados. But his lasting renown rests not with this, or with bloody raids on Spanish forts, but in the capture of 'a great Book full of Sea-Charts and Maps'.

Sharp landed on the coast of Darien in 1680 with 330 buccaneers, intending to cross the isthmus and sack Panama again. The small pirate army included all manner of war-weary rogues and educated men too: the studious Basil Ringrose, whose journal was later printed, and the ever-curious swashbuckler William Dampier, who went on to explore parts of Australia and became the first person to navigate the world three times. It is said Dampier waded through the rivers of Darien with his journal watertight inside a bamboo cane.

Guided through the jungle by local Kuna, the buccaneers made their way on foot and in canoes. They then overcame several armed ships, which allowed them to roam the coast at will, preying on smaller craft. After defections and mutiny, Sharp rose to overall command. On 28 July 1681, in what are now Ecuadorian waters, he captured the Spanish vessel *Santo Rosario*, shot its captain and seized a book the Spaniards were about to heave overboard. It was a *derrotero*, or wagoner: a secret collection of charts and sailing directions, detailing all the anchorages from California to Cape Horn. When Sharp returned to London he was put on trial for murder, but was acquitted. It is believed King Charles II intervened to spare his life having been given a beautiful copy of the stolen charts.

Sharp was later appointed captain of the respectable Admiralty sloop *Bonetta*, but never took up the job. According to one source he bought a cheap boat in the Thames, filled it with cheese, beer and beef, and escaped down river. He used it to board a French vessel in the Channel and with his prize sailed on to the Caribbean. Twice again he was captured and was put on trial on charges of piracy, but managed to wriggle free. In 1688 he appeared in Anguilla in the Leeward Islands, having declared himself governor. Ten years later, the last mention of his life records that he had been caught by the Dutch and thrown into jail in a fort on St Thomas. About this time he was described as being lame and without the use of his hands. We have no information as to whether he died there, or if his fellow pirates helped him make yet another escape.

It describes all the ports, roads, harbours, bayes, Sands, rocks and riseing of the land and instructions how to work the ship into any port or harbour between the Latt. of 17d.15'N to 57.S Latt. They were goeing to throw it overboard but by luck I Saved it.

Opposite: 'The Isle of Juan Fernandes' was Sharp's pirate hideout and became notorious for its many castaways, long before Daniel Defoe's *Robinson Crusoe*. Sharp's band retired there at the end of 1680 – with a good water supply, and plenty of wild goats, this was 'a very refreshing Place to us'.

Overleaf, left: Sailor-cartographer William Hack prepared elaborate copies of many sea journals, adding colourful illustrations that he often drew directly from the Spanish chart book seized by Sharp.

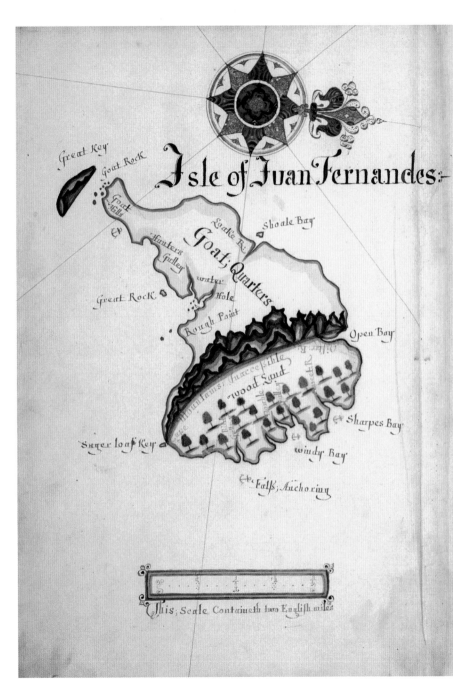

Isle of Juan Fernandes:

Great Key

Goat Rock

Goat Hills

Goat Quarters

Snake B.

Shoale Bay

Hunters Gulley

water

Hole

Great Rock

Rough Point

Open Bay

Inaccessible

Wood Land

high Mountains

Sharpes Bay

Suger loaf Key

Windy Bay

Falls Anchoring

This Scale Containeth two English miles

This Island in the Lat: of 33: 40: S; it is 20 miles in Circumference very high land & steep every where to the sea side only where you find som few Gullyes (where is good rideing) the SW side is barren land not haveing one stick of wood true Tuft of Gras or one drop of sweet water: but the NW side of it makes amends for that: by reason it is stored w.th excellent timber good gras & incomparable good water; the clime of this Island is exceeding moderate (& healthy) on the barren side run thousands of the fattest Goats I ever saw or tasted; there are plenty allso on the other side but eat not so sweet neither are they so fatt as the other; the Low Land is extraordinary good; & without doubt will produce any sort of Graine: the Hills tops are plentifully stor'd with a sort of trees whose tops eat as well as any westindia Cabbinge; here is allso store of silk wormes which thrive Naturally very well, Silver here is for I have taken of the ore out of a Rock the worst is by reason of the scragged mountains it is not possible to travell by Land from one side to the other; The bays of this Island are Cover'd with seel's: & Likewise another sort of Amphibious creatures w.ch wee may call sea Lyons; theire heads being in forme to a Lyons & theire cry Answerable they are about 12 or 14 foot in Length & 11 or more in Circumferen:ce they have short thick bristles of a mouse Callour: here is plenty of good fish of severall sorts I have caught them with a bare hook in the surfe of the water; here is Conveniency to build or refit a Vessell to wood water & take in fresh provisions; it is not inhabited but if it were it would prove the sharpest thorn that ever tourcht the Spaniard; for it is naturally fortified: & with a 100: charge & good managment 100 men may keep it from 1000 if it should be invaded: it lyes 110 Leagues west from Valpariso

In a word if this Isle was inhabited it would be very profitable in matter of trade in time of peace with the Spaniard; & if a war very usefull to the English:

 Finis

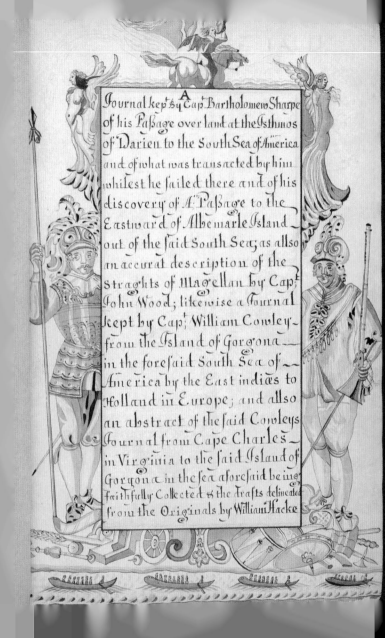

A

Journal kept by Capt. Bartholomew Sharpe of his Passage over land at the Isthmos of Darien to the South Sea of America and of what was transacted by him whilest he sailed there and of his discovery of A Passage to the Eastward of Albemarle Island out of the said South Sea; as allso an accurat description of the straghts of Magellan by Capt. John Wood; likewise a Journal kept by Capt. William Cowley from the Island of Gorgona in the foresaid South Sea of America by the East indies to Holland in Europe; and allso an abstract of the said Cowleys Journal from Cape Charles in Virginia to the said Island of Gorgona in the sea aforesaid being faithfully Collected & the drafts delineated from the Originals by William Hacke

ACAPULCO
NICOYA
POPAYAN
ÆQUINOC TIALIS
MAR
PERU
DEL
TROPICUS CAPRICORNI
Potosy
ZUR
Coquimbo
CHILI

Above: This South Sea chart, the 'Mar del Zur', was inked in 1685 and presented to James II. Sharp's track is clearly marked, as is the silver mine at Potosí.

Opposite: On 6 November 1681 Sharp headed for the Strait of Magellan, but a storm pushed him far south of his intended track, and he had no option but to weather the Horn instead, becoming the first English

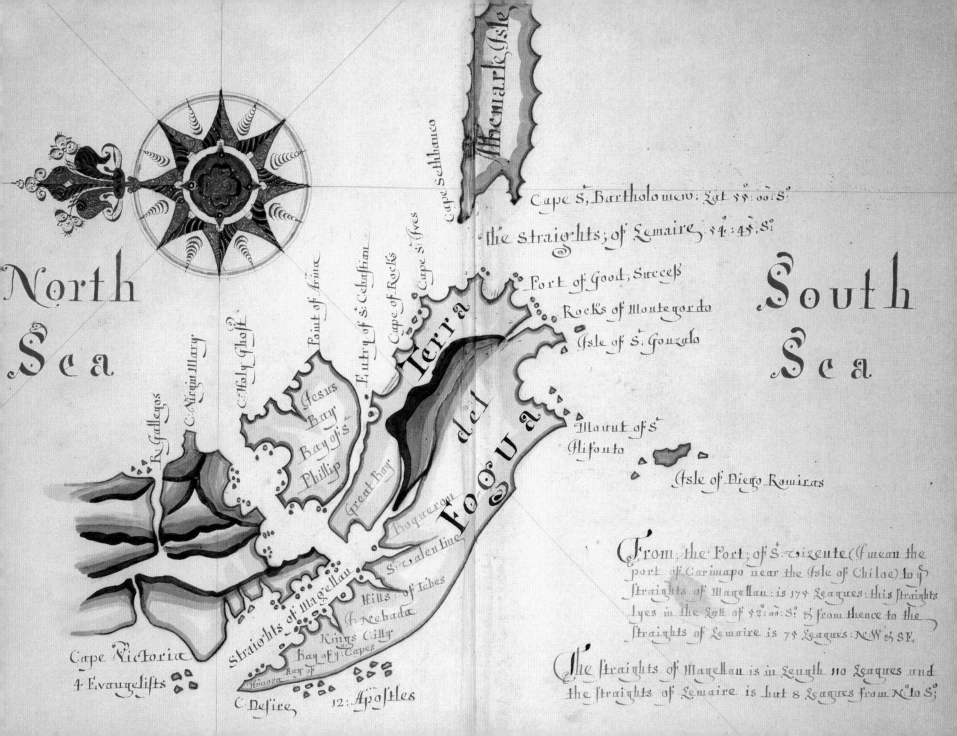

North Sea

South Sea

Albemarle Isle

Cape Setthanco

Cape S. Bartholomew: Lat 55:00:S.

the straights; of Lemaire, 54:45:S.

Cape S. Ives

Port of Good; Success

Cape of Rocks

Rocks of Montegordo

Entry of S. Sebastian

Isle of S. Gonzalo

Point of Anna

Cattely Ghost

Terra

Maruk of S. Alifonto

C. Virgin Mary

R. Gallegos

Jesus Bay

Bay of S. Phillip

del

Isle of Diego Ramiras

Great Bay

Boquereon

Fogua

S. Valentine

From; the Port; of S. vizente (I mean the
port of Carimapo near the Isle of Chiloe) to y
Straights of Magellan: is 175 Leagues: this straights
lyes in the Latt of 52:00:S. & from thence to the
straights of Lemaire is 75 Leagues: N.W. & S.E.

Hills; of tobes

Straights of Magellan

F. Nehada

Kings Citty

The straights of Magellan is in Length 110 Leagues and
the straights of Lemaire is but 8 Leagues from N. to S.

Bay of 4 Capes

Cape Victoria

4 Evangelists

Himosa Bay of

C. Desire

12: Apostles

WILLIAM SMYTH 1800–1877

We were helpless and immovable, fixed
in the solid mass as if in a block of marble.

*T*error left England confidently in the summer of 1836 – the latest naval expedition in search of a Northwest Passage – with a strengthened hull and food for eighteen months. Many of the crew were volunteers, including whalers from the Greenland fishery attracted by the double pay and good rations. Among the others was a lively and cheerful young officer, first lieutenant William Smyth.

Like so many sailors of the day, Smyth had gone to sea as a boy, entering the navy at thirteen. His first major voyage was as a mate on *Blossom*, under Frederick Beechey, exploring the Pacific and Bering Strait from 1825 to 1828, and he was advanced to lieutenant for his survey work along Alaska's northern coast. In the early 1830s he was on *Samarang*, first based at Rio, then cruising on anti-slaving patrols along western coasts as far north as the Gulf of California. Ever adventurous, Smyth led a two-man expedition by mountain track across the Andes, working his way through the jungle from Peru to the mouth of the Amazon. His sketches and maps were considered a great advance on knowledge of the region, and he won a place on the new Arctic voyage.

Under the command of Captain George Back, *Terror* headed north to Hudson Bay, but no channel could be found to the west beyond Southampton Island, just a barrier of solid sea ice. *Terror* was to remain stuck in the ice and drifting with it, in 'almost hourly danger of destruction', for the next ten months. Daily the men tried in vain to force channels and work the ship clear with axes and handspikes. Some evenings Smyth helped to run a school for the sailors, or he would retire to his berth to sketch, updating his journal. He also managed the 'Arctic Theatre' on board, painting backdrops on old bed sheets.

By the middle of May, open lanes at last began to appear, although it was not until July that *Terror* broke clear, severely damaged and leaking badly. Sailing and drifting across the Atlantic, they made for the nearest land, Lough Swilly in Ireland, where the ship was beached and the crew tumbled wearily out on to the sand.

Smyth rose to commander, but never headed north into the ice again. Instead he went off to chase more slaving ships, patrolling in warm waters from the Cape of Good Hope up to Mozambique. On Christmas Day in 1843 he was promoted to captain, though did not see more active service, instead retiring to a happy life of painting, surrounded by his family, and eventually rose to the rank of Admiral. *Terror* later sailed on the pioneering Antarctic voyage under James Clark Ross in 1839-43 with the *Erebus*, and both were then refitted for John Franklin's Arctic expedition, leaving London in 1845. The ships were last seen by whalers heading north in Baffin Bay. The 129 men of the expedition never returned; the wreck of *Terror* was finally located in 2016.

The cover of Smyth's journal and 'Winter Amusements'
in 1836. As their ship *Terror* was trapped in the
ice, the men often played football out on the floe:
'the whole crew were made to play at this active
and amusing diversion with the officers'. The main
challenge was keeping body and mind active, while
many began to suffer the early symptoms of scurvy.

PITCAIRN

PITCAIRN I.ⁿ

These pages and overleaf: Smyth's sketchbooks from his earlier voyage on *Blossom* also survive, in which he recorded exploring the Pacific and as far north as the Bering Strait under Captain Beechey. The pages include delicate drawings of the landscapes and people of the Northwest Coast, the early settlement at San Francisco, the island of Pitcairn and its inhabitants, Tahitians and tattoos.

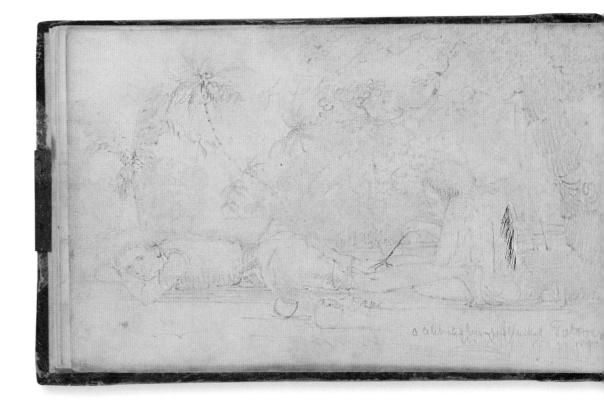

Until the voyage of the *Blossom*, it was not generally known that the lagoons in these islands were of such depths, or that the wall of coral which encircles them was so narrow and perfect ... nor that the islands were of such dimensions, as they were designated groups, or chains of islands, in consequence of the wall being broken by channels into the lagoon.

CAPTAIN F. W. BEECHEY, 1831

WILLIAM SPEIDEN 1835-1920

This evening some Japanese officers came on board
... they have been exceedingly anxious to see the
ship on account of her formidable appearance.

Eyewitness to events that shaped the future of great nations, at just sixteen William Speiden was the youngest member of Commodore Matthew Perry's naval mission, authorized by the American President, to open trade with Japan. The country had been closed to outsiders for hundreds of years, but the Americans were keen to be at the vanguard of a great wave of change. It was a voyage of financial speculation and diplomacy, backed by gunboats.

Speiden joined the flagship *Mississippi* in the spring of 1852 as an assistant to his father, a veteran naval purser. The side-wheel steamer *Mississippi* was already renowned – constructed to Perry's specifications and successful in the Mexican War under his command. Young Speiden wrote his first journal entries at the Philadelphia Navy Yard, several months before they left, and joined a short cruise that summer in advance of the expedition. He then sailed outward from Virginia across the Atlantic in late 1852, to the Madeira islands, St Helena, Cape Town, Mauritius and Singapore, before reaching coastal areas of China and Japan.

As most teenagers would, Speiden enjoyed the adventure. He sneaked to the grave of Napoleon with his shipmates on St Helena, saw his first Buddhist temple in March 1853 in Sri Lanka and his first Chinese junks in Singapore a few days later, and 'had a jolly time' setting off firecrackers in the streets of Canton. Arriving in Hong Kong in April, he began collecting pith paintings, which he tucked in his journal.

Perry transferred his command to *Susquehanna* in May 1853. The squadron left Shanghai and reached the Ryukyu Islands in May, arriving on 8 July at Edo Bay, now Tokyo.

It was not until the following March that negotiations with the Shogunate were concluded, despite the intimidating military presence of the American 'black ships' that belched fire. After centuries of isolation, Japan was reluctantly open to business. Within five years other trading treaties were forged with Britain, Russia and France.

Speiden returned home in 1855, but sailed away once more to take up a job as naval storekeeper in Hong Kong. From 1870 to the end of his life he worked as customs agent at the Port of New York. Commodore Perry had died there long before, in 1858, from rheumatic fever, gout and heavy drinking, having written a book about the historic voyage. The final lines in Speiden's journal form an ode to two dogs lost off Chile on the homeward leg, apparently gifts from the Japanese to Perry: 'Happy dogs to die, upon the broad blue sea, for there your bones will lie, buried, and forever be.'

The two stout volumes that comprise Speiden's journal contain drawings in his hand, as well as those by other shipmates, Japanese artworks he collected on the voyage, and sketches and delicate watercolour paintings on pith created by unknown Chinese artists.

Wm. Speiden Jr 1852.

JOURNAL OF A
CRUISE
IN THE
U.S. STEAM
FRIGATE MISSISSIPPI
BY
WM. SPEIDEN JR
VOL. I.

Actors &
Sleight of hand
men & women.

Soldiers

Freight Junk.

Soldiers

Bomb Boat
Cape Town

~Signals~

Correct.

Int'g

Ans'g

Ref.

Distinguishing Pennants

Diagram of the Landing.

These screens were all ornamented with what seemed to be heraldic devices.

canvas screen enclosing the ground.

these dots represent Japanese Soldiers.

Space included about 20 acres.

1 Entrance to hall
2 Relieving Room
3 Reception hall
4 kitchen
5 Sleeping ship
6 house for presents

Villages

Japanese Boats

Our Boats

Com. Boats

Japanese Boats

Japanese Reg. Boats

General Order No. 15.

In conformity with General Order No. 1, all notes, journals, manuscripts, drawings &c., &c. kept or collected by the officers of the Squadron for the year 1853, must be sent in by the 15th of February 1854, to be safely deposited with the Store Keeper at Macao until they can be transmitted to the Navy Department.

By order of the Commander in Chief.
H. A. Adams.
Chief of the Fleet.

Japanese Junk.

...crew were walking about on shore, the Japanese took great in that concerned their dress and appearance generally, and to make drawings of their Epaulets, Pistols, Swords endage attached to their persons. The Japanese also ...selves in recording the Officers names in their books

Japanese Freight Junk.

Mt. Fusi bearing
W by N ½ W

Morning of
Feb. 13th 1854

Saddle Hill

Pt. Sagami Entrance
N E ½ E to Bay
of Yedo

Morning of Feb. 13th
1854

Island of Oso-sima
Opposite the entrance of
Bay of Yedo
Centre of volcano bearing SW by S ½ S

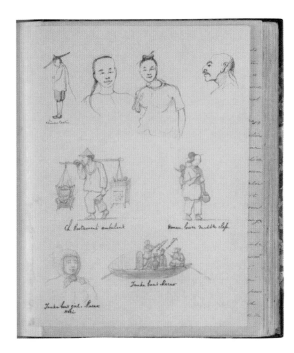

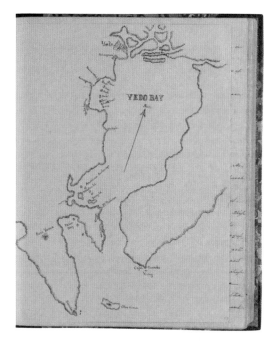

Commodore Perry's mission was a historic cruise to the far edges of the map. Speiden describes the first reception of Perry in Japan in his journal entry for 14 July 1853, and on 8 March 1854 he sketched a diagram of the second landing and also pasted into his journal a drawing of the Commodore by an unnamed Japanese artist. Later entries describe his experiences ashore at Yokohama and the 'House of Reception', where Perry held a conference with elders of the Tokugawa Shogunate to negotiate a 'Treaty of Peace and Amity', later known as the Kanagawa Convention. Speiden also drew Mt Fuji on 13 February 1854 (opposite), and one of the earliest western maps of Yedo Bay.

OWEN STANLEY 1811–1850

Had the ship struck, a few minutes would have ended our survey ... such are the pleasures of exploring!

In a time of expanding maritime interests, Australia's Great Barrier Reef was proving a graveyard for shipping. In 1846 the ageing British frigate *Rattlesnake* was repurposed to tackle the complexity of the Coral Sea once and for all. 'Every reef, every shoal, every rock hazard' had to be located and charted with extreme accuracy. British sea power, and the fortunes of a new colony, were said to be at stake.

The leader of this enterprise was Captain Owen Stanley, the ambitious eldest son of the Bishop of Norwich, and the nephew of a landed politician, Lord Stanley of Alderley, who both encouraged him to follow his dreams of a life at sea. Though short in stature, and somewhat unstable in constitution, he was by most accounts an excellent hydrographer and zealous in his pursuit of this new nautical science.

After training at the Royal Naval College, Stanley shipped as a volunteer in the frigate *Druid* in 1826, shortly after his fifteenth birthday. He was soon appointed midshipman in *Ganges* and spent four years off South America, learning the art of surveying. He would be at sea for the next two decades, with just a few months of leave ashore. In the Mediterranean he served under the celebrated explorer John Franklin, surveying the Greek archipelago. In 1836 he was on *Terror* on its fateful voyage to find a Northwest Passage (p. 224), given charge of astronomy and magnetic observations.

At twenty-six Stanley secured his first command, in the brig *Britomart*, and left for Australian waters, where he helped to establish a foothold amid the crocodile-infested swamps at Port Essington. Duties also took him to New Zealand where, sailing under secret orders, he helped fend off French hopes of settling at Akaroa, taking possession of the Banks Peninsula for the Crown. Further north, he surveyed Waitemata Harbour, upon whose shore the new capital, Auckland, was to be established. In 1844 he was back in England and was offered a position on Franklin's tragic Arctic expedition, but got command of his own ship instead, the *Rattlesnake*.

His task was to find a passage through the inner shoals of the Great Barrier Reef and explore the islands of the Torres Strait, opening new shipping routes for the East Indies trade. He also continued north to survey the unknown southern coast of New Guinea and created the first detailed charts of the region. By this time, though not yet forty, he was nearing breaking point, weighed down by fears of cannibalism ashore, dealing at turns with a leaking ship and disgruntled crew, and the pressures he placed upon himself to deliver the most accurate chart ever attempted.

With the mission completed, *Rattlesnake* returned to Sydney, though Captain Stanley was in failing health, having just suffered a paralytic fit. A boat came alongside with a bundle of letters, bearing bad news. Both his father in England and his brother then working in Tasmania had died within a month of each other; this was probably too much for his weakened mind to bear. He was found a few weeks later unconscious on the floor of his cabin.

Stanley's sketches from the *Rattlesnake* voyage survive in an album of some 125 drawings and the journal with this wonderful title-page. Opposite is a sketch from Stanley's polar voyage in 1837.

10 P.M. March 15 1837.

Only those who have known the intense anxiety attendant on a cruise amongst a mass of shoals and reefs, can understand the delight with which I went to sleep, when we were fairly clear. The nature of the reefs amongst these Islands is such that the lead gives no warning whatsoever ... and it does not add very much to one's happiness to know that if you hit them hard enough you have every prospect of going down in deep water.

These pages and overleaf: Stanley used his sketches of his voyages both north and south to create larger watercolours. He had sailed on *Terror* to the Arctic in 1837, keeping a daily diary and making sketches of life on board. The ship was caught in the ice and drifted helplessly for ten months. He was later offered a position on Franklin's tragic Arctic expedition which set out in 1845, but took command of *Rattlesnake*. The most intricate part of *Rattlesnake's* work was the new survey of the Inner Passage, from Rockingham Bay north to the Torres Strait. *Rattlesnake* was the floating headquarters, from which boats were sent out under junior officers to trace shorelines and find anchorages.

Jetty boat Swamped when lowered to

Situation in which HMS Terror remained
from March 16 to July 13 1837

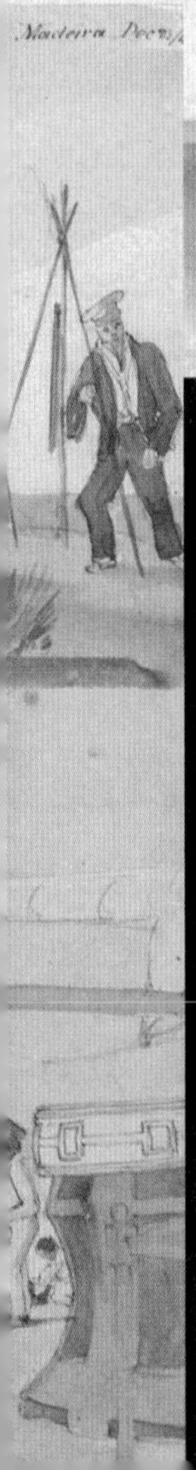

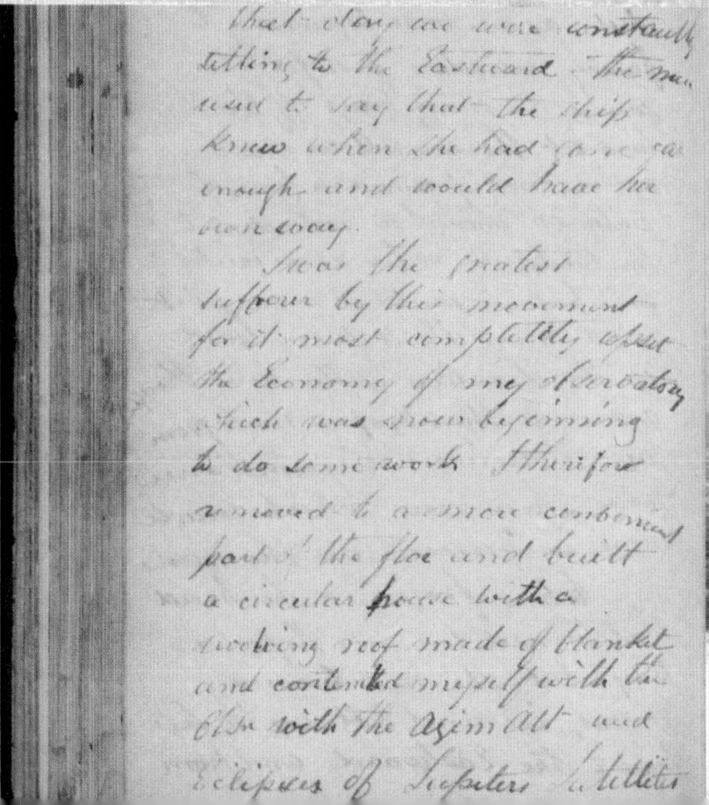

Madeira Dec.

that day we were constantly
setting to the Eastward — the men
used to say that the ship
knew when she had come far
enough and would have her
own way.

I was the greatest
sufferer by this movement
for it most completely upset
the Economy of my observatory
which was now beginning
to do some work I therefore
removed to a more convenient
part of the floe and built
a circular house with a
revolving roof made of blanket
and contented myself with the
Obs with the Azimuth and
Eclipses of Jupiters Satellites

HMS Rattlesnake bartering with native Canoes off the Brig Island Louisiade Archipelago — June 1849

FARTHEST SOUTH

Rodney Russ

... that which we are, we are,
One equal temper of heroic hearts,
Made weak by time and fate, but strong in will
To strive, to seek, to find, and not to yield.

ALFRED, LORD TENNYSON, 1842

Directly ahead of us is a vast wall of ice. It is 26 February 2017 and our satellite positioning system puts us precisely at 78°44'008 South. I have learnt to navigate a ship by a sextant and can plot a course using the stars, but today we don't need these backups. I know exactly where we are. We can't go any further.

I'm Expedition Leader of the *Professor Khromov*. The ship is owned by the Far-Eastern Hydrometeorological Research Institute in Vladivostok, and I've spent the last three decades operating her in some of the most challenging waters in the world. Ice-strengthened and crewed with Russian sailors, she's a tough ship. Now deep in Antarctica's Ross Sea we are at the very limits of what is possible. Our bow points due south, and we have nudged our way right up to the Ross Ice Shelf. It is not humanly possible to take a ship any nearer the South Pole. In fact, we have just set a new world record for the most southerly voyage ever made.

Few get into this life at sea for records or riches. For me, and other mariners like me, setting out on the ocean and exploring its wilderness regions is the inspiration. That's not to say things are always easy: far from it. I've feared for my life many times, felt as sick as a dog in storms and worried if our ship would make it through the night. And yet, with luck, hard work and patience, we always pull through. If you want to experience the very best Antarctica has to offer, you have to put up with unfriendly weather and uncertainty. The sea ice stops us in our tracks, our charts have unexplored areas with no soundings and storm spray entombs our ship in rime unless we hack it away. Temperatures here can break bones and tear the skin off your face. This life is not for everyone.

I grew up around boats, but my earliest ocean crossing – the first time I lost sight of land – was in 1972, when at eighteen I joined an expedition to the Auckland Islands, off New Zealand, as a trainee wildlife manager. This was on the 60-foot *Acheron* and I almost literally drowned in the excitement of it. My first voyage to Antarctica didn't come for another seventeen years, when I was hired as a zodiac driver on *World Discoverer*. At the time, I didn't really know where my life would lead, but when I saw the coast rising up from the horizon I felt in my heart I had arrived at the start of something.

Antarctica has now come to define my life, and all the while I've kept journals, diaries, notebooks, ships' logs, sketchbooks – all kinds of records, for all kinds of reasons. But essentially they serve the same purpose. Like the focus ring on a camera, they help sharpen my memories of a journey and locate me when I'm making it. Where the sea meets the shoreline, a journal is indispensable. It is at this interface – the rich seascapes, the landscapes and wildlife, where people live or have lived – that it is important to try to record something of the experience.

The first recorded entry into Antarctic waters was in January 1773, when James Cook with *Resolution* and *Adventure* sailed within the Antarctic Circle. The ships would actually cross 66° three times in various parts of the Southern Ocean, and in doing so they also became the first to circumnavigate Antarctica. Cook's journals are a marvellous source of information. Then in January 1841 James Clark Ross navigated his way further south still with *Erebus* and *Terror*, stout ships with only sails and courage to propel them onwards.

Our ice-strengthened *Khromov* has engines capable of a combined 3,120 horsepower, not huge by comparison to today's modern icebreakers, but vastly more than the explorers of old could rely on. We also carry with us six inflatable zodiacs, stacked on the stern deck and lashed down until needed, each with a 60hp outboard motor. When Shackleton pushed his way south into the Ross Sea in 1908, his ageing wooden sealer *Nimrod* was driven by a single 60hp screw propeller. It's remarkable he got as far as he did.

In today's world at sea everyone relies on satellite and navigation technologies, but I don't get excited by electronic charts. The cold does not like them either. It's always necessary to have a Plan B. Original accounts and first-hand diaries are essential resources when going somewhere little visited, particularly a remote place like Antarctica. And a sea journal is still one of the most important things to pack. Binoculars are a close second. But the most crucial thing to take is *patience*. Always give yourself plenty of time, and have the courage to do so. This might sound strange – and as sailors we so often have to move fast and respond rapidly to things as they unfold – but usually there is a real virtue in taking time. So, my advice for a future seafarer is simple: *don't rush*.

We operated our very first expedition to the Auckland Islands for a group of penguin-lovers from Japan. Their passion for the birds got them through the roughest weather. Further south still, Antarctica has always drawn explorers, from the first in wooden ships to modern travellers on cruises. My heart lies in small expeditions and remote islands: the New Zealand Sub-Antarctics with their rich flora and fauna and the Russian Far East. Yet I also feel, like many other explorers, exactly what the Frenchman Jean-Baptiste Charcot wrote of in his journal, the 'strange attraction' of the polar regions. 'So powerful, so overwhelming, that once safely home we forget the moral and physical fatigues and feel the urge to go back.'

So, why make a voyage? For me it's ultimately about sharing and empowering. Locking away areas of wilderness is not conservation; empowering people so that they want it preserved and protected is. Voyaging to distant places can benefit research in myriad ways, but as important is the potential in inspiring people to become ambassadors for the environment.

These frozen oceans and remote islands inspire us with their fragile beauty and challenging geography. The more we see the more we should want to know. It was certainly true of the great voyages in history – like Darwin with Captain FitzRoy in the *Beagle*, Ross in *Erebus* and *Terror* – and with the right approach it can also be said of wilderness travel today. The power and promise of a voyage to change the way people think is limited only by the imagination. A giant ice shelf need not always stop your progress.

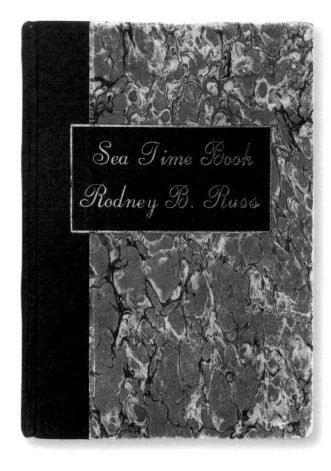

Rodney Russ' notebook, logging his time at sea as expedition leader on many vessels, from the Russian Arctic to the most southerly points possible to reach by ship. In recent years, he has been joined in the Antarctic by artist Spider Anderson, whose map made of their voyage in the footsteps of Scott and Shackleton, and plan of Shackleton's hut at Cape Royds, are seen opposite.

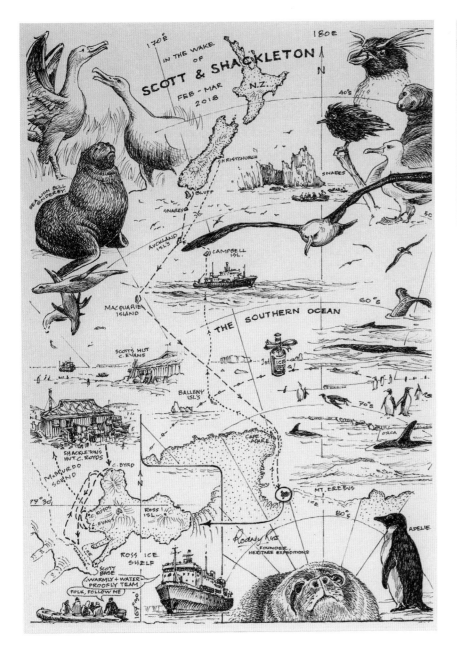

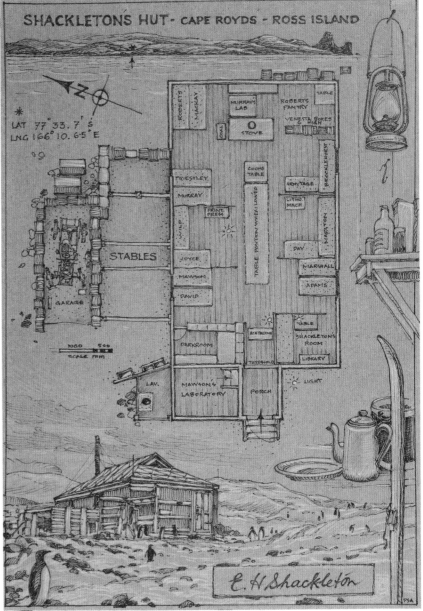

GEORG STELLER 1709-1746

No one who has studied the life of the lands doubts
that the vast ocean is full of unknown creatures.

The 'Great Northern Expedition' was an immense eighteenth-century enterprise, which set out from St Petersburg in 1733 led by Danish captain Vitus Bering. With him were hundreds of sailors and a vast retinue of officials and scientists, even wives and children, all trekking thousands of miles to the far eastern coast of Russia. There they would have to build the ships for the voyage to explore and chart the Arctic coasts of Siberia and North America. Everything needed for the voyage – from shipbuilding gear and supplies, to anchors, sails and cannonballs – had to be hauled overland.

A diligent young German physician and naturalist named Georg Wilhelm Steller joined the expedition in 1740 as Bering's ships, *St Peter* and *St Paul*, were nearing completion. For much of the stages at sea Bering, nearing sixty years old and sick and tired, was rarely seen on deck. His diaries do not appear to have survived, but we do have two remarkable first-hand accounts: a manuscript by his second in command, the Swede Sven Waxell, and the journals of Steller. Steller's efforts to pursue science were usually at odds with naval requirements, and time ashore was precious. For Steller, a coastline looming from the mist represented opportunity; for the crew, it was an uncharted hazard. Landing at Kayak Island, Steller's explorations there mark the first scientific discoveries in western North America, yet he complained that ten years of preparation had resulted in just ten hours of investigation as the ships' water barrels were replenished.

The two ships had become separated, and Bering's was later shipwrecked in the Commander Islands, where the crew had to overwinter in harsh conditions. But Steller now had time for more lengthy observations. He described several new species: sea lions and fur seals, a large flightless cormorant, and a 'special eagle with a white head and tail', today known as Steller's sea eagle. It is said he also prepared a catalogue of birds and plants, though the Arctic foxes would sometimes carry off his papers or knock over his inkstand. Steller transforms over the odyssey, from dry savant to lifesaver, with his intimate knowledge of flora and fauna rescuing his starving, scurvy-ridden comrades. Many died, however, including Bering himself.

The survivors built a vessel from the wreck of the ship and finally reached safety. Steller's untimely death on the winter sleigh journey back to St Petersburg meant that his contributions saw little light that century. Yet the voyage quickly caught the attention of entrepreneurs. The following year hunters returned with a cargo of 'sixteen hundred sea otter, two thousand fur seal, and two thousand blue fox skins'. Steller's sea cow, discovered in 1741 on the island that now bears Bering's name, was hunted to extinction in just twenty-seven years, as was the spectacled cormorant Steller first observed. The story of Bering's voyage shows the great lengths to which humans are driven by their curiosity, but also too the environmental consequences of human greed.

Manuscript map of the Kamchatka peninsula and the coast of the Sea of Okhotsk, 1734. Bering's journals have not survived and the majority of Steller's drawings were lost. The sketch opposite is a detail from a chart made in 1744 by Sofron Chitrow, based on Steller's observations.

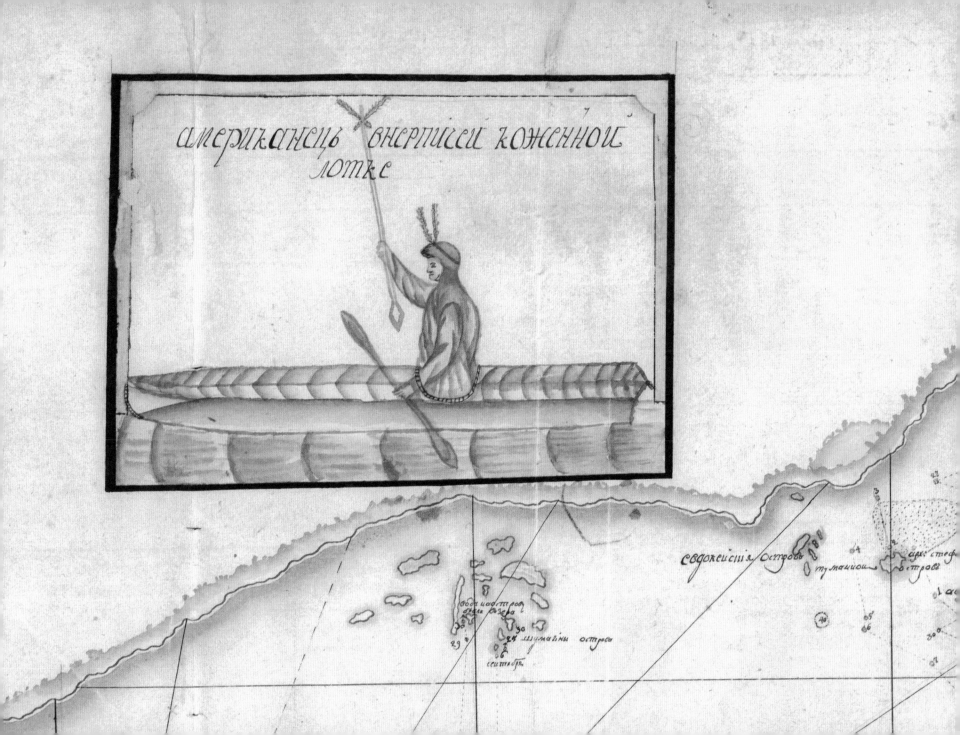

Американець внерписеи коженнои лотке

сведокейскiя Острова
туманнои острова
острова

TOMÁS DE SURÍA 1761–1844

Their eyes are sparkling and alive, although always manifesting a wild and untamed air.

Until the voyages of Vitus Bering, Alaska was an un-inked emptiness on the chart. Mariners came north into these waters drawn by reports of its rich economic potential, and artists regularly joined them. In the summer of 1791 the indigenous Tlingit of Yakutat awoke to find ships rounding the headland of their bay. On board one of these strange craft was a Spanish artist, his journal at the ready.

Born in Madrid, Tomás de Suría had studied at Spain's Royal Art Academy of San Fernando. In 1778 he moved to Mexico with his teacher, Jerónimo Antonio Gil, to help found the Academy of San Carlos, the first museum and art school in the Americas. He was enjoying a quiet career as an engraver at Mexico City's mint when naval officer Alessandro Malaspina recruited him for his expedition that had set out from Spain in 1789 to explore the Pacific Northwest. The official artists had become sick, and an emergency replacement was needed.

In Mexico, Malaspina received a dispatch from the king of Spain ordering him to search for a Northwest Passage and to try to forestall Russian advances in the region. He took his corvettes, *Descubierta* and *Atrevida,* north from Acapulco to 'Port Mulgrave' in Alaska, where a passage was rumoured to exist. Finding only an inlet, Malaspina carefully surveyed the coast west to Prince William Sound, then sailed south in order to resupply the Spanish trading outpost on Nootka Sound, Vancouver Island. Suría's sea journal, the only surviving private diary of the adventure, provides a candid counterpoint to official accounts.

Later crossing the Pacific to Guam and the Philippines, the expedition followed in James Cook's wake by touching in on New Zealand and the new British colony at Port Jackson. Besides the thorough charting and scientific observations, one great success of Malaspina's expedition was that it was the first major long-distance voyage to experience virtually no scurvy. His medical officer, Pedro González, recognized that oranges and lemons were essential, and while other seafarers had tried to store citrus juice, Spain's large empire and many ports of call made it easier to acquire fresh fruit.

After a stop in the Vava'u Tongan group the expedition sailed to Peru, then back to Europe by way of Cape Horn, arriving in Cádiz on 21 September 1794 after a voyage of over five years. Malaspina's involvement in a conspiracy to overthrow the government later saw him arrested, imprisoned and eventually banished to Italy. Much of the botanical and ethnological material collected by the expedition was locked away as a result, and has only recently been rediscovered.

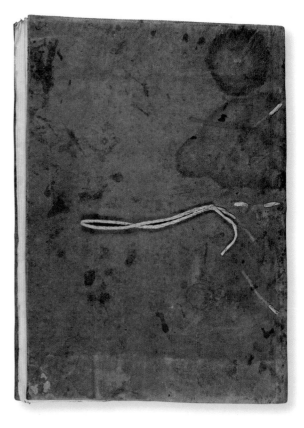

Tomás de Suría's private sea journal fortunately survived the long voyage. The sketch opposite shows a first encounter, or 'discord with the natives', on 5 July 1791. It was a short-lived misunderstanding over some stolen goats.

Discordia con los Naturales del P.to Mulgrabe en 5 de Junio de 1791

Other sketches in Suría's journal include this Tlingit warrior in his bearskin coat, a Spaniard in his 'exploring dress', and the Chief Ankaiui with a traditional septum piercing, and hat woven from spruce root and a sea-lion coat.

The chief was an old, venerable and ferocious looking man with a very long beard, in a pyramidal form, his hair flaccid and loose over his shoulders ... A large [sea] lion skin for a cape was gathered in at the waist.

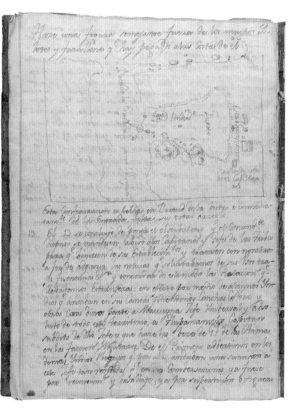

A 'warrior from Nootka' and a Tlingit 'warrior armed for war'. The latter wears a wooden helmet carved like a mask, with a wooden collar to protect his throat. Armed with bow and arrow, and a dagger at his waist, he also has a cuirass of wooden slat armour that hangs to his knees. Far right is a description and map of a shore landing.

GUILLAUME LE TESTU 1509–1573

This Land is part of the so-called Terra Australis,
to us Unknown, so that which is marked herein
is only from Imagination.

A buccaneering explorer who drew some of the finest charts of his day, Guillaume le Testu was born in Le Havre in Normandy, France, and studied navigation in Dieppe. Here, talented artist-cartographers such as Johne Rotz and the hydrographer Pierre Desceliers were making some of the finest maps ever created, for wealthy patrons including Henry II of France and Henry VIII of England. Rotz had joined an expedition to Sumatra in 1529, and later one to Brazil, and Le Testu himself sailed the Atlantic.

In 1550 Le Testu was commissioned by the French king to create a map of new areas of the Americas, where France wanted to trade. He sailed to Brazil on a dangerous reconnaissance mission in the ship *Salamandre*, reaching some way beyond present-day Rio, and was later caught up in a firefight with two Portuguese ships near Trinidad. He sketched charts and the information contained in his sea journals had huge economic and strategic value. Le Testu created his great atlas, the *Cosmographie Universelle,* in 1555, containing all the latest knowledge of the maritime world.

In the turmoil of the French Wars of Religion, Le Testu sided with the Protestants and made privateering raids against the Catholics. He was captured and thrown in prison for four years, but was released on royal orders. In 1573 he was in command of the 80-ton warship *Havre* on a secret mapmaking mission off Panama when he met Francis Drake (p. 112) and the pair joined forces. Together they led a raid against a Spanish mule train laden with treasure heading to the city of Nombre de Dios. Ambushing the Spaniards on the edge of the jungle, it is said they captured nearly 30 tons of gold and silver. With too much to carry, they had to bury the rest, and in the meantime, an enemy fleet was approaching.

Drake stashed his silver and escaped to safety by building a raft and sailing to a nearby island. Le Testu was seriously injured and, resting at the roadside, was captured by soldiers. Though Drake's men returned as a rescue party they were too late to save him. Le Testu was executed and his head was carried into the city and displayed on a pike in the marketplace.

Le Testu's remarkable world atlas, *Cosmographie Universelle* of 1555, was drawn in France, and he was later awarded the title of Pilote Royale by Henry II. One page, left, shows the Red Sea and Persian Gulf while opposite right, the known world unfurls outwards in a four-petalled projection.

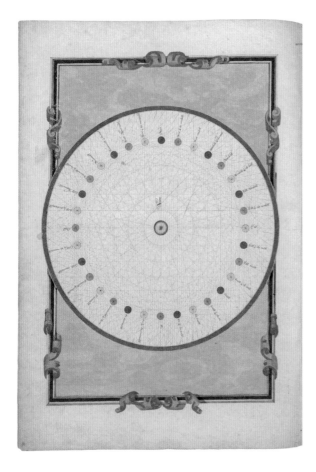

Le Testu based his illustrations for his *Cosmographie Universelle* on charts he sketched on his voyages, as well as Spanish and Portuguese journals he managed to obtain.

Opposite: A detail from Le Testu's depiction of 'Terra Australis'. Some have suggested that birds in the margins resemble black swans and cassowaries, both native to Australia, but Le Testu's maps also show purple lions, unicorns, basilisks and satyrs. He also denied the place existed: 'there is no account of anyone having yet found it, and therefore nothing has been remarked of it but from Imagination.'

GEORGE TOBIN 1768–1838

An Artist was to have accompanied this Expedition, but he was left in ill health ... this obliged us all to work with our pencils as well as we were able.

Two years after the mutiny on the *Bounty*, Captain Bligh (p. 48) was sent back to the South Pacific. This time, with two ships, a proper officer corps and a detachment of marines to keep order, he succeeded in completing his original mission of transplanting breadfruit to the West Indies. Matthew Flinders, later one of the pioneer explorers of Australia, accompanied him. Also chosen for the voyage was a young officer named George Tobin, a keen amateur artist.

Tobin was the son of sugar planters on the small island of Nevis in the West Indies. He joined the navy as a captain's servant and had sailed to many parts of the world before being selected in April 1791 as third lieutenant of *Providence* for Bligh's second breadfruit voyage. When the official artist withdrew, Tobin rose to the challenge of painting the journey to Tahiti and beyond. The journal he kept reveals him to be an interested and sensitive observer of Tahitian life and an enthusiastic natural historian. His sketches from his fifteen days at Adventure Bay are among the first European records of Tasmania.

In 1793 Tobin was second lieutenant on the frigate *Thetis*, under Alexander Cochrane. Many of his sketches from this time survive, as do some from his service in George Murray's flagship *Resolution* in the Halifax squadron. From 1798 he spent some years harrying French coastal trade off Brittany before being paid off in October 1801. Although he married in 1804, within weeks he was back at sea. In 1805 on the frigate *Princess Charlotte* he was in the West Indies chasing the French fleet. By disguising his ship as a merchantman he managed to capture the French corvette *Cyane*.

On *Princess Charlotte*, later renamed *Andromache*, Tobin saw action in Irish waters, off the north coast of Spain and in the Channel. In July 1814 he retired from the sea to Teignmouth, a fishing town in Devon, and continued to sketch and paint naval scenes. For a few years he commanded the royal yacht *Prince Regent*, until it was sold in 1836, and he was later promoted as Rear Admiral of the White. Despite such an eventful career at sea – on voyages of exploration, and in fierce ship-to-ship fighting – Tobin was one of the lucky ones, able to come home and spend his final years with family and friends. He is buried in Teignmouth in the church of St Michael the Archangel, the 'church by the sea'.

Opposite: A scene at Matavai Bay in Tahiti in 1792, close to the spot where James Cook had landed over twenty years earlier.

Below: This chart of the Torres Strait, based on one drawn by Captain Flinders, was enhanced by Tobin over the years. Flinders was a young midshipman with Tobin on the *Providence*.

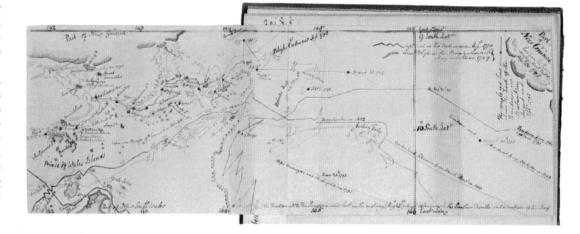

Matavai Bay, Island of Otahytey.... Sun set.... 1792 Page 163.

Mounts Bay fishing Boat _ 1808 _ Pss Charlotte

Rokal

Rokal

Virginia P.L. boat GT 1795

The 2d and staysail only used in very foul weather

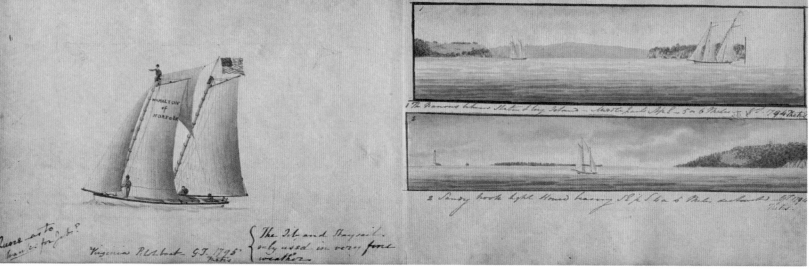

Opposite: In this early sketchbook Tobin has drawn
a Mounts Bay fishing boat when serving on *Princess
Charlotte* in 1808. Below is a Virginia pilot boat,
seen in 1795 when on the *Thetis*, with a detail showing
Sandy Hook lighthouse.

Providence stayed for almost four months in Tahiti,
and Tobin gives lengthy descriptions of many aspects
of life there and an unrivalled sequence of views of
the island. Here are his sketches of a 'Mother Cary's
Chicken' - a storm petrel - a Portuguese Man-of-War
and the 'Flying Fish of St Jago'.

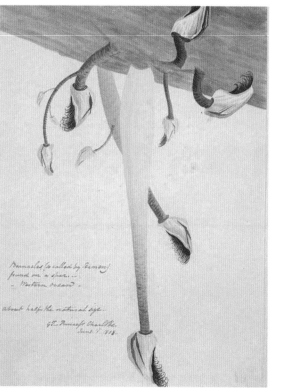

Tobin's drawing of 'The Bread Fruit of Otahytey' (above left): on *Providence* Bligh was able successfully to transport breadfruit from Tahiti to the West Indies. Other drawings from Tobin's journal here show barnacles found growing on the underside of a spar, some tropical fish of Adventure Bay, and, opposite, coastal profiles of Bligh's Islands and the New Hebrides.

Blighs Islands &c.

Island G, or
WB

S 73 W. 6 or 7 leagues
One of Blighs islands. Page 248.

Island F or
WB

S 3 W.

One of Blighs islands, 4 or 5 leagues distant ..... Sunday island, at the time F had

S 25 W.

these bearings, bore SEbE ½ E 8 or 9 leagues. — Page 248.

New Hebrides.

Island B or
A few minutes after this view was taken, another island opened above the hill ✗
WB

One of the northern of the New Hebrides. — SSE 5 or 6 miles distant

— Page 253. —

1792

N e E

N 16 N

The Western part (seen from the Providence) of Blighs Islands, 4 or 5 leagues distant. Page 252.
WB.

TUPAIA 1725–1770

By means of Tupaia you would always get people to direct you from Island to Island and would be sure of meeting with a friendly reception.

On the small island of Edam off the north coast of Java is a lighthouse to guide ships, but no trace can be seen of the grave of a priest who was a skilled Polynesian navigator. His name was Tupaia, and he was born on Raiatea, an island in the heart of the Pacific, enclosed by a coral reef. It was a place also known as Havai'i, the homeland of the Māori people. In time Tupaia became a leading priest trained in the ways of learning. Passed down through generations, his knowledge encompassed the size and location of scattered islands, and the stars and swells needed to navigate between them.

Tupaia's peace was shattered in 1763 when Bora Bora warriors invaded the island, forcing him to take refuge in Tahiti. It was here, in the summer of 1767, that Tupaia met Samuel Wallis and the crew of his ship *Dolphin*, the first Europeans to reach Tahiti's shores. Tupaia befriended Wallis, learnt a little English and helped him observe the solar eclipse. In 1769 another ship arrived, the *Endeavour* of James Cook, and Tupaia would soon be supporting the botanist Joseph Banks in collecting botanical specimens. The wealthy young Banks was keen to take Tupaia back to England as a kind of human 'curiosity', while the adventurous Tupaia wanted to see more of the world, and he joined the ship on its onward journey.

Cook and Banks both recognized Tupaia's skills. At each landing he went ashore as first contact and interpreter, facilitating more positive encounters and helping Banks improve his collections. When asked for details of the regions through which they sailed, Tupaia helped Cook draw a chart showing some 130 islands stretched over 3,200 km (2,000 miles). The expedition turned south for New Zealand, then unknown to Europeans except for a small line of coast traced by Dutch seafarer Abel Tasman in the century before. Tupaia was welcomed by some Māori as a *tohunga* – an expert to be respected, a living link to the culture of their ancestors. They gave him many gifts including a dog-skin cloak.

After New Zealand and then Australia, the *Endeavour* and its crew sailed on to Batavia (Jakarta), where they stayed to make repairs to the ship. In the unhealthy conditions there many became ill. Tupaia died sometime before Christmas from dysentery, weakened also by scurvy and perhaps malaria, and was buried on Edam. Twenty-eight more would die on the journey back to England, their bodies thrown overboard. On Tupaia's death, Cook wrote in his journal: 'He was a Shrewd, Sensible, Ingenious Man'. Irish sailor John Marra called him 'a man of real genius, a priest of the first order, and an excellent artist'.

When Cook returned to New Zealand on a second voyage in 1773, the Māori approached him shouting 'Tupaia! Tupaia?' As Cook wrote that night, his name 'was so popular among them that it would be no wonder if at this time it is known over the great part of New Zealand'.

Although not certain, this portrait of a 'High Priest of Raiatea' probably depicts Tupaia. It is based on a sketch by the artist Sydney Parkinson, who was on the *Endeavour*. Tupaia sketched the Tahitian scene opposite in 1769, with a sailing canoe and two war canoes offshore. Either side of the longhouse are pandanus, breadfruit, banana and coconut palms.

A sketch map in pencil, ink and wash of the Society Islands - an intricate working drawing. Tupaia gave Joseph Banks the place names, which he carefully added, crowded round the islands' coastlines.

Below: Tupaia joined the *Endeavour* when it left Tahiti and travelled on with Cook to New Zealand and Australia. This drawing by him shows indigenous Australians fishing from bark canoes; one man is using a three-pronged spear.

Above: Four musicians on Tahiti, two playing nose-flutes and two drummers.

Right: Tupaia's sketch shows Joseph Banks bartering for crayfish in New Zealand in 1769. 'Above all the luxuries we met with,' Banks observed, 'the lobsters or sea crawfish must not be forgot.' For many years, the artist was unknown, until a letter by Banks came to light: 'Tupaia the Indian', he wrote, has 'the genius for Caricature which all wild people Possess.'

JOSEPH TURNER 1775-1851

I got the sailors to lash me to the mast to observe it;
I was lashed for four hours, and I did not expect to
escape, but I felt bound to record it if I did.

Whether or not Turner really had himself tied to a mast in a storm to paint it, he certainly experienced rough seas at close quarters and went to great lengths to sketch his subjects. His finished oil on canvas, *Snow Storm*, was exhibited in 1842 at London's Royal Academy, with the added note 'the author was in this storm on the night the *Ariel* left Harwich'. Turner was sixty-seven and in indifferent health – if he had been lashed to the mast he would probably have been dead by the time they cut him free.

Turner wanted to move beyond mere depiction, to place his audience in the centre of a great drama and to bring the power of the sea into the gallery space in a way few had ever attempted. Some hailed the painting as his masterpiece, while others could not quite fathom it. The *Athenaeum*'s art critic described it as a 'frantic puzzle' and another dismissed it as all 'soap-suds and whitewash', to which Turner is said to have replied: 'What would they have? I wonder what they think the sea's like? I wish they'd been in it!'

Prolific and original, Turner possessed skills that were second to none and his range was unprecedented. Admired in his day for his landscapes in watercolour and grand historical allegories, his move to abstraction in his later career, which foreshadowed the modernists, saw some of his finest seascapes; often, like *Snow Storm*, these were explorations of colour and light.

Turner was born in London, and throughout his life water, and the River Thames in particular, had a magnetic attraction. He rowed on it, fished in it and eventually had his own inshore sailing boat, which he designed himself. His youth

was spent within sight and sound of the Pool of London, and at the Bristol docks, Margate, Deal and Folkestone he intently watched boats at work. The first oil he ever exhibited, in 1796, was of fishermen and the work he was painting in the months before his death, the story of Aeneas, embraced 'the myth of the sea in a dream'. His most beloved picture, *The Fighting Temeraire*, exhibited in 1839, shows the old wooden warship, a veteran of Trafalgar and a last reminder of the Napoleonic war at sea, being towed by a steam-tug belching smoke up the Thames to the breaker's yard. It was the passing of an era and the advent of a new one.

In his last years Turner lived discreetly with his partner in a small house on the edge of the Thames in Chelsea. To the few locals who knew him, he was 'Admiral Booth', a kindly old figure who had a waterman row him and his 'wife' on the river as he sketched away and sipped gin from a bottle. Though he had children by another mistress decades earlier, he neither married, nor sought a family life, nor enjoyed the attention that his talent brought him. From Turner's point of view, his achievements could be understood easily enough: 'the only secret I have', he once declared, 'is damned hard work'. Even to the end of his days he was sketching, always observing. Most mornings he would climb to his roof to sit, wrapped in a blanket, and watch the sun rise.

Turner's first exhibited oil painting, in 1796,
was *Fishermen at Sea*, for which these are some
preparatory studies. Opposite is an early sketch from
1793 - 'Dover: the Pier, with a Ship at Sea in a Storm'.
Though incomplete it is important as possibly the
first storm from nature that he attempted.

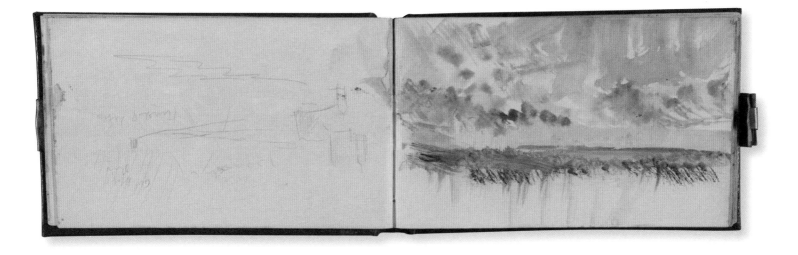

Opposite: Turner was drawn overwhelmingly to coasts, including Margate, the Cornish peninsula, Scotland and the northeast of England. This is a watercolour of a paddle-steamer and an approaching storm.

Above and below: When touring, Turner carried pocket-sized sketchbooks which he would fill with pencil drawings and descriptions, often working across both pages. He kept no diary, but his sketchbooks are intensely autobiographical.

Overleaf: An array of Turner's sea and sky studies, none ever intended for exhibition. These sketches show Turner working, playing, experimenting. Many of these studies, or 'colour beginnings', were painted very rapidly.

SUSAN VEEDER 1816-1897

Going along nicely toward home. I hasten the time when we may arrive.

By the middle of the nineteenth century American whaling was at its peak. Thousands of men were leaving ports on the northeastern seaboard each year to try their luck in pursuing creatures 'twenty times the size of an elephant in small wooden boats'. It was frightening and dirty work, and yet also filled with long months of tedium in an often fruitless search. From the earliest days, American whaling crews were a mixed bunch, with Basque harpooners and other European seaman adding their experience and muscle. Into the nineteenth century, ships increasingly included the energies of African-Americans, Native Americans and Pacific Islanders too.

But the narrative of a thrilling and solely masculine endeavour is not the whole picture. Not often told are the stories of the women who also came along. As whale numbers declined in the Atlantic, ships had to explore new grounds. Greater distances meant longer voyages, usually of two to four years, and though regular sailors remained separated from their families, the wives of ships' captains increasingly joined their husbands on board.

One of these extraordinary women is Susan Veeder. In 1848, aged thirty-two, she sailed from Nantucket on *Nauticon* with her husband Captain Charles Veeder and their sons, bound for the Pacific. It was a voyage that was to last almost five years, and Susan Veeder's account bears witness to both her joy and hardship. For Susan was pregnant, and after the ship had rounded Cape Horn, they went to port in Talcahuano in Chile, where her baby girl was born. After several months on shore, mother and child rejoined the ship. There are fleeting

The title-page of Susan Veeder's journal and pages for November 1849 when they were at the Tuamotus, in what is now French Polynesia.

glimpses of life on board in Susan's journal. On 31 December 1849, she recorded that 'Mary Frances is 11 months old has 7 teeth creeps all about the ship and is very cunning.'

All was well until March, when at Tahiti the baby girl was ill. Guessing she was teething, her parents took her to a local doctor to have her gums lanced. He said it just a cold, and prescribed a powder. But that night the baby grew very sick and she died the following morning. The idea of leaving little Mary in Tahiti was out of the question: 'we must take her with us away, so we have had a lead coffin made and the corpse embalmed to take home with us'.

The voyage took them to Pitcairn and the Tuamotus and they even headed north to the Arctic. Little is known of Susan after *Nauticon* finally returned to Nantucket in the spring of 1853. They buried baby Mary in the cemetery there, where her gravestone still stands. Charles returned to sea, and the couple had another daughter, named Marianna, a few years later. But it is also believed that Charles later quit his ship in Tahiti, in the middle of a voyage in 1872. In love with his Polynesian mistress, he never came home.

November th 2d 1849 Paumota Society
to day we have seen Greig Isld
and saw a white flag set on it and could
see some of the residents and suppose them to
be French from the Society Islds,
29 th nothing of any note all well
30 th to day we are near Deans Isld Stearing E
December th 1 st to day we are of Krusensteins Isld
one Boat went in and caught a lot of fish
2 d to day nothing of any note Stearing S
3 d the same Stearing SSo
4 th to day saw a Shoal of Sperm Whales
going quick to windward we lowered our
boats but get none
5 th Strong wind nothing of any note
6 th saw Sperm whales lowered our boats
and we was fortunate to get one 90 bbls
7 th to day cut in the whale
8 th saw three more whales but they was going
very quick to the windward
9 th strong winds nothing of any note
10 th to day it is rather Squally seen nothing Stearing N
11 th 12 th nothing of any note
13 th 14 th strong winds and very squally Latt 13°46´ = Long 144°43´
15 th 16 th nothing of any note wind not so strong
17 th 18 th weather fine again
19 th to day we have seen the Isld of Ahii
20 th weather fine nothing of any note Latt 14°5´ = Long 145°6´
21 th this morning saw a Ship and Barque
22 d to day seen the Islds of Oura all well
23 d saw Wilson Isld at 8 Pm one boat went in
fishing they saw some of the Natives got a few Coconuts

Some off the Paumota Group

E. Side of Albemarle

Ditcisons Island as Seen bearing S. W. Dist 2 Miles

Sales Rock   Dist 3 Miles

Payta Harbor   Distance 1 Mile

Opposite left: Albemarle, now Isabela, in the Galapagos islands, which were a popular destination for whalers. The *Nauticon* called there in 1850.

Opposite right: In April 1850 the Veeders were at Pitcairn for three days, where they visited the house of *Bounty* mutineer Fletcher Christian. 'We had not been there many minutes before the house was full of People every one in the place came to see me I think they are the kindest people I have ever meet with', Susan wrote.

Left: Paita (Payta) in Peru was another favourite port of call for whalers. Susan Veeder was not the only captain's wife who accompanied her husband on a whaling ship, but on the whole the ordinary sailors resisted, even resented it, and were often hostile to finding 'petticoat whalers' on board.

WILLEM VAN DE VELDE 1611–1693

I go with Royal appointment to make Draughts of sea fights, and my son to put said Draughts into Colours.

Willem van de Velde rose to fame as one of the finest, and bravest, artists of the Dutch Golden Age. He was born in Leiden, the Netherlands, the son of a Flemish skipper, and it is said that 'he was bred to the sea'. In the Second Anglo-Dutch War he was the official war artist of the Dutch fleet and was in the thick of the Four Days' Battle in June 1666 and the St James' Day Battle later that summer, making sketches of the fierce engagements in which ships of both sides were lost and many thousands died. He had his own nimble galley so he could follow the fleets and come to very close quarters.

His efforts won him admirers among the enemy too, and he moved to England in 1672 at the invitation of King Charles II. He was joined by his artist son, also called Willem, and on their arrival in London they began their first major commission – designs for a set of tapestries of the recent Battle of Solebay in the Third Anglo-Dutch War. The two men worked together from a studio in the Queen's House, Greenwich, and were paid salaries by the king – the father for his drawings, the son for his paintings.

Over the next twenty years they painted pictures of ships, battles and the sea for the court, the aristocracy and naval officers. Willem the Elder usually followed his sketches with intricate monochrome pen paintings in ink, known in the Netherlands as *penschilderingen*, but in later years he also worked in oils. When he died in London, his son continued to oversee the work of their studio and a growing band of assistants, copyists, trainees and paint-mixers. Many other marine artists were also producing versions and variations of his paintings. One of his own daughters, Sara, worked in the studio too. Willem van de Velde's pioneering techniques laid the foundation for the practice of marine painting in England, and his work influenced celebrated seafaring artists including Nicholas Pocock (p. 210), Dominic Serres and, most famously, Joseph Turner (p. 266).

Willem van de Velde's drawings, mostly in pen and grey wash, provide an extraordinarily complete record of the ships and small craft of the Netherlands and England in the seventeenth century. During the Second Anglo-Dutch War, the English Rear Admiral Robert Holmes raided the Vlie estuary in August 1666, setting fire to a large Dutch merchant fleet (opposite).

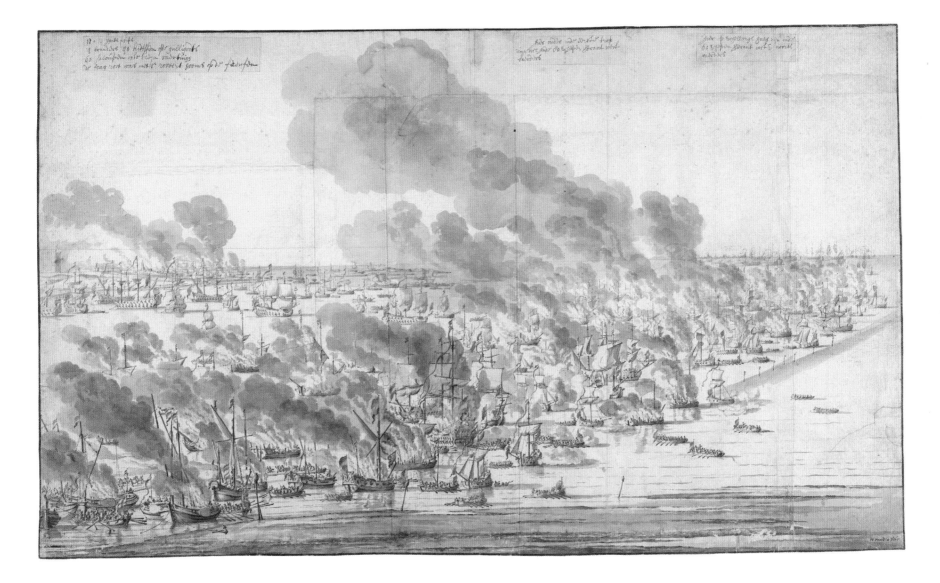

Above: 'Council of War' aboard *The Seven Provinces*,
the flagship of Michiel Adriaenszoon de Ruyter,
10 June 1666, preceding the Four Days' Battle,
during the Second Anglo-Dutch War.

Opposite: Willem van de Velde sketched scenes in
the Anglo-Dutch wars from close quarters - from his
own galley and also from both sides in the conflict.
He was first official war artist for the Dutch and
then moved to London, working for King Charles II.

PAPER AND ICE

Kari Herbert

Now I hear the sea sounds about me; the night high tide is rising, swirling with a confused rush of waters against the rocks below my study window.
RACHEL CARSON, 1955

We live at the edge of the land, in a house that may one day slip into the sea. When the sun is out, the beach below us is filled with happy people. On more usual mornings, when the fog rolls in and the rain drums against the window, we still see people walking their dogs, or surfers sitting out beyond the break. In the winter, when the storms blow in from the Atlantic, the waves tear at the bottom of the cliff and the sands of the beach disappear offshore to reveal boulders and rock. The roof of the house rattles. Here, I often dream of Greenland.

My father, Wally Herbert, took me to Greenland when I was a baby to grow up with the Inuit in a hunting community. My earliest memories are of the sea ice, of sledge trips and journeys out into the bay in small boats. By then, the 1970s, my father had already come to know the pleasures and the hardships of this place well. He was the first man to cross the Arctic Ocean. His ship was a sledge and his crew a team of huskies he had reared and trained himself. For sixteen months, and over 5,800 km (3,600 miles), he made his way across the frozen surface, each day in danger and with rescue next to impossible should it have been necessary. And why? Because he wanted to prove that something that so many said was impossible could be done. And, more importantly I suppose, because he *loved* being out on the ice. That is where his heart sang.

Last summer I joined a voyage to the North Pole. It was incredible to stand on the ice, floating in the middle of the frozen ocean. To reach it was relatively easy: an experienced ice captain, a powerful Russian icebreaker, and incredible effort from a team of guides and sailors. There were photographs and celebrations, of course, but I also found a quiet spot to sit still and breathe in the emptiness, to think of the past and the future. I sketched in my journal, simple drawings, personal memories. In 1969 when my father stood at the same spot, he huddled in his furs for a photograph and raised a flag on a harpoon tied on the back of his sledge. It was the first time the Union Jack had flown there, but within a few minutes he carefully rolled it back into his bag and got going again. The ice is always moving. Had he left his flag there it would have simply floated away. His goal was not just to reach the Pole, but the far greater challenge of crossing from coast to coast. Ahead of him, safe landfall was hundreds of miles away and another six weeks of effort and uncertainty. And yet, even when he had finished his journey – his ocean voyage – he still loved the ice and wanted more. His respect for the environment and the Inuit was genuine and lifelong, and he spent many years championing the Arctic, that beautiful and fragile part of the world that many call home.

As well as all the remarkable seafarers of ages past who made intrepid and dangerous polar voyages, there are others who stayed behind but are just as important. Jane Franklin left no ship's log or sea journal, but when her famous husband, John Franklin, sailed off the edge of the chart in 1845 and didn't return, she campaigned for almost two decades and raised funds for search efforts. She never went to the Arctic, but sailed to Scotland to encourage the whalers to go to look for him. Many voyages were sent out because of her and large parts of northern Canada were charted for the very first time. Josephine Peary did sail to the Arctic with her explorer husband Robert Peary, and gave birth in northern Greenland, but she also kept the home fires burning for many years when her husband was away, chasing his dreams. As their children grew up, she wrote endless letters carried on numerous ships in the hope he might one day write back.

The sea causes heartbreak. Many women were left alone when their husbands decided to remain with Polynesians on the other side of the world or were lost in Atlantic storms just a few days from home and happy retirement. And what of María Caldera Beatriz Barbosa? She was married to Ferdinand Magellan, and supported him unwaveringly, suffering the discomforts of court politics, penury and slander. When he didn't return home she was bankrupt, with no reward or assistance, and her name was dragged through the mud. There were other brave wives who joined their husbands on ships in order to keep their families together, or who emigrated with them to America, to Australia. They survived shipwreck and other dangers to start new lives in foreign lands.

For the lucky few, seafaring in the Arctic brought rich rewards, but it remained a risky business. Of the more than 700 whaling ships launched from New Bedford during the nineteenth century nearly 300 sank or were wrecked. Whalers' journals are filled with the adventure of the hunt as much as the terrors of the trade. They were mostly men, but not all. Susan Veeder (p. 272) was just one of many incredibly courageous and supportive women, adventurers in their own right. In 1871, more than thirty whaling ships were trapped and crushed by pack ice off Alaska. Miraculously, all 1,219 people aboard – including many wives and children – made it to shore alive, although the fleet was a total loss.

Just a couple of years earlier, in July 1869, the painter William Bradford embarked with two photographers on one of the earliest Arctic art expeditions. In the course of the voyage in steamship *Panther*, Bradford made hundreds of pencil drawings and oil sketches in preparation for the larger paintings he would complete on his return. His photographers John Dunmore and George Critcherson, meanwhile, took over 400 photographs using the painstaking wet-plate collodion technique, a process made all the more challenging by the extreme weather conditions they faced. The resulting remarkable paintings and photographs found a hungry audience, eager to see landscapes few Europeans or Americans had ever witnessed. Queen Victoria became the principal sponsor of a book Bradford published in 1873 called *The Arctic Regions*. And in what became known as the 'Bradford Recitals', the artist took to the lecture circuit, telling stories of his polar adventures accompanied by magic lantern slides of the photographs projected on to screens, his paintings resting on easels at the side.

Ice might not be for you: just too cold, remote and lifeless? Yet as an artist and writer myself, I find the sea, and ice in particular, a source of real inspiration, with its ever-changing colours and its fragility. Beauty can be found abundantly at sea, but it is also possible to witness the damaging effects humans are having. Some experts predict ice-free Arctic summers as early as 2020 and sea levels could rise by up to 3 m (10 ft) by the century's end. While most people can't travel to such remote places, art has the power to raise awareness of the urgency of climate change. Behavioural psychology tells us that we take action and make decisions based on our emotions. Art can move us in a way that statistics may not.

In recent years, other artists have been drawn to the ice. Zaria Forman joined NASA as an artist on Operation IceBridge. The mission has been running for almost a decade, the longest airborne survey of Earth's polar ice, using a DC-8 aircraft outfitted with radar and laser altimeters as a kind of flying laboratory, and also making amazingly detailed photographic maps, a mosaic of images. 'I realized that I'm one of the first artists to witness these landscapes from this perspective', Forman says, 'and so I feel compelled more than ever to document this change.'

Forman creates portraits of ice by working soft pastel on to paper with her fingertips. They take months to complete once she's back from a voyage. She starts with a very simple pencil sketch and then painstakingly layers with colour. 'My hope is that my drawings bring awareness and invite viewers to share the urgency meaningfully', she says.

Art can facilitate a deeper understanding of any crisis, helping us to find meaning and optimism in shifting landscapes. Images have the power to rouse us to action. For many seafarers in the past, ice was all about danger. For many artists now, it has come to stand for creativity, but also as the symbol for everything we stand to lose in a warming climate.

Page 280: This hand-tinted glass lantern slide shows William Bradford sketching at the edge of Karsut Fjord in 1869. It was an Arctic voyage 'made solely for the purposes of art'.

Opposite: Zaria Forman at work in her New York studio on her vision of 'Whale Bay, Antarctica, no. 4, 2016'. 'I make art to connect people to landscapes that are distant', she says, 'and yet so important to our shared future.'

ROBERT WEIR 1836–1905

We are far very far out of sight of land – of sweet Ameriky. I was sent aloft on the lookout for whales and whatnots.

Like many young men both before and after him, one night Robert Weir ran away to sea. Some left for adventure and the chance to see exotic shores, others to escape a personal crisis – a broken heart or perhaps financial woes. Their stories are mostly lost to us, but Weir is exceptional in that he kept a detailed journal of his first voyage, and it is studded with beautiful sketches of activities aboard ship.

His father, the artist Robert Walter Weir, was for almost four decades the Professor of Drawing at the United States Military Academy at West Point. As one of sixteen children, it's perhaps no surprise that Robert junior tried his chances at sea, but he had also 'shamed' his family by running up a gambling debt. So, with just the shirt on his back and a few dollars in his pocket, he made his way to the whaling boomtown of New Bedford, Massachusetts. Using the name 'Walla', he signed with the bark *Clara Bell*.

It would be a voyage of nearly three years across the South Atlantic, round the Cape of Good Hope and deep into the Indian Ocean, chasing sperm whales. When the going was good it was all hands to action: out in the boats during daylight and often working through the night to render the blubber into oil, covered head to toe in blood, fat and soot, with the furnaces on deck blazing in the darkness. Weir took his chances to sketch or ruminate in his diary. His opinion of the tough whaling life didn't improve over time, and he experienced all the loneliness, exhilaration and dangers of the trade, so well described in Melville's *Moby-Dick*. 'Tumbled into my bunk with exhausted body and blistered hands', he wrote, and added a final word, with some irony: 'Romantic.'

On his twenty-first birthday he managed to harpoon a whale with his own hands. 'Oh I wish I was somewhere near civilization', he wrote that night. 'To remain here 18 months more seems awful, but I've battled it so far ... If father could see me now!'

Did Weir's father forgive him? We can only guess, because his journals never tell us, but we do know he survived the voyage. He returned to sea in 1862, enlisting in the Union Navy during the Civil War, serving as an engineer on the USS *Richmond* under Rear Admiral David Farragut at the fierce Battle of Mobile Bay. During this time he also acted as a kind of war correspondent, penning short stories and sketching for *Harper's Weekly*. Records show he later found work on the Croton aqueduct into New York and as an engineer with the new Union Subway Construction Company. A restless soul, he seems finally to have settled down.

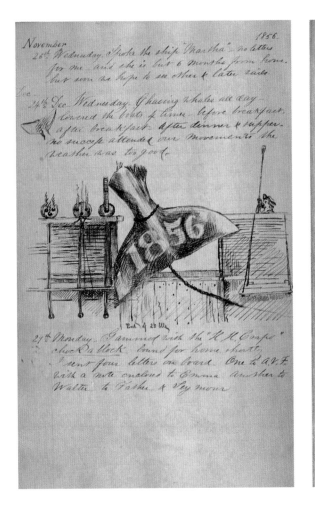

On Christmas Eve in 1856 Weir and the crew of the *Clara Bell* were busy on the hunt all day, and on 29 December they 'gammed', or socialized, with another ship which was homeward bound, and Weir took the opportunity to send letters.

'Too Late', three harpooners stand ready to deliver their deadly thrusts, but the whale has 'turned flukes' and gone into a deep dive.

'Extracting Ivory': the sailors are pulling a line of teeth from a whale's lower jaw. The best teeth were highly prized for they could be transformed with patience and skill - and some ink, a sharp point and a steady hand - into a piece of scrimshaw.

GERRIT WESTERNENG 1858-1959

Before we left we made a speech about our forefathers who discovered these islands and gave them their names. It was cold and chilly.

In 1878, relatively speaking, the Arctic was a busy place. Though the peak of the whaling trade was long past, the British sent some twenty-two ships north that season, and sealers from the United States were active too, while others were hunting walrus in the Kara Sea. The Norwegians were conducting deep-sea research in the North Atlantic, the Danish were surveying the west coast of Greenland, the Russians were hoping to open up trading routes to the river Ob, the Swedish were trying to navigate a Northwest Passage, and in Alaska yet more expeditions were prospecting for gold.

Meanwhile, the wanderlust of a headstrong young Dutch fisherman born in the village of Durgerdam was drawing him over the horizon. Gerrit Westerneng had grown up afloat, sailing the little wooden botters in the Zuiderzee for anchovy and herring. It is said he was gazing at an atlas in the window of a bookseller in Amsterdam when he first heard that a Dutch voyage was being fitted out to head into the ice, and he went to the docks to apply in person.

The recent discovery of relics of the expedition of legendary explorer Willem Barentsz on the remote island of Novaya Zemlya had wakened Dutch interest in the country's polar exploring past. Aware that other competing nations were also looking north, the newly founded Dutch Geographical Society had helped to co-ordinate efforts and a new schooner was launched, named *Willem Barents* (see also p. 22). This had the dual task of placing memorial stones at sites where the Dutch had operated in earlier centuries, as well as making contributions to the emerging field of oceanography. This was science and nationalism hand in hand: a chance to engage in a new kind of Arctic exploration and re-establish a claim in the region, in the inspirational sense if not in practice.

Westerneng joined the *Willem Barents* as a sailor, and though just nineteen years old and the youngest on the ship, his experience at sea was far greater than many others aboard. His keen eye and curiosity meant he was later assigned to assist the zoologist with dredging and identifying marine life. Although he never had a drawing lesson in his life, throughout his three Arctic voyages he kept a diary and sketched with coloured crayons and homemade inks.

Ice conditions made progress difficult, but Westerneng was part of the team that placed a memorial marker ashore at the Orange Islands, off the north cape of Novaya Zemlya on 23 August 1881. Back home, he later married a woman from the island of Urk and settled there, working his own boat until an accident prevented him from fishing. Instead, he opened a coffee house – the aptly named 'Willem Barents' – and there he entertained guests with increasingly elaborate sea tales well into his nineties.

'An excited seal did the high jump. He wanted to see what we were doing on deck. He was a perfect pearl colour, with white, and only the front claws and tail were black with a narrow black region on the back.'

Opposite: 'Bear Island' surrounded by ice floes, with a small *Willem Barents* in the foreground to give a sense of scale.

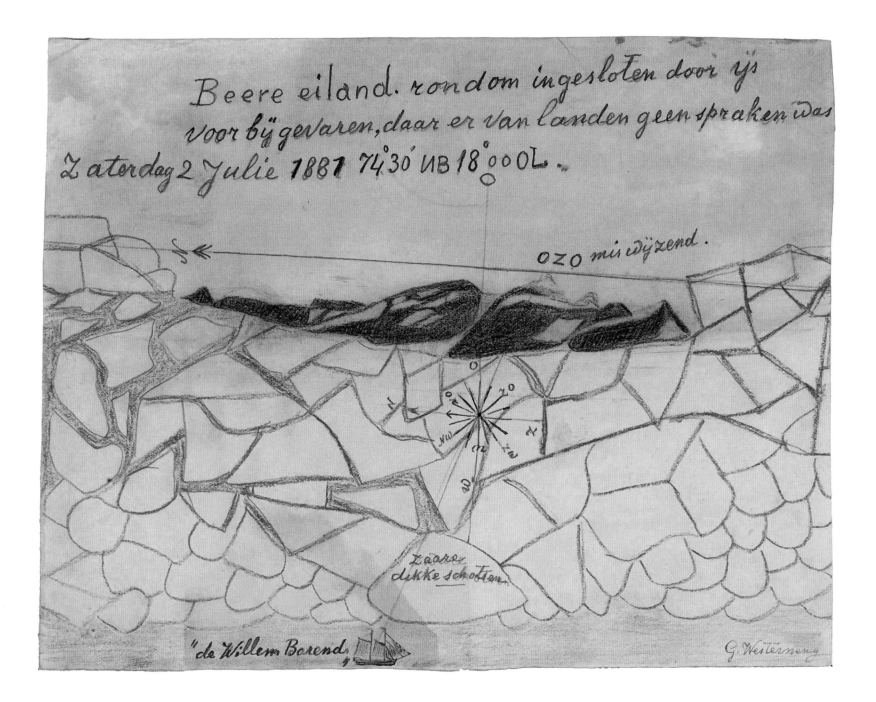

De "Willem Barends. in de Noordelijke
" ijsZee. aan het pak ijs
gemeerd.

Overleaf: Westerneng's sketches of sea creatures,
including a sea tomato, a sea cucumber, a worm and
sea star, caught with the cod in the Barents Sea;
fish caught in the Matochkin Strait in 1879, between
the islands of Novaya Zemlya, including Arctic
flounder, salmon and sturgeon; and the Northern
Lights, 14 September 1880.

The *Willem Barents* was a schooner built as a research
vessel to explore polar seas and with the aim of
reaching the islands of Novaya Zemlya, where famed
Dutch explorer William Barentsz had overwintered with
his crew in 1596. Unfortunately, the voyages coincided
with heavy sea ice and they did not reach their goal.

een ijs schots met een speelonk
25 voet bove water.

in de Barends Zee 16...

25 voet bove water

30 voet hoog.

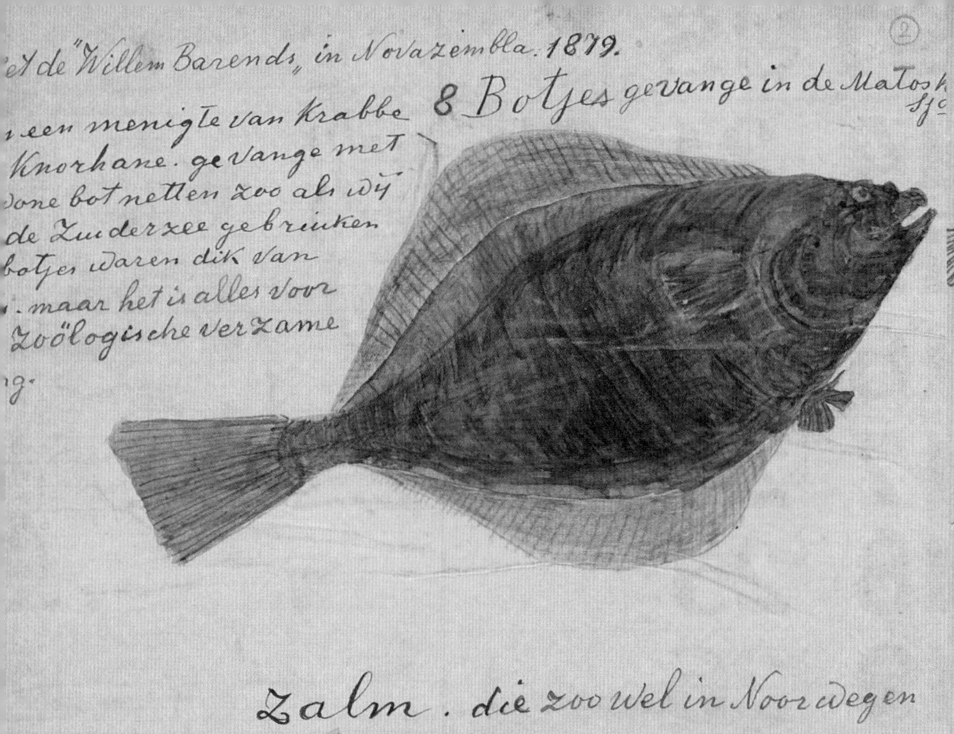

②

et de "Willem Barends, in Novazembla. 1879.

8 Botjes gevange in de Matosk...

een menigte van krabbe
Knorhane. gevange met
...ne bot netten zoo als wij
de Zuiderzee gebruiken
botjes waren dik van
... maar het is alles voor
Zoölogische verzame
...ng.

Zalm. die zoo wel in Noorwegen

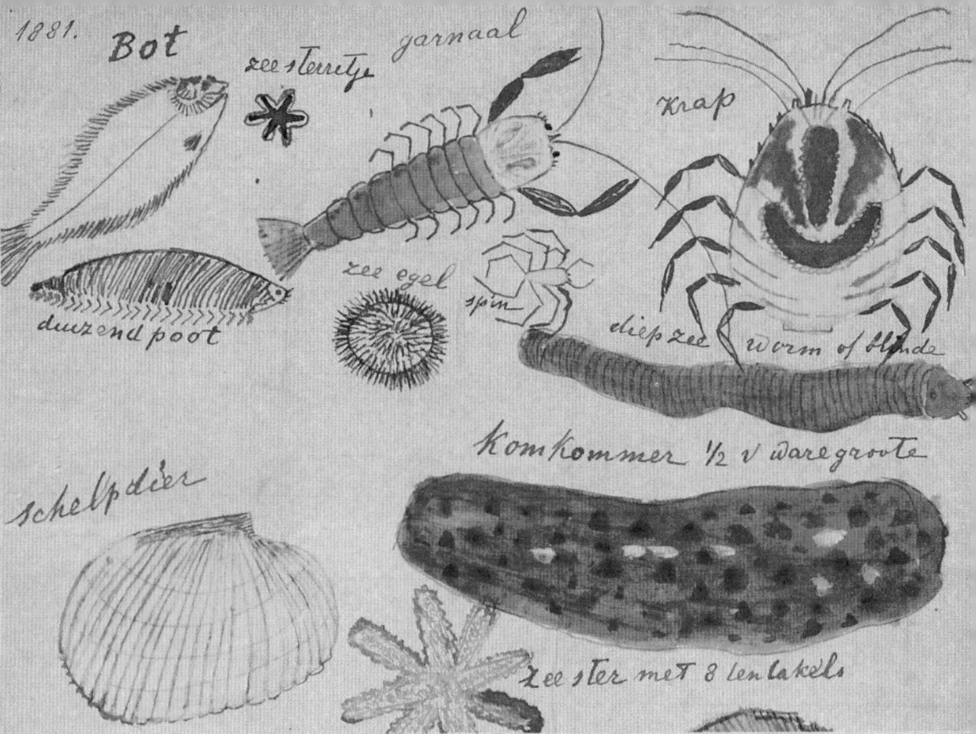

1881. Bot   zee sterretje   garnaal

krap

duizend poot   zee egel   spin   diep zee worm of slinde

schelp dier   Komkommer ½ v ware groote

Zee ster met 8 tentakels

...llem Barends, in de Spitsberg Zee. 1881. 6 Julie. dit is de grootste en h...
...ts, als onder aan gegeven.

± 80 voet.

met de "Willem Barends in de
Noordelijke ijs Zee. voor de petsjora.
1879

een Walrusch op het ijs liggende. maar waak zaa...

WILLIAM WYLLIE 1851–1931

The man who strives to rival Turner must go
out and study nature face to face as he did.
On the mountainside, in crowded cities,
or afloat on the ever-changing ocean.

For William Lionel Wyllie the sea was a lifelong source of happiness and inspiration. He was a man who 'seemed to live entirely for boats' – he designed them, raced in them, drew from them and 'never ceased to paint them in every size and shape and in all weathers', with a small sketchbook, a wedge of green India-rubber and a stub of pencil always tucked into the pocket of his waistcoat.

Wyllie's father was an artist, his mother a singer, and both nurtured his talents. The family wintered in London, where Wyllie attended art school, and spent the summers in a ramshackle house on the water's edge at Wimereux in the Pas-de-Calais, with its miles of empty beaches and dunes. Wyllie roamed the coast by sail with his brothers and mastered the ebb and flow of Channel tides as an amateur lifeguard. On one occasion he swam with a rope to the rescue of a schooner, as a crowd, including Napoleon's nephew, watched from the shore. The prince invited Wyllie on to his yacht for a glass of brandy.

In 1866, aged fifteen, he went to London's Royal Academy schools and won the Turner gold medal at eighteen for *Dawn after a Storm*. He married in 1879, and his wife Marian shared his love of the sea. On their honeymoon the newlyweds sailed across the Channel from France in a flat-bottomed punt. For many years they lived on a sailing boat, the *Ladybird*, which Wyllie had built in Boulogne and converted into a studio, surviving mostly on ship's biscuit and whelks before his paintings started to sell. In time they settled in a house on the banks of the Medway, where the world's shipping passed before Wyllie's eyes. This was the Thames in its heyday, when London was the biggest and richest port in the world.

Wyllie's sketchbooks are filled with all manner of craft, from fishing smacks to frigates, battleships and barges, and myriad scenes too: sailors on the yardarm furling canvas, women at their shrimping nets, men on the conning towers of submarines, or at work, at the oars or caulking the hulls. He also spent considerable time away, including voyages ranging from Trinidad to Spitsbergen, regularly sailing across to Holland, or creating work on transatlantic liners for White Star and other merchant lines. In 1907 the family moved to a house overlooking the entrance to Portsmouth harbour, and Wyllie became more involved with the Royal Navy. He painted countless scenes of the First World War, sailing with the fleet by special licence. He was for some time at Scapa Flow, the base of the British fleet, and was on *Revenge* during the armistice, escorting German ships to their internment.

In 1930, at the age of eighty and still energetic, Wyllie spent a year creating a panorama of the Battle of Trafalgar to raise funds for the maintenance of Nelson's *Victory*, working for free as his bequest to the nation. It was the culmination of a happy career, and he was painting, sailing and exhibiting to the end. 'This, the dream of my life, has come to pass.'

Wyllie sailed to Holland on many sketching trips. This quick watercolour, with windmills silhouetted between sea and sky, was probably created on his cruise of the Dutch waterways in 1888. Opposite, the racing yachts *Valkryie* and *Britannia* off Spithead, 1893.

With his own yacht as a floating studio, Wyllie avidly painted the Thames and the vessels he saw upon it. Spritsail barges evolved with a very simple rig, despite their size, which could normally be easily managed by just two people.

Above: 'Lord Dufferin's yacht racing', possibly from around 1894 and typical of the many sketches Wyllie prepared for newspapers and magazines, notably the *Graphic*. Dufferin, former Governor General of Canada and Viceroy of India, was a talented yachtsman.

Opposite: *Davy Jones's Locker* was one of four paintings Wyllie exhibited at the Royal Academy in London in 1890. He made sketches for it while cruising with his family in the Firth of Clyde in the summer of 1889, going underwater with a diving helmet improvised from a biscuit tin.

BIOGRAPHIES

Author
HUW LEWIS-JONES is a historian and expedition guide with a PhD from the University of Cambridge. He was Curator at the Scott Polar Research Institute, Cambridge, and the National Maritime Museum, London, and is now an award-winning author. When not creating books and photography exhibitions, Huw spends much of his time navigating little boats in Antarctica and the Pacific. Now published in fifteen languages, his books include *Imagining the Arctic*, *Ocean Portraits*, *Explorers' Sketchbooks*, *The Conquest of Everest*, which won the History Award at the Banff Festival, and most recently *The Writer's Map*, an atlas of imaginary lands. He lives in Cornwall.

Contributors
PETER 'SPIDER' ANDERSON is an Australian master mariner and artist. He was second mate on the square-rigger *Eye of the Wind* during its scientific circumnavigation 'Operation Drake', and sailed around the world a second time, on his honeymoon, in the ketch *Skerryvore*. His first daughter was born in Trinidad along the way. He has since joined numerous voyages, building a traditional ocean-going canoe in Papua New Guiena and following ancient trading routes, and as co-pilot in *Endeavour* he crossed Australia in the world's first manned super-pressure helium balloon. When not painting in his studio in Brisbane, Spider looks after zodiacs on expedition ships, regularly travelling to the New Zealand Sub-Antarctic Islands and Antarctica's Ross Sea.

ARVED FUCHS is a renowned mariner, filmmaker, author and explorer who trained with the merchant navy, sailing on ships like *Clipper*, *Albatross* and *Thor Heyerdahl*. As a young man he paddled round Cape Horn in a collapsible kayak. Later he bought and renovated his own ship, a Danish fishing cutter *Dagmar Aaen*. He became the first German to reach the North Pole on foot in 1989. Most famously, with mountaineer Reinhold Messner, he was the first to reach the South Pole without dogs or vehicles. Over the last twenty years he has made countless voyages in polar waters, repeating the routes of many historic expeditions, and retracing Shackleton's voyage of survival across the Southern Ocean.

KARI HERBERT is an author, artist and educator. She grew up in Greenland, but is now living in Cornwall, where she writes a blog for the Newlyn School of Art. She has written four books on exploration, women's history and visual culture including *Heart of the Hero* and *In Search of the South Pole*. She voyages regularly to the polar regions as a speaker and artist. Her father, Sir Wally Herbert, was the first man to cross the Arctic Ocean.

SIR ROBIN KNOX-JOHNSTON is the pre-eminent mariner of his generation. In 1969 he became the first person to sail single-handed and non-stop around the world. He is currently President of the Cruising Association and Chairman of Clipper Ventures. Previously ISAF Sailor of the Year and winner of the Jules Verne Trophy for the fastest circumnavigation of the globe, he was one of the first inductees into world sailing's Hall of Fame.

PHILIP MARSDEN is a sailor and the award-winning author of ten books including *The Crossing Place*, *Rising Ground* and *The Levelling Sea*, which elegantly traced the history of the port of Falmouth. His most recent book, *The Summer Isles* (2019), is the account of sailing single-handed up the west coasts of Ireland and Scotland. His work has been translated into more than a dozen languages. He lives in Cornwall with his wife and family and a number of boats.

RODNEY RUSS is a proud New Zealander and is rightly described as 'a living legend'. He is a conservation pioneer turned master mariner, whose early work in protecting rare birds became a lifelong passion for the wilderness. With over a hundred voyages south, he has led more expeditions to the Ross Sea than any man in history, as well as opening up parts of the Russian Far East for responsible tourism. He is currently building his own ship – *Strannik*, a 75-foot expedition ketch – and planning more voyages to little visited regions.

ROZ SAVAGE is a record-breaking ocean rower and environmental campaigner. The first woman to row solo across three oceans – the Atlantic, Pacific and Indian – she has spent over five hundred days of her life at sea in a 23-foot rowboat. Named *National Geographic's* 'Adventurer of the Year' in 2010, Roz is now a United Nations Climate Hero, an ambassador for the BLUE Oceans and Climate Project, and a recent recipient of a Yale World Fellowship.

DON WALSH is a true American legend, a submarine captain, war veteran and renowned marine explorer. Most famously, in 1960 he and Jacques Piccard piloted the US Navy's bathyscaphe *Trieste* to the deepest point in the world's oceans: seven miles down in the Mariana Trench. After graduation from the US Naval Academy, he served in both the Korean and Vietnam wars, and became the navy's first deep submersible pilot. He commanded *Trieste* from 1958 to 1962. For over fifty years he has remained active in the design, construction and operation of deep submersibles. In addition, he has also made nearly sixty voyages to the polar regions. Antarctica's 'Walsh Spur', a remote mountain ridge, is named in his honour.

SELECTED READING

GEORGE ANSON

Anson, George, *A Voyage Round the World*, compiled by Richard Walter (Knapton, 1748)

— *A Voyage Round the World*, edited by Glyn Williams (Oxford University Press, 1974)

Knight, Frank, *Captain Anson and the Treasure of Spain* (Macmillan, 1959)

Williams, Glyn, *The Prize of All the Oceans* (Viking, 1999)

LOUIS APOL

Croiset van der Kop, Anna, 'A painter of winter, Louis Apol', *The Art Journal* (1893), 353–56

Mörzer Bruyns, Willem, 'The Dutch in the Arctic in the late 19th century', *Polar Record*, 23 (1986), 15–26

SIGISMUND BACSTROM

Bacstrom, Sigismund, 'Account of a Voyage to Spitsbergen in the Year 1780', *The Philosophical Magazine* (1799), 139–52

Henry, John Frazier, *Early Maritime Artists of the Pacific Northwest Coast* (University of Washington Press, 1984)

O'Brian, Patrick, *Joseph Banks* (Harvill, 1997)

JEANNE BARET

Dunmore, John, *Monsieur Baret: First Woman Around the World* (Heritage, 2002)

— *Storms and Dreams: The Life of Louis de Bougainville* (University of Alaska Press, 2008)

Dussourd, Henriette, *Jeanne Baret: Première Femme autour du Monde* (Pottier, 1987)

EDWARD BARLOW

Course, Alfred, *A Seventeenth Century Mariner* (Muller, 1965)

Lubbock, Basil (ed.), *Barlow's Journal of his Life at Sea in King's Ships* (Hurst & Blackett, 1934)

FRANCIS BEAUFORT

Courtney, Nicholas, *Gale Force 10: The Life and Legacy of Admiral Beaufort* (Headline, 2002)

Friendly, Alfred, *Beaufort of the Admiralty* (Random House, 1977)

Huler, Scott, *Defining the Wind* (Crown, 2004)

CHARLES BENSON

Bolster, Jeffrey, *Black Jacks: African American Seamen in the Age of Sail* (Harvard University Press, 1997)

Creighton, Margaret, *Rites and Passages* (Cambridge University Press, 1995)

Sokolow, Michael, *Charles Benson: Mariner of Color in the Age of Sail* (University of Massachusetts, 2003)

PETER BLAKE

Blake, Peter, *An Introduction to Sailing* (Aurum, 1994)

— *The Last Great Adventure of Sir Peter Blake* (Adlard Coles, 2004)

Sefton, Alan, *Sir Peter Blake: An Amazing Life* (Sheridan, 2005)

WILLIAM BLIGH

Bligh, William, *A Voyage to the South Sea* (George Nicol, 1792)

Dening, Greg, *Mr Bligh's Bad Language* (Cambridge University Press, 1992)

Salmond, Anne, *Bligh: William Bligh in the South Seas* (University of California Press, 2011)

ELSE BOSTELMANN

Beebe, William, *Half Mile Down* (Harcourt, Brace and Company, 1934)

Bostelmann, Else, 'Notes from an Undersea Studio off Bermuda', *Country Life* (1939), 67–68

ANNIE BRASSEY

Brassey, Annie, *A Voyage in the 'Sunbeam'* (Longmans, 1880)

— *In the Trades, the Tropics, the Roaring Forties* (Longmans, 1885)

— *The Last Voyage, to India and Australia, in the 'Sunbeam'* (Longmans, 1889)

GABRIEL BRAY

Chatterton, Keble, *King's Cutters and Smugglers, 1700–1855* (G. Allen & Co./Lippincott, 1912)

Johns, Jeremy, *Smuggling in Cornwall* (Amberley, 2016)

Platt, Richard, *Smuggling in the British Isles* (The History Press, 2011)

Winfield, Rif, *British Warships in the Age of Sail, 1714–1792* (Seaforth, 2007)

JOHNNY BROCHMANN

Babcock, Lawrence, *Spanning the Atlantic* (A. A. Knopf, 1931)

Børresen, Jacob, *The Norwegian Navy: A Brief History* (John Grieg, 2012)

Brochmann, Diderik, *Med norsk skib i Verdenskrigen* (N. H. & S. T., 1928)

Espeland, Velle, *Blow Boys Blow: Sjanties frå Diderik Brochmanns samlinger* (Tiden, 1981)

FRANCIS CHICHESTER

Chichester, Francis, *Alone Across the Atlantic* (Allen & Unwin, 1961)

— *The Lonely Sea and the Sky* (Hodder & Stoughton, 1964)

— *Gipsy Moth Circles the World* (Hodder & Stoughton, 1967)

Strathcarron, Ian, *Never Fear: Reliving the Life of Sir Francis Chichester* (Unicorn Press, 2016)

LOUIS CHORIS

Chamisso, Adelbert, *A Voyage Around the World*, edited by Henry Kratz (University of Hawaii Press, 1986)

Choris, Louis, *Voyage pittoresque autour du monde* (Didot, 1822)

Forbes, David, *Encounters with Paradise: Views of Hawaii and its People, 1778–1941* (Honolulu Academy of Arts, 1992)

Mornin, Edward, *Through Alien Eyes* (Lang, 2002)

FREDERIC CHURCH

Carr, Gerald, *Frederic Edwin Church: The Icebergs* (Dallas Museum of Fine Arts, 1980)

— *In Search of the Promised Land: Paintings by Frederick Edwin Church* (Berry-Hill Galleries, 2000)

Harvey, Eleanor Jones, *The Voyage of the Icebergs* (Dallas Museum of Art, 2002)

Noble, Louis Legrand, *After Icebergs with a Painter* (Appleton, 1861)

WILLIAM COATES

Carlyon, Les, *Gallipoli* (Doubleday, 2002)

Coates, William, *The Old 'Country Trade' of the East Indies* (Imray, 1911)

— *The Good Old Days of Shipping* (Times of India Press, 1900)

Moorehead, Alan, *Gallipoli* (Aurum, 2015)

Opposite: This 'Devilfish' was caught by naturalist Johann Reinhold Forster on 10 May 1774 in Matavai Bay, Tahiti, during Cook's second Pacific voyage. His son Georg made this beautiful sketch the following day.

ADRIAEN COENEN

Egmond, Florike (ed.), *The Whale Book: Whales and Other Marine Animals* (Reaktion Books, 2003)

Magnus, Olaus, *Historia de Gentibus Septentrionalibus* (Gregg, 1971)

JOHN KINGSLEY COOK

Lane, Tony, *The Merchant Seamen's War* (Manchester University Press, 1990)

Mitchell, William Harry, *The Empire Ships* (Lloyds of London Press, 1990)

Slader, John, *The Red Duster at War: A History of the Merchant Navy During the Second World War* (Kimber, 1988)

EDWARD CREE

Bickers, Robert, *The Scramble for China: Foreign Devils in the Qing Empire, 1832–1914* (Penguin, 2012)

Cree, Edward, *The Cree Journals*, edited by Michael Levien (Webb &Bower, 1981)

Platt, Stephen, *Imperial Twilight: The Opium War and the End of China's Last Golden Age* (Atlantic Books, 2018)

AARON CUSHMAN

Bockstoce, John, *Whales, Ice, and Men* (University of Washington Press, 1986)

Ellis, Robert, *Men and Whales* (Knopf, 1991)

Nichols, Peter, *Final Voyage* (Putnam, 2009)

Starbuck, Alexander, *History of the American Whale Fishery* (Waltham, 1878)

JOSEPH DESBARRES

Blake, John, *The Sea Chart* (Conway, 2009)

Hornsby, Stephen, *Surveyors of Empire* (McGill-Queen's University Press, 2011)

Whitfield, Peter, *Charting the Oceans* (British Library, 2017)

FRANCIS DRAKE

Kelsey, Harry, *Sir Francis Drake: The Queen's Pirate* (Yale University Press, 1998)

Sugden, John, *Sir Francis Drake* (Pimlico, 2006)

Wilson, Derek, *The World Encompassed: Drake's Great Voyage 1577–1580* (Hamilton, 1977)

JOHN EVERETT

Everett, Katherine, *Bricks and Flowers* (Constable, 1949)

Knight, Laura, *Oil Paint and Grease Paint* (Nicholson & Watson, 1936)

Riding, Christine (ed.), *Art and the War at Sea, 1914–45* (Lund Humphries, 2015)

Yarker, Gwen, *Inquisitive Eyes: Slade Painters in Edwardian Wessex* (Sansom, 2016)

EDWARD FANSHAWE

Berry, Warren, *The Pre-Dreadnought Revolution* (The History Press, 2013)

Fanshawe, Alice, *Admiral Sir Edward Gennys Fanshawe* (Spottiswoode & Co., 1904)

Padfield, Peter, *Rule Britannia: The Victorian and Edwardian Navy* (Pimlico, 2002)

Parkinson, Roger, *The Late Victorian Navy* (Boydell Press, 2008)

ROSE DE FREYCINET

Bassett, Marnie, *Realms and Islands* (Oxford University Press, 1962)

Clode, Danielle, *Voyages to the South Seas* (State Library of Victoria, 2007)

Rivière, Marc (ed.), *A Woman of Courage: The Journal of Rose de Freycinet* (National Library of Australia, 2003)

VASCO DA GAMA

Cliff, Nigel, *Holy War* (Harper, 2011)

Crowley, Roger, *Conquerors* (Faber, 2015)

Subrahmanyam, Sanjay, *The Career and Legend of Vasco da Gama* (Cambridge University Press, 1997)

Watkins, Ronald, *Unknown Seas* (John Murray, 2003)

JOSEPH GILBERT

Beaglehole, John Cawte (ed.), *The Journals of Captain James Cook on His Voyages of Discovery* (Cambridge University Press, 1955–74)

Kaeppler, Adrienne and Fleck, Robert, *James Cook and the Exploration of the Pacific* (Thames & Hudson, 2009)

KONRAD GRÜNENBERG

Aercke, Kristian (ed.), *The Story of Sir Konrad Grünemberg's Pilgrimage to the Holy Land in 1486* (Centro interuniversitario di ricerche sul viaggio in Italia, 2005)

Denke, Andrea, *Konrad Grünembergs Pilgerreise ins Heilige Land 1486* (Böhlau, 2011)

ZHENG HE

Dreyer, Edward, *Zheng He: China and the Oceans in the Early Ming Dynasty, 1405–1433* (Longman, 2007)

Levathes, Louise, *When China Ruled the Seas: The Treasure Fleet of the Dragon Throne, 1405–1433* (Oxford University Press, 1994)

Yamashita, Michael, *Zheng He* (White Star, 2006)

ERIK HESSELBERG

Andersson, Axel, *A Hero for the Atomic Age* (Peter Lang, 2010)

Hesselberg, Erik, *Kon-Tiki and I* (Allen & Unwin, 1950)

Heyerdahl, Thor, *The Kon-Tiki Expedition* (Allen & Unwin, 1950)

Kvam, Ragnar, *Thor Heyerdahl* (Gyldendal, 2005)

GLORIA HOLLISTER

Beebe, William, *Half Mile Down* (Harcourt, Brace and Company, 1934)

— *Adventuring with Beebe* (Bodley Head, 1956)

Matsen, Brad, *Descent: The Heroic Discovery of the Abyss* (Pantheon, 2005)

Welker, Robert, *Natural Man: The Life of William Beebe* (Indiana University Press, 1975)

FRANK HURLEY

Frank Hurley, *Argonauts of the South* (Putnam's 1925)

— *Shackleton's Argonauts: A Saga of the Antarctic Ice-Packs* (Angus & Robertson, 1948)

— *The Diaries of Frank Hurley, 1912–1941*, edited by Robert Dixon (Anthem Press, 2011)

KUMATARO ITO

Hedgpeth, Joel W., 'The Steamer Albatross', *Scientific Monthly*, 65 (1947), 17–22

Smith, David and Williams, Jeffrey, 'The Great Albatross Philippine Expedition and Its Fishes', *Marine Fisheries Review*, 61 (1999), 31–41

Springer, Victor, 'Kumataro Ito, Japanese Artist on Board During the U.S. Bureau of Fisheries Steamer *Albatross* ...', *Marine Fisheries Review*, 61 (1999), 42–57

ROCKWELL KENT

Kent, Rockwell, *Wilderness: A Journal of Quiet Adventure in Alaska* (G. P. Putnam's Sons, 1920)

— *Voyaging Southward from the Strait of Magellan* (G. P. Putnam's Sons, 1924)

— *N by E* (Harcourt, 1930)

Melville, Herman, *Moby-Dick*, with illustrations by Rockwell Kent (Random House, 1930)

BENJAMIN LEIGH SMITH

Capelotti, Peter, *Shipwreck at Cape Flora* (University of Calgary Press, 2013)

Credland, Arthur, 'Benjamin Leigh Smith: A Forgotten Pioneer', *Polar Record*, 20 (1980), 127–45

Jones, Alfred, 'Benjamin Leigh Smith: Arctic Yachtsman', *Musk-Ox*, 16 (1975), 24–31

HENRY MAHON

Bown, Stephen, *Scurvy: How a Surgeon, a Mariner and a Gentleman Solved the Greatest Medical Mystery of the Age of Sail* (Summersdale, 2003)

Lamb, Jonathan, *Scurvy: The Disease of Discovery* (Princeton University Press, 2016)

National Archives, *Tales from the Captain's Log* (Adlard Coles, 2017)

NEVIL MASKELYNE
Dunn, Richard and Higgitt, Rebekah, *Finding Longitude* (Collins, 2014)
Howse, Derek, *Nevil Maskelyne: The Seaman's Astronomer* (Cambridge University Press, 1989)

WILLIAM MEYERS
Meyers, William H., *Naval Sketches of the War in California*, introduction by Franklin D. Roosevelt (Random House, 1939)
— *Sketches of California and Hawaii*, introduction by John Kemble (Book Club of California, 1970)
Palmquist, Peter and Kailbourn, Thomas, *Pioneer Photographers of the Far West* (Stanford University Press, 2002)

GEORG MÜLLER
Bown, Stephen, *Merchant Kings: When Companies Ruled the World, 1600–1900* (Conway, 2010)
Boxer, Charles, *The Dutch Seaborne Empire 1600–1900* (Knopf/Hutchinson, 1965)
Burnet, Ian, *East Indies* (Rosenberg, 2017)

HORATIO NELSON
Nicolas, Nicholas (ed.), *The Dispatches and Letters of Vice Admiral Lord Viscount Nelson* (Colburn, 1844–46)
Oman, Carola, *Nelson* (Hodder & Stoughton, 1947)
Pocock, Tom, *Horatio Nelson* (Bodley Head, 1987)
Sugden, John, *Nelson: The Sword of Albion* (Bodley Head, 2012)

PAUL-ÉMILE PAJOT
Decron, Benoît (ed.), *Paul-Émile Pajot: Le Journal* (Éditions 303, 2008)
Duviard, Dominique and Gruet, Noël, *Histoire d'un bateau de pêche* (Gallimard, 1981)
Gérard, Alain, *Mes Aventures: Journal inédit de Paul-Émile Pajot* (Centre Vendéen, 2015)

Huguet, Jean, *Paul-Émile Pajot* (Le Chasse-Marée, 1989)

JULIUS PAYER
Payer, Julius, *New Lands within the Arctic Circle* (Macmillan & Co., 1876)
Weyprecht, Karl, *Die Metamorphosen des Polareises* (Moritz, 1879)

ANTONIO PIGAFETTA
Bergreen, Lawrence, *Over the Edge of the World* (HarperCollins, 2003)
Pigafetta, Antonio, *Magellan's Voyage: A Narrative Account of the First Circumnavigation*, edited by R. A. Skelton (Yale University Press, 1969)
Zweig, Stefan, *Conqueror of the Seas: The Story of Magellan* (Literary Guild of America, 1938)

NICHOLAS POCOCK
Cordingly, David, *Nicholas Pocock* (Conway, 1986)
Duffy, Michael and Morriss, Roger, *The Glorious First of June 1794* (Liverpool University Press, 2001)
Greenacre, Francis, *Marine Artists of Bristol* (City of Bristol Museum and Art Gallery, 1982)

PIRI REIS
McIntosh, Gregory, *The Piri Reis Map of 1513* (University of Georgia Press, 2000)
Soucek, Svat, *Piri Reis and Turkish Mapmaking After Columbus* (Oxford University Press, 1996)

BARTHOLOMEW SHARP
Howse, Derek and Thrower, Norman (eds), *A Buccaneer's Atlas: Basil Ringrose's South Sea Waggoner* (University of California Press, 1992)
Lloyd, Christopher, 'Bartholomew Sharp, Buccaneer', *The Mariner's Mirror*, 42 (1956), 291–301
Williams, Glyndwr, *The Great South Sea: English Voyages and Encounters 1570–1750* (Yale University Press, 1997)

WILLIAM SMYTH
Back, George, *Narrative of an Expedition in H.M.S. Terror* (John Murray, 1838)
Beechey, Frederick, *Narrative of a Voyage to the Pacific and Beering's Strait* (Colburn, 1831)
Smyth, William, *Narrative of a Journey from Lima to Para* (John Murray, 1836)

WILLIAM SPEIDEN
Hawks, Francis L., *Commodore Perry and the Opening of Japan* (Nonsuch, 2005)
Houchins, Chang-Su, *Artifacts of Diplomacy* (Smithsonian Institution Press, 1995)
Speiden, William, *With Commodore Perry to Japan* (Naval Institute Press, 2013)
Wiley, Peter Booth, *Yankees in the Land of the Gods* (Viking, 1990)

OWEN STANLEY
Goodman, Jordan, *The Rattlesnake: A Voyage of Discovery to the Coral Sea* (Faber, 2005)
Lubbock, Adelaide, *Owen Stanley RN, 1811–1850* (Heinemann, 1968)

GEORG STELLER
Littlepage, Dean, *Steller's Island* (Mountaineer's Books, 2006)
Stejneger, Leonard, *Georg Wilhem Steller. The Pioneer of Alaskan Natural History* (Harvard University Press, 1936)
Steller, Georg, *Journal of a Voyage with Bering, 1741–1742*, edited by Orcutt Frost (Stanford University Press, 1988)

TOMÁS DE SURÍA
Engstrand, Iris, *Spanish Scientists in the New World* (University of Washington Press, 1981)
Inglis, Robin (ed.), *Spain and the North Pacific Coast* (Vancouver Maritime Museum Society, 1992)
Serrano, Carmen Sotos, *Los pintores de la Expedición de Alejandro Malaspina* (Real Academia de la Historia, 1982)

Wagner, Henry, 'Journal of Tomás de Suría of His Voyage with Malaspina ...', *Pacific Historical Review*, 5 (1936), 234–76

GUILLAUME LE TESTU
Eisler, William, *The Furthest Shore: Images of Terra Australis from the Middle Ages to Captain Cook* (Cambridge University Press, 1995)
Lestringant, Frank, *Mapping the Renaissance World: The Geographical Imagination in the Age of Discovery* (University of California Press, 1994)
Le Testu, Guillaume, *Cosmographie Universelle* (Arthaud, 2012)

GEORGE TOBIN
Oliver, Douglas (ed.), *Return to Tahiti: Bligh's Second Breadfruit Voyage* (University of Hawaii Press, 1988)
Schreiber, Roy (ed.), *Captain Bligh's Second Chance* (Chatham, 2007)

TUPAIA
Druett, Joan, *Tupaia: Captain Cook's Polynesian Navigator* (Praeger/Random House, 2011)
Salmond, Anne, *Aphrodite's Island: The European Discovery of Tahiti* (University of California Press, 2010)
Smith, Bernard, *European Vision and the South Pacific* (Yale University Press, 1985)
Williams, Glyn, 'Tupa'ia: Warrior, Navigator, High Priest', in *The Global Eighteenth Century*, edited by Felicity A. Nussbaum (Johns Hopkins Press, 2003), 38–51

JOSEPH TURNER
Butlin, Martin and Joll, Evelyn, *The Paintings of J. M. W. Turner* (Yale University Press, 1984)
Hamilton, James, *Turner: A Life* (Hodder and Stoughton, 1997)
Riding, Christine and Johns, Richard, *Turner & the Sea* (Thames & Hudson, 2013)
Warrell, Ian, *Turner's Sketchbooks* (Tate, 2014)

SUSAN VEEDER

Druett, Joan, *Petticoat Whalers: Whaling Wives at Sea, 1820–1920* (University Press of New England, 2001)

Garner, Stanton (ed.), *The Captain's Best Mate. The Journal of Mary Chapman Lawrence* (University Press of New England, 1966)

Norling, Lisa, *Captain Ahab Had a Wife: New England Women & the Whalefishery* (University of North Carolina Press, 2000)

WILLEM VAN DE VELDE

Daalder, Remmelt, *Van de Velde & Son, Marine Painters* (Primavera, 2016)

Quilley, Geoffrey, *Empire to Nation* (Yale University Press, 2011)

Robinson, Michael, *Van de Velde Drawings* (Cambridge University Press, 1958, 1974)

ROBERT WEIR

Creighton, Margaret, *Rites and Passages* (Cambridge University Press, 1995)

Gilje, Paul A., *To Swear Like a Sailor* (Cambridge University Press, 2016)

Wardle, Marian, *The Weir Family, 1820–1920* (University Press of New England, 2012)

GERRIT WESTERNENG

Bosman, Cécile, 'Matroos en Visserman op de Noordelijke Ijszee', *Jaarboek* (Scheepvaartmuseum, 2016), 44–51

Wildeman, Diederick, 'De Belofte Van Gerrit Westerneng', *Zeemagazijn*, 35 (2008), 8–9

WILLIAM WYLLIE

Quarm, Roger and Wyllie, John, *W. L. Wyllie: Marine Artist, 1851–1931* (Chris Beetles, 1981)

Wyllie, William Lionel, *Marine Painting in Water-Colour* (Cassell & Co., 1901)

— *Nature's Laws and the Making of Pictures* (Edward Arnold, 1903)

— *Sea Fights of the Great War* (Cassell, 1918)

ILLUSTRATION CREDITS

a = above; b = below; c = centre; l = left; r = right

1 Australian National Maritime Museum, Sydney. Gift from Garry Weir, reproduced courtesy of Michael Hope; 2al, 2ar, 2bl, 3ac, 3ar, 3bl Beinecke Rare Book and Manuscript Library, Yale University, New Haven; 2ac Used by permission of the Folger Shakespeare Library, Washington, DC (Call No. STC 6370); 3al Library of Congress, Geography and Map Division, Washington, DC; 3br Walters Art Museum, Baltimore; 2bc, 3bc Nicholson Collection (Wh W7183 1852j), Providence Public Library Special Collections, Rhode Island; 4, 6 National Maritime Museum, Greenwich, London; 10 J. Paul Getty Museum, Los Angeles. Digital image courtesy Getty's Open Content Program; 12a State Library of New South Wales, Sydney; 12b Nicholson Collection (Wh S193 1859j), Providence Public Library Special Collections, Rhode Island; 13 Courtesy of the Nantucket Historical Association, MA; 14 Courtesy of the New Bedford Whaling Museum, MA; 15 James Cook, National Library of Australia, Canberra (nla.obj-228963089); 17 Art Collection 3/Alamy Stock Photo; 18 British Library, London/British Library Board. All Rights Reserved/Bridgeman Images; 19 Rijksmuseum, Amsterdam; 20 Courtesy Antipodean Books, David & Cathy Lilburne, Garrison, NY; 21 National Maritime Museum, Greenwich, London; 22 Rijksmuseum, Amsterdam; 23, 24, 25br Collection Het Scheepvaartmuseum, Amsterdam; 25–27 Rijksmuseum, Amsterdam; 28 NHM Images; 29–33 Western Americana Collection, Beinecke Rare Book and Manuscript Library, Yale University, New Haven; 34 Leemage/Universal Images Group/Getty Images; 35 Bibliothèque nationale de France, Paris; 36, 37 National Maritime Museum, Greenwich, London; 38–40 National Meteorological Archive © Crown copyright, National Meteorological Library and Archive. 41 The Huntington Library, San Marino, CA (Sir Francis Beaufort Papers, FB 17); 43–45 General Collection, Beinecke Rare Book and Manuscript Library, Yale University, New Haven; 46, 47 Sir Peter Blake Collection, New Zealand Maritime Museum/Hui Te Ananui A Tangaroa, Auckland; 48 National Library of Australia, Canberra (nla.obj-233760933-1); 49l State Library of New South Wales, Sydney; 49r National Library of Australia, Canberra (nla.obj-233730330-1); 50–53 State Library of New South Wales, Sydney; 55–57 © Wildlife Conservation Society. Reproduced by permission of the WCS Archives, New York; 58 Rijksmuseum, Amsterdam; 60, 61 Photos Huw Lewis-Jones. Courtesy Robin Knox-Johnston; 62 From Brassey, A. *A Voyage in the 'Sunbeam'* (Chicago, 1881); 63 Lady Annie Brassey Photograph Collection (photCL 331 v. 62), The Huntington Library, San Marino, CA; 64, 65 National Maritime Museum, Greenwich, London; 66–71 Vancouver Maritime Museum, 1984.226.010, 1984.226.004, 1984.226.002, 1984.226.006, 1984.226.005, 1984.226.007; 72, 73 Sir Francis Chichester, by kind permission of the Chichester family (photos Florian Michelet); 74–79 Western Americana Collection, Beinecke Rare Book and Manuscript Library, Yale University, New Haven; 80 Beinecke Rare Book and Manuscript Library, Yale University, New Haven; 81 Gift of Louis P. Church (1917-4-294-a). Photo Matt Flynn. Cooper-Hewitt, Smithsonian Design Museum/Art Resource, NY/Scala, Florence; 82–85 Mystic Seaport Museum, CT; 86–89 National Library of the Netherlands, The Hague (78 E 54); 90 National Maritime Museum, Greenwich, London; 93 Mitchell Library, State Library of New South Wales, Sydney; 94–103 National Maritime Museum, Greenwich, London; 104–07 Courtesy PBA Galleries, San Francisco, CA; 108 Granger Historical Picture Archive/Alamy Stock Photo; 109, 110l Courtesy the Norman B. Leventhal Map Center, Boston Public Library; 110r New York Public Library; 111 National Maritime Museum, Greenwich, London; 112–14 Library of Congress, Washington, DC; 115 Bibliothèque nationale de France, Paris; 116–23 National Maritime Museum, Greenwich, London; 124 State Library of New South Wales, Sydney; 125 State Library of Western Australia, Perth (ACC 5907A/4); 126 Morgan Library & Museum, New York, 2018. Photo Morgan Library & Museum/Art Resource, NY/Scala, Florence; 127 Bibliothèque nationale de France, Paris; 128 Morgan Library & Museum, New York, 2018. Photo Morgan Library & Museum/Art Resource, NY/Scala, Florence; 129l Municipal Library of Porto; 129r G. Dagli Orto/De Agostini/Diomedia; 130, 132, 133 © Spider Anderson; 134, 136r, 137 The National Archives, Kew, London (ref. ADM 55/107 (137)); 135 UK Hydrographic Office (www.gov.uk/the-ukho-archive); 136l The National Archives, Kew, London (ref. ADM 55/107 (205)); 138, 139 Badische Landesbibliothek, Karlsruhe; 140 Philadelphia Museum of Art, Gift of John T. Dorrance (1977-42-1); 141l Library of Congress, Washington, DC; 141ar, br Reproduced by kind permission of the Syndics of Cambridge University Library (FC.246.5, Wade Collection C114); 142, 143 Photos courtesy Kon-Tiki Museum, Oslo. © Estate of Erik Hesselberg; 144, 145 Courtesy Kon-Tiki Museum, Oslo; 146, 147 © Wildlife Conservation Society. Reproduced by permission of the WCS Archives, New York; 148–51 State Library of New South Wales, Sydney; 152 National Library of Australia, Canberra (nla_obj-223377083-1); 153l National Library of Australia, Canberra (nla.obj-223387160-1); 153r National Library of Australia, Canberra (nla_obj-223371792-1); 154–57 Smithsonian Institution Archives, Washington, DC (SIA2017-024473, SIA2017-024502, SIA2017-024483, SIA2017-024535, SIA2017-024580, SIA2017-024596, SIA2017-024526, SIA2017-024550); 158 National Gallery of Art, Washington, DC. Rights courtesy of Plattsburgh State Art Museum, State University of New York, Rockwell Kent Collection, Bequest of Sally Kent Gorton. All rights reserved; 159 Image courtesy Boston Rare Maps Inc., Southampton, MA. Rights courtesy of Plattsburgh State Art Museum, State University of New York, Rockwell Kent Collection, Bequest of Sally Kent Gorton. All rights reserved; 160, 162, 163 State Library of New South Wales, Sydney; 164 Alexander Turnbull Library (MSX-4088-03), Wellington, New Zealand; 165 Beinecke Rare Book and Manuscript Library, Yale

University, New Haven; 166–67 Rijksmuseum, Amsterdam; 168 Courtesy Somerset & Wood Fine Art Ltd; 169l Scott Polar Research Institute, University of Cambridge; 169r Illustrated London News Ltd/Mary Evans; 170 The National Archives, Kew, London (ADM 101/119/3); 171 The National Archives, Kew, London (ADM 101/7/8); 172 The National Archives, Kew, London (ADM 101/119/3/10); 173 The National Archives, Kew, London (ADM 101/119/3); 174 Reproduced by kind permission of the Syndics of Cambridge University Library (RGO 14/36); 175 Reproduced by kind permission of the Syndics of Cambridge University Library (RGO 4/1); 176l Reproduced by kind permission of the Syndics of Cambridge University Library (RGO 4/312); 176r Reproduced by kind permission of the Syndics of Cambridge University Library (RGO 4/196); 177 Reproduced by kind permission of the Syndics of Cambridge University Library (RGO 4/321); 178–81 New York Public Library; 182–87 Abbey Library, St Gallen (Cod. Sang. 1311); 188–91 National Maritime Museum, Greenwich, London; 192–97 Collection musée de l'Abbaye Sainte-Croix, Les Sables-d'Olonne; 198 Collection Het Scheepvaartmuseum, Amsterdam; 201 British Library, London; 202 Osterreichische Nationalbibliothek, Vienna (E 22.534-D); 203 Osterreichische Nationalbibliothek, Vienna (Inv. +Z115192600); 204l, 205al, 205bl, 205br From Payer, J. *New Lands within the Arctic Circle* (New York, 1877); 204r Kriegsarchiv, Osterreichisches Staatsarchiv, Vienna; 205ar Osterreichische Nationalbibliothek, Vienna (PK 3001, 1428); 206, 207, 209 General Collection, Beinecke Rare Book and Manuscript Library, Yale University, New Haven; 208 Library of Congress, Washington, DC; 210–15 National Maritime Museum, Greenwich, London; 217l Topkapi Palace Museum Library, Istanbul; 217r, 218, 219 Walters Art Museum, Baltimore; 221, 222r, 223 National Maritime Museum, Greenwich, London; 222l Morgan Library & Museum, New York, 2018. Photo the Morgan Library & Museum/Art Resource, NY/Scala, Florence; 224, 226–29 State Library of New South Wales, Sydney; 225 Hudson Bay Company, Canada/Bridgeman Images; 230–35 Library of Congress, Washington, DC; 236 State Library of New South Wales, Sydney; 237, 238 Thomas Fisher Rare Book Library, University of Toronto; 239 National Library of Australia, Canberra (nla. obj-138502863-1); 240ac, 240ar, 240bl, 240br, 240cr, 241al, 241ar, 241br State Library of New South Wales, Sydney; 240al, 240bc, 241bl Thomas Fisher Rare Book Library, University of Toronto; 242 State Library of New South Wales, Sydney; 244 Photo Huw Lewis-Jones. Courtesy Rodney Russ; 245 © Spider Anderson; 246 Russian State Archive of Ancient Documents/ Rossiyskiy Gosudarstvennyy Arkhiv drevnikh aktov, Moscow (F. 248, op. 160, d. 140). Image courtesy of Prof. Natalia Lind; 247 Russian State Archive of the Navy, St Petersburg (F. 1331, op. 4, d. 79); 248–50 Western Americana Collection, Beinecke Rare Book and Manuscript Library, Yale University, New Haven; 251l Museo de América, Madrid; 251c, 251r Western Americana Collection, Beinecke Rare Book and Manuscript Library, Yale University, New Haven; 252–55 Bibliothèque du Service historique de la Défense, Paris; 256, 257 Mitchell Library, State Library of New South Wales, Sydney; 258 Mystic Seaport Museum, CT; 260, 261 Mitchell Library, State Library of New South Wales, Sydney; 262 Dixson Library, State Library of New South Wales, Sydney; 263–5 British Library, London/© British Library Board. All Rights Reserved/Bridgeman Images; 266, 267 Tate, London 2019; 268, 269, 270bl, 271bl Paul Mellon Collection, Yale Center for British Art, New Haven; 270al, 270ar, 270cl, 270br, 271al, 271ar, 271br Tate, London 2019; 272–74 Courtesy Nantucket Historical Association, MA; 276, 277, 278, 279al, 279bl, 279br Rijksmuseum, Amsterdam; 279ar National Maritime Museum, Greenwich, London; 280 Courtesy of Peary-MacMillan Arctic Museum, Bowdoin College, Brunswick, ME; 283 Courtesy Zaria Forman; 284, 285 Mystic Seaport Museum, CT; 286–91 Collection Het Scheepvaartmuseum, Amsterdam; 292–95 National Maritime Museum, Greenwich, London; 296 Natural History Museum, London/Alamy Stock Photo; 301 Courtesy Dartmouth College Library, Hanover, NH.

ACKNOWLEDGMENTS

This book would be nothing without the incredible seafarers. They opened the eyes and the minds of their contemporaries through new discoveries. I've also been lucky enough now to drive little boats through Arctic ice, among reefs in the Pacific and along some of Antarctica's remote coasts. I appreciate these stories all the more for it. I'm thankful to my companions on these many voyages, in particular Rodney Russ, and new friend Spider Anderson, who I'm pleased to include here. I'm glad to have Don Walsh, Robin Knox-Johnston, Roz Savage, Arved Fuchs and Philip Marsden on our crew too.

At Thames & Hudson, my stalwart editor Sarah Vernon-Hunt has been worth her weight in Spanish gold once more, and Johanna Neurath and Sophy Thompson ably steered the ship. Thanks also to designer Avni Patel, production controller Rachel Heley, and Pauline Hubner, who followed my research trail again through international archives. From his beautiful corner of the Pacific, Yosef Wosk supported this project with wisdom.

To Kari, for making it possible and for making it better. And lastly, to our Nell, growing up fast, and now joining me on ships to the ice. Last year the North Pole, so where next?

In 1840, a fourteen-year-old boy went to sea on the whaler *Sussex*, sailing from London for the South Seas Fisheries. Twenty-five years later he sat down to write 'his yarn' as a means of guiding his children through 'many a shoal and quicksand'. He included this sketch of the time he almost got eaten by a shark.

INDEX